# DINUZULU

*By the same author*

THE LAST ZULU KING:
The Life and Death of Cetshwayo

C. T. BINNS

# DINUZULU

*The Death of the House of Shaka*

LONGMANS

LONGMANS, GREEN AND CO LTD
48 Grosvenor Street, London W1
*Associated companies, branches and representatives*
*throughout the world*

© *C. T. Binns 1968*
*First published 1968*

*Printed in Great Britain*
*by Ebenezer Baylis and Son, Limited*
*The Trinity Press, Worcester, and London*

To the Memory of

KILLIE

# CONTENTS

## Contents

# ILLUSTRATIONS

# MAPS

# ACKNOWLEDGEMENTS

SINCE my writing *The Last Zulu King* the death of Dr Killie Campbell of Durban has occurred and her passing has been a severe blow to countless students and research workers; to myself the loss is irreparable, for it was not merely her magnificent library but her encyclopaedic knowledge of the Zulus and their history and her gracious and freely given encouragement and assistance that are so sadly missed and leave a gap in life which can never be filled. It is with great pride that I look back upon those many, many happy days spent in close friendship with this selfless woman and this book, inspired by her, is therefore dedicated to her memory.

There are others, too numerous to mention individually, who have also been of great assistance in volunteering information, in kindly giving me hospitality in my wanderings over many parts of Zululand, and in loaning letters, documents and books which have often proved of great value.

Particular mention must be made of the following:

Mrs M. M. K. Robinson, the daughter of Sir Charles Saunders, for the loan of her father's diary for the critical year 1906 and for innumerable documents, papers and photographs which have proved invaluable in the writing of this book and for her friendship and assistance during the past ten years.

Mr and Mrs George Buntting of Fugitives Drift for valuable assistance and generous hospitality on many occasions.

The Librarian and Staff of the Natal Society Library, with particular mention of Miss H. Baudert of the Reference Section.

The Archivist and Staff, Natal Archives, Pietermaritzburg.

Lt-Col. J. E. Fairlie of Pietermaritzburg for the use of a black and white sketch drawn by his uncle Lt-Col. W. F. Fairlie.

## Acknowledgements

Mr J. L. Smail of Durban for his maps and general co-operation.

Mr Ian Lewis of Kranzkop for taking me on a flight over the Mome Gorge.

Father Ignatius of the Benedictine Hospital, Nongoma, and the many other Catholic Fathers and Sisters up and down Zululand who have helped in so many ways and ever shown unfailing hospitality.

To my loyal and happy comrades on many delightful treks, Shelagh, Brian, Malcolm and Rusty.

To my numerous Zulu friends I wish to pay tribute for their personal knowledge of this period which has been freely imparted, much of which has thrown new light on some of the incidents recorded in this book. Particular mention must be made of:

The Princess Magogo Buthelezi, daughter of Dinuzulu.
The Princess Kusabhede Soneni, daughter of Cetshwayo.
Chief Mangosuthu Buthelezi and his wife.
Chief Zwizwe Ziyatengwa, son of Sibebu and guardian of the grave of Maphitha.
Mr Otty E. H. Nxumalo, Zulu writer, of Pietermaritzburg.

Finally I am grateful to Macmillan & Co. Ltd for permission to quote from *A History of the Zulu Rebellion* by J. Stuart.

PIETERMARITZBURG                                          C.T.B.

NATAL and ZULULAND

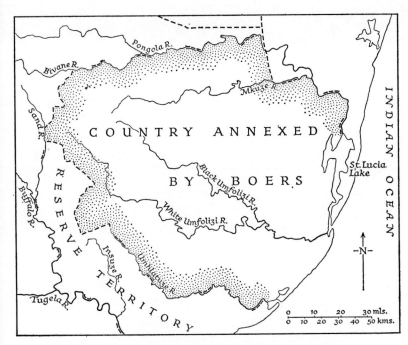

*Zululand showing acquisition of territory by the Boers*

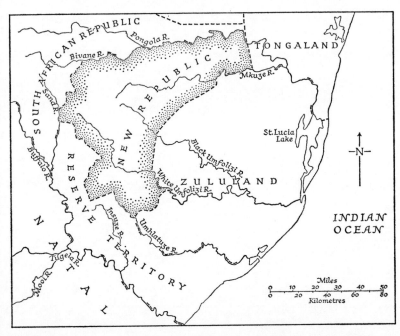

*Boundaries of Zululand and the New Republic, and the line marked off by the Boundary Commission of 1886–87*

## CHAPTER I

# The Boyhood of Dinuzulu

DINUZULU, the eldest son and heir of Cetshwayo, was born in 1868, four years before the death of his grandfather Mpande. For several years before Mpande's death, though he was still King in name, all real power was vested in his son Cetshwayo. Thus during his early and most impressionable years Dinuzulu was surrounded by all the pomp of the Zulu nation : he witnessed the revival of the great military system of Shaka and his young eyes became accustomed to the sight of his father's regiments drilling, parading and dancing before him in all their barbaric splendour. When only five years old he was privileged to see one of the most amazing events that ever occurred in Zululand, the coronation of his father by a British official, Theophilus Shepstone, a spectacle embodying a strange mixture of Zulu pageantry at its best and of the military discipline and might of the British army.

As a child Dinuzulu sat with his father at the annual Feasts of the First Fruits which every man in the land was bound to attend; saw the warriors in their thousands proclaiming their loyalty, and men wrestling bare-handed with savage black bulls as part of the ceremonies and bringing them down to their death; heard the music of the flutes as messengers went forth piping their lilting notes confirming that now the First Fruits could be eaten, for as their King had broken his fast his subjects could also join in the feast.

He was present at one of these feasts when a fight took place between the Tulwana and the Ngobamakosi regiments as a result of the young men of the former taunting the seasoned veterans of the latter, a fight which resulted in much bloodshed and many deaths. Thus early in his life he became accustomed to the sights and sounds of war.

No doubt there were also many occasions when he overheard discussions between his father and his councillors on the bitter land disputes between the Zulu nation and the Boers and, more ominous still, their protracted talks about the massing of British troops on their borders beyond the Tugela. Cetshwayo and his older chiefs were anxious to avoid the gathering clouds of war but they were often overruled in their councils by the younger and more irresponsible element of the nation who were only too anxious to blood their spears.

When only eleven years of age he saw his father's armies at the zenith of their power set forth from Ondini, regiment on regiment, to match their skill against the mighty British Empire, soon, at Isandhlwana, to inflict upon that Empire one of the most crushing defeats in her history, a defeat brought about by the utter incompetence of the British Commander-in-Chief. Other humiliating defeats followed, but in the end superiority of arms prevailed and the boy saw the return of the Zulu warriors, now shattered and defeated as never before in their long history of conquests; he learnt with sorrow of his father's flight and relentless pursuit by British troops; saw the home of his forbears razed to the ground and left a smoking ruin whilst he himself, in the care of his uncle Ndabuko, had to flee; later he heard of his father's capture, banishment and imprisonment at Capetown.

Then began a very different life for Dinuzulu. No longer feted and treated with the deference due to a prince, he was placed under the guardianship of Ndabuko who together with Novimbi Msweli, Dinuzulu's mother, acted as Regent during the King's exile. The Regents in turn fell under the rule of their enemy, Chief Sibebu; the enmity intensified, partly on account of his harsh treatment of all members of the royal family and partly because Ndabuko strongly supported the restoration of Cetshwayo, to which Sibebu was bitterly opposed, for he knew that should this take place the Usutus would quickly attempt to take their revenge. It was during this period that the seeds of a lasting hatred were sown in the heart of Dinuzulu. Not only was he personally humilated on every possible occasion, he was also compelled by force of circumstances to stand idly by whilst this arrogant chief, taking full advantage of

2

Cetshwayo's absence, plundered the royal herds which were the property of the nation and, worse still, tampered with the King's harem, even going so far as to seize a number of Cetshwayo's wives and force them to submit to him. Such outrages burned into Dinuzulu's very soul and remained with him to the day of his death, for they were of such gravity that in the days of his father's rule they would have been punished by instant death. Even members of Sibebu's own tribe, the Mandhlakazi, were so shocked by their chief's conduct and its effects upon Dinuzulu that the aged Mnyamana, Cetshwayo's prime minister, was informed and the boy was quietly spirited away to Opisweni, Mnyamana's kraal; there is little doubt that Sibebu's own brothers offered their assistance in this move, for even they turned against him.*

The escape of his royal prisoner roused Sibebu to fury and numerous attempts were made to recapture him, without success; Mnyamana himself was threatened with the direst consequences but, loyal to his exiled King, he flatly refused to hand Dinuzulu over. Raiding parties were sent out and a ruthless persecution of those loyal to the King was launched; cattle were seized, men were killed and the whole countryside was in turmoil. Dinuzulu meanwhile kept on the run but so faithful were his adherents that his numerous hiding-places were never disclosed to the vengeful Sibebu.

These experiences undoubtedly had a great effect on Dinuzulu's character: they sharpened his wits, familiarised him with hardship and fitted him in great measure for the rough and difficult life which lay ahead of him in the next few years. That he was a remarkably intelligent youth is beyond question; his father had already noted this, for when he was only eleven Cetshwayo referred to him as 'a sharp boy' in his conversation with Bishop Colenso during his visit to the King at Capetown Castle.

It was during this period that an incident occurred which reveals something of the spirit of daring in Dinuzulu, showing undoubtedly that there ran in his veins the blood of his ancestors.

While still on the run Dinuzulu in disguise went alone to

* This was confirmed by one of the sons of Sibebu, still alive, whom I visited a short time ago.

Sibebu's kraal at Bangonomo. Not being recognised, he told the chief that he was the son of Dabulamanzi and as he was passing through Sibebu's territory he thought it only fitting to pay a call on him. The chief presented the young traveller with the customary choice piece of meat as food for the journey and after bidding him '*Hamba kahle*' Dinuzulu proceeded on his way. Shortly after leaving Bangonomo he met one of Sibebu's men on his way to the chief's kraal. Having exchanged the usual saluta-tions with him he handed over the meat recently given him, saying: 'This is from Sibebu, please give it back to him with my compliments.' On being asked who he was he replied unhesi-tatingly, 'I am Dinuzulu', and before the man could recover from his astonishment the youth had vanished. Very soon he was over the hills, for at that time he had the reputation of being one of the swiftest runners in the country.*

In addition to his uncle Ndabuko another great influence over Dinuzulu during these difficult years was his mother, Novimbi Msweli. In a recent interview which I had with Princess Kusabhede, a daughter of Cetshwayo,† Dinuzulu's mother was described as 'a very able woman indeed'; in support of this the Princess quoted two lines from the *Isibongo* (Praise Song) of Dinuzulu:

> *Ithole LokaMsweli*
> *Elanyisa liguqile.*
>
> (The Okamsweli's calf
> which sucks kneeling down.)

Dinuzulu himself she spoke of as 'A very handsome young man, fond of the girls and of hunting. He was used to the handling of a gun and was quite a good shot. The first time he returned from a hunt, when people saw the amount of game he had killed they sang his praises and a dance was held in his honour. He was always conscious of his position and enjoyed the privileges of being a prince, even at an early age. By nature he was very short-tempered and when he became angry his eyes turned red. He

---

* For this story I am indebted to Chief Gatsha Buthelezi, son of the Princess Magogo, a daughter of Dinuzulu.

† See Appendix I for an account of this interview.

hated Sibebu and when in later years he was called to Eshowe to meet and be reconciled with him, as Sibebu stood up and started to walk towards him to shake hands Dinuzulu's eyes blazed so red with fury that the Europeans advised Sibebu to sit down.'

At the beginning of 1883 Cetshwayo returned to Zululand and on 26 January was reunited with his children at Emtonjaneni. Fortunately there is a record of this reunion which though brief is descriptive. After he had met his prime minister and other officials, we read:

Last of all the children, led by the son and heir, entered the tent. The son merely shook hands with his father, whilst the four girls saluted their parent much as English children would have done. They remained with him for a considerable time. Their appearance bore witness to the good treatment they had met with during his exile.[1]

At this time Dinuzulu was about sixteen, a fine, big, strapping lad, already developing the large hips and heavy muscular build so common among his male forbears. Frances Colenso tells us: 'He is the image of his father and was evidently fully alive to his position for he trod the earth as if he owned it. In receiving the congratulations of his numerous Indunas he maintained a sang-froid worthy of his birth.'[2]

Cetshwayo returned to an impossible situation: the whole country was in a state of chaos, yet his own powers were so restricted through the machinations of the Natal officials that no military force whatsoever was allowed him by which he could possibly restore order; on the other hand, the official favourite Sibebu, his bitterest enemy, was given every facility to make use of his *impis*, with no restrictions on their arms. The result was inevitable. Ndabuko, against the will of the restored King, determined on revenge, assembled his forces and marched against the Mandhlakazi. The clash occurred on 30 March 1883 around the Msebe Valley where, thanks to the vastly superior generalship of Sibebu, the Usutu suffered a crushing defeat.

Confusion now became worse confounded and on 21 July of the same year Sibebu in a surprise attack on Ulundi took his revenge.

The cream of the Zulu nation were annihilated, Cetshwayo was wounded, his kraal burnt to ashes and he himself driven to seek refuge in the fastnesses of the Nkandhla Forest, a broken and ruined man largely through his endeavours to remain faithful to the impossible conditions of his restoration.[3]

Dinuzulu was fortunately rescued by Sitshitshili, a fine chief, faithful to Cetshwayo through all the vicissitudes and trials of the preceding years. Together they managed to make their escape, later joining the King in his hiding-place at the Stronghold, overlooking the Mome Gorge.

After spending some weeks in this almost inaccessible spot Cetshwayo was finally persuaded to go to Eshowe under the jurisdiction of Osborn, the Resident Commissioner, who treated him more or less as a prisoner, restricting both his actions and his movements, and it was here that the exiled monarch died by poisoning on 8 February 1884.* In the meantime Dinuzulu had remained in the Nkandhla Forest which was considered by Ndabuko and his brothers the safest spot for him to remain until the advent of a more settled state of affairs.

During the last few months of Cetshwayo's life considerable pressure had been brought to bear upon him to treat with the Boers. Such intervention had been strongly supported by his brothers, led by Ndabuko, but just as strongly opposed by Cetshwayo himself who, when it had been suggested to him that he should obtain the services of a number of Boers equal to the number of white men fighting for Sibebu, had sternly replied, 'Do not dare to treat with the Boers for if you once get them into the country you will never get rid of them.'[4] Nonetheless he had exchanged certain courtesies with them and after his final defeat at Ulundi had sent a messenger, Lugagani, to them, stating that 'Sibebu was killing him.' On receipt of this message the Boers had replied that 'They were coming to help him against Sibebu.'[5] The King at once sent a second messenger, Mboxaludaka, informing them that such assistance was not required and that his former message had been sent merely to tell them what had happened.[6]

Then came his sudden death. Hardly had he breathed his last

* See Appendix II, p. 259.

6

when Mboxaludaka returned with the news that the Boers were coming in spite of Cetshwayo's refusal of their assistance. Ndabuko, remembering the late King's warning against such help, sent back a message to say that 'Cetshwayo would not accept their assistance during his life and if they wished to help him in any way they must represent it to the Government of Natal.'[7]

The King's unexpected death caused great confusion throughout the country. Sir Henry Bulwer, Governor of Natal, worried at the turn of events, again urged Britain to take over the whole country:

There appears to be no alternative course open that holds out a promise of peace and order except the establishment of our rule. . . . There is reason to believe that the greater portion of the Zulu people will gladly accept our authority. . . . It will prove the one arrangement that will best secure their interests and welfare.[8]

The British Government turned a deaf ear to his pleading; under no circumstances would they interfere with the affairs of Central Zululand.

The Boers, closely watching events, realized that Cetshwayo's death had presented them with a splendid opportunity for intervention, particularly in view of Britain's renewed avowal to refrain from any direct action. Accordingly, they sent their own messenger, Kamasana, to Ndabuko with the request that he be allowed to bring Dinuzulu back with him to the Transvaal, giving as their reason for this action, 'The very great sorrow felt by them and because they did not desire the House of Mpande to become extinct as long as they [the Boers] were there.'[9] This unexpected and subtle request met with a curt refusal from Ndabuko, particularly as Dinuzulu was still at the Nkandhla.

The royal brothers, overburdened with anxiety as to the future of their people, endeavoured to assess the situation. A stupendous problem faced them. Their King was dead; the succession was in doubt; their country was torn with strife; the menace of Sibebu hung over them, he had destroyed all their crops and famine stared them in the face; the Natal officials were hostile and Britain had disregarded all their appeals. Their only ray of hope appeared to be the offer of assistance from the Boers. What action must they take in the best interests of their people?

Obviously their first duty was to get a successor to the throne *officially appointed*. Naturally, their choice fell upon Dinuzulu although he was only a boy of sixteen, for they knew it had been Cetshwayo's wish that Dinuzulu should succeed him. Meanwhile Ndabuko as the full brother of Cetshwayo would have to act as Regent till the boy came of age. It was imperative that these appointments be made without delay, for at any time another claimant to the throne might appear and thus cause further disruption.

It was common knowledge that Cetshwayo's chief wife was at that time well advanced in pregnancy. She might produce a son – which actually happened – and thus a section of the people might turn to him, for it must be remembered that Dinuzulu was the son of a minor wife, Novimbi Msweli, a commoner.* To forestall anything of this nature Dinuzulu's succession must be officially announced as soon as possible. Such a proclamation, they anticipated, would act as a rallying point and possibly draw the nation together.

Having decided upon their first move the brothers made their way to Osborn, the Resident Commissioner, and with Dabulamanzi acting as spokesman, they submitted their request in the following somewhat startling form:

We, the brothers of Cetshwayo who is now no more, come to tell you the words spoken by Cetshwayo in the forenoon of the day on which he died. 'I am now in this state you see me in and I want you to tell Mr Osborn the words I now speak. . . . Mpande, my father, left the country to me; I, Cetshwayo, leave the country to my son Dinuzulu for him to have when I am no longer here. . . . Take these words to

* Manzolwandhle, named thus 'Water of the Ocean' in memory of his father's voyage to England, was born posthumously of Cetshwayo's chief wife. His claim to the chieftainship has always been regarded by many Zulus as superior to that of Dinuzulu. Cetshwayo had also had another son, Inyonientala, born after Dinuzulu. As a small child he had been murdered by Sibebu's warriors at the disastrous battle of Ulundi on 21 July 1883. His mother, Majiya, though severely wounded, managed to escape. (B.B. C3705 Encl. 71.)

Mr Osborn and ask him to send them to the Governor with the request that he would send them to the Queen.'[10]

It was a most unwisely phrased statement, especially to a man who was already prejudiced against the Usutus, for it was wholly inconsistent with the circumstances of Cetshwayo's sudden death which had left no time for him to make any arrangements regarding his successor. Furthermore, if the King had given such instructions why had the brothers allowed three days to elapse before reporting them? The Commissioner cannot be blamed for treating their report with some suspicion. It must not be overlooked that his authority extended not only over the Reserve, but in some measure also over Sibebu. Thus on Osborn's shoulders rested the heavy responsibility of maintaining peace between these three hostile factions. It is not surprising therefore that in his dispatch to the Governor he commented adversely on the acceptance of Dinuzulu as the future heir.

Sir Henry, naturally supporting his subordinate, telegraphed the following to London: 'I find myself at the present time and under the present circumstances unable to recommend this course because I see in it only the prolongation of the troubles and contests that have for many years afflicted the Zulu people.'[11] A few days later a reply was received confirming his action.

This refusal to recognise Dinuzulu was a serious rebuff to Ndabuko and his brothers. Now, to add to their difficulties, one of their own messengers arrived from Nkandhla with the news that Kamasana had turned up in the forest more or less demanding that Dinuzulu accompany him to the Transvaal. Here again he was told in no uncertain terms that this was impossible. Nevertheless it was disquieting news to the brothers, for it aroused their suspicions that possibly a plot was afoot to seize Dinuzulu and get him away to the Transvaal. Consequently they sent an urgent message to the Nkandhla that Dinuzulu must be moved secretly, by night, from that area and taken to Mnyamana's kraal where they knew he would be well guarded.[12]

The bearer of this confidential message, Siziba, was one of their most trusted agents, a man who had frequently been employed on matters of state both by the royal brothers and by Mnyamana, the late King's prime minister. On fulfilment of his mission at the Nkandhla he was then to proceed without delay to Shumayeleni (near the Ngome Forest) and there report to Mnyamana himself all that had happened both at Eshowe and in the forest.

Before he had completed the first part of his task he found out that Kamasana had now decided to push on to Mnyamana's kraal. Siziba decided to accompany him, no doubt with a view to keeping a watchful eye on his movements. On reaching his destination he was somewhat taken aback to find two Boers, Conrad Meyer and Jacobus van Staden, engaged in close conference with Mnyamana. The latter, being informed of the arrival of Siziba and no doubt anxious to hear his news, immediately dismissed the Boers and summoning the messenger to his hut received from him a full account of Kamasana's exploits and the Usutu reaction to his request. Meanwhile the Boers, evidently disappointed at the non-arrival of Dinuzulu with their messenger, sought another interview with Mnyamana.

It appears that they had introduced themselves by saying that they had come to mourn with the Zulus and to offer the nation their condolences. After a few desultory remarks, they came without further ado to the main object of their visit, stating that they felt it their duty, in common humanity, to try and put a stop to the incessant strife caused by Sibebu's party; moreover they considered that Cetshwayo had been badly treated by the British Government, which had allowed bloodshed to continue unabated, adding, 'Have you forgotten how peacefully and happily Mpande lived after the Boers made him King? Have you forgotten that it was the English who took Cetshwayo and killed him? Whose fault is it Zululand is in such disorder today? Is it not the fault of the English? If you wish to see Dinuzulu killed, then take him to the English but if you would like him to be King like Mpande then give him to us.'[13]

Considerable argument followed but Mnyamana, sensing an ulterior motive behind the Boers' offer of help, firmly refused to hand Dinuzulu over, excusing his non-compliance with their request by stating, 'How can I give him away since his mother and uncles are not here?' Informing them that the brothers would be summoned in due course he closed the discussion and dismissed the Boers. Immediately they had left, ostensibly to return to the Transvaal, he sent an urgent message to Ndabuko and his brothers bidding them come to his kraal without delay.

Some days later Dinuzulu arrived safely, greatly to Mnyamana's relief, for it transpired later that the Boers had not returned to the Transvaal but had made their way to the Nkandhla where they hoped to get hold of Dinuzulu.[14] Finding that he had left, but determined if possible to catch up with him, they followed his tracks which led them right back to Shumayeleni.

In the meantime as soon as Dinuzulu's uncles had received Mnyamana's summons they set out with all speed for his kraal. In spite of their haste they found on arrival that the Boers had preceded them and were already engaged in further discussion with the aged chief for the possession of Dinuzulu. The royal brothers' approach having been announced, the Boers were dismissed until such time as all could reassemble for a round table conference. Before this could take place, however, it was necessary for the brothers and Mnyamana to meet privately to consider the critical situation, particularly in view of Osborn's refusal to accept the nomination of Dinuzulu as Cetshwayo's heir.

The problem of supreme importance at that moment was to restore peace in the land. Everywhere there was desolation, anarchy, suffering; kraals were in ruins; crops destroyed; women and children hiding in caves and holes, living on roots and any odd scraps of food they could scrape together, most of them dragging out a miserable existence little better than death itself. In addition, numerous marauding bands, driven desperate by hunger, roamed the country, plundering cattle and murdering.

As the discussion went on the state of their country receded into the background, giving way to the question of how to crush Sibebu, for their hatred of him was of such intensity as to blind them to all else. The main reason for this was their firm conviction that he had been the cause of Cetshwayo's death. Knowing to their cost Sibebu's ability as a general, the assistance he could obtain from his white filibusters and the favouritism shown him by the Natal officials, they fully realised the dangers of the situation and the uncertainty of victory unless aided by the Boers. Thus when they met Meyer and van Staden there can be little doubt that, though Mnyamana was hesitant, the others were favourably inclined to accept Boer help.

Van Staden shrewdly opened the discussion by striking at the weakest spot in their armour: 'We are commissioned to come and take Dinuzulu away because if we do not take him Sibebu will come and kill him.'[15] Asked from whom they received this authority the Boers replied, 'By the authority of Mr Krogh, Landdrost of Wakkerstroom, by the big Amakosi from Pretoria and by the authority of H.M. the Queen.'*

In spite of these sources of authority quoted by the Boers, Mnyamana refused to allow Dinuzulu to accompany them, stating that 'he understood that Dinuzulu was placed under the feet of the British Government by his father'.[16] The brothers also withheld their consent, saying that 'They first wanted to bury Cetshwayo.'[17]

Van Staden, grasping this opening for another telling blow, answered: 'Where will you remain whilst Dinuzulu is without protection? We only want to make him King, we don't want any payment at all. We want to do this on account of our sorrow for the Zulu nation.'[18]

Mnyamana and the brothers, still unconvinced of the sincerity of the Boers, yet anxious to obtain their assistance against Sibebu, now questioned them as to their reason for wishing to take

* Their statement regarding the authority of the Queen was vouched for by Tshingana, by Siziba, by Santingi, brother of Mnyamana, by Hemulana speaking on behalf of and with the authority of Mnyamana, and by Mfunzi, an accredited messenger serving since the time of Mpande. (See B.B. C4913, Encl. 1 in 50, p. 78 and Encl. 2 in 50; B.B. C4645, Encl. 1 in 56, pp. 80–4, and Encl. 4 in 61; B.B. C4913, No. 25, p. 44; B.B. C4587, Encl. 2 in 106, p. 103.)

Krogh later flatly denied that he had ever given authority to van Staden to use his name in this connection: 'How can you say that you had not mentioned my name to the Zulus and told them that you had been sent by me on behalf of the Transvaal Government; you know yourself that it is not true and that I never gave you an order to do such a thing.' (B.B. C4645, Encl. 1 in 56, pp. 80–4; see also B.B. C4913, Encl. 1 in 50, p. 78.)

Van Staden himself later admitted to Hemulana that he had used the words 'by the authority of the Queen' and that he had sworn an oath that the Boers wanted no land. (B.B. C4913, Encl. 2 in 50, pp. 87ff.)

Dinuzulu with them and received the reply that 'They were only taking him in order that the other Boers might be satisfied that we really wanted them to help us against Sibebu.'[19] Determined to press home their request by any and every means, van Staden and Meyer now collected together a heap of stones, placed a stick with a hat on top and swore a solemn oath that they told the truth and that the Transvaal Government would, within one month, subdue all the enemies of the Zulus and restore to them their kraals and cattle;[20] further, that they wanted neither cattle nor lands.[21]

After lengthy discussion it was finally decided, in view of the callous indifference of the British authorities and the hostile attitude of the Natal officials, to accept the offer of Boer aid on condition that not more than twenty-five men would come to their assistance to counteract Sibebu's white filibusters.

The Boers had won the day and Dinuzulu was allowed to accompany them to the Transvaal on condition that he be taken for protection to Krogh, the Landdrost of Wakkerstroom, as the official representative of the Transvaal Government, and later be returned when his safety in Zululand was assured.

Another important question now claimed the attention of the Zulu leaders, the burial of their late King. This was a matter of extreme urgency, for his death had taken place on 8 February and it was now nearing the end of March. Consequently it was decided that Ndabuko and his brothers should return immediately to Eshowe and interview Osborn with a view to obtaining his consent for this to take place in the usual burial ground of their Kings, the Emakosini Valley.

On submitting their request to the Resident they met with a flat refusal; Osborn would not countenance such an idea, offering as an excuse the unsettled state of the country. When the brothers suggested that a military escort might be provided to guard against any trouble they were peremptorily told that such a course was out of the question.

Hardly had they retired from this interview when they suffered an even greater shock. News reached them that the Resident was endeavouring to persuade the Governor to apply to the British Government to enlarge the Reserve territory so as to embrace the whole of Central Zululand and at the same time to extend the boundaries of Sibebu's and Uhamu's land down to the Black Umfolosi River. As news of this spread among the people it roused the anger of the nation to such an extent that many who previously had submitted to Osborn now repudiated his authority and offered their allegiance to Ndabuko. So great was the swing in this direction that henceforward the Usutus became known as the National Party.

Some days later the brothers again approached Osborn about the pressing matter of the King's burial, this time asking to be allowed to conduct the ceremony at the kraal of Lohunu in the Nkandhla. Again they met with a point-blank refusal on the grounds that they had only selected this place in order to enlist popular support for a general movement against Sibebu. (Osborn's action was later supported by the Governor.[22])

What was to be done? Already the smouldering fires of revolt were breaking into flame as reports of Osborn's obstinacy went out over the country; skirmishes broke out; two of the lesser tribes of Uhamu were attacked and defeated by the AbaQulusi (a section of the Usutus), whilst near the coast Sokwetyata, a supporter of the Resident, suffered a severe defeat. These raids were indicative of the feeling that was sweeping over the nation and as the tide of that emotion swept onwards it produced a reaction in a most unexpected quarter.

The widows of Cetshwayo, angered beyond endurance at the protracted delay in the funeral arrangements of their royal master, took the law into their own hands. On the afternoon of 8 April they set out and made their way in a body to the man who was responsible for all their disappointments. Sweeping every obstacle aside they thronged into the Residency demanding the late King's immediate burial. So excited were they and so violent did they become that Osborn had to beat an ignominious retreat, leaving them in full possession of the building.*

---

* When I visited the Princess Magogo, the grand-daughter of one of the wives who was actually in the hut when Cetshwayo died, she told me, referring to this incident, that the women commented on Osborn's flight: 'He is like the ants, he has lots of exits to his home so that he can escape.'

A few hours later official sanction was granted for the removal of the remains to the kraal of Dabulamanzi. That night the funeral cortège, consisting of about a hundred people, proceeded on the first lap of its journey to the last resting place of their King. A handful of determined women had succeeded in a task which the combined efforts of the royal brothers had failed to accomplish. The official dispatch, though making no mention of this incident, stated tersely: 'The Resident Commissioner *found it necessary to give his consent* [author's italics] to the removal of the remains to a kraal belonging to Dabulamanzi, distant some 6 miles from Eshowe.'[23]

CHAPTER 2

# The Boer Committee

THE report of the unexpected success of Cetshwayo's widows soon spread and as the funeral procession advanced the small following grew rapidly to a big crowd, all eager to pay their last respects to their King who had been held in much esteem by the majority of the nation.

It was a difficult journey for a lumbering ox-wagon and as it bumped its way over mountainous tracks it was soon realised that the place selected by the Resident for the burial was unapproachable owing to the bad state of the road. Consequently a message was sent to him requesting permission to proceed to another locality; this was granted and a spot somewhat further afield was suggested. After several hours of heavy going the tired travellers reached the appointed kraal only to be met by a hostile body of men who refused to give them either shelter or hospitality. Their reply to questions about this unheard-of discourtesy was 'that they were to deny all hospitality by order of superior authority'.[1] After a hurried consultation Ndabuko and his brothers decided to continue to Entumeni and spend the night there; the following morning they would proceed to the Nkandhla as originally planned, in spite of the Resident's opposition to their selection of this site.

By next day the crowd had greatly increased and after several miles it was unexpectedly confronted by an armed force under the command of Mavumengwana, one of Osborn's chiefs, who informed the brothers that he had orders to stop them. As he took no steps to enforce this order, probably because he was so outnumbered, the cortège moved on unconcernedly and Mavumengwana and his men gradually disappeared over the hills, not one of them having ventured to oppose the movements of the funeral party.

16

As the procession drew nearer to its destination progress became slower due to the very broken and rugged nature of the country; hills became steeper, valleys and streams more difficult to negotiate. Eventually the wagon could go no further, the weary oxen had to be unyoked and the great coffin was lifted on to the shoulders of loyal and willing helpers; in this way, at long last, it reached the kraal of Lohungu, situated in one of the most remote and beautiful spots in Zululand.

It was now 10 April but before the interment could take place much had to be done, for the hasty decision regarding the King's last resting place had allowed no time for the usual preparations to be made. A huge grave had to be prepared, the wagon had to be broken to pieces – for it must not be profaned by any future use – and every part of it carried those last few miles. After the interment had taken place those pieces would reverently be laid on the grave itself; they remain untouched to this day. Then followed a lengthy and intricate ceremonial lasting several days during which all the oxen which had pulled the wagon had to be slaughtered as a sacrifice to the spirit of their departed King.

Whilst these ceremonies were taking place a force of Native police, sent by Osborn, burst in upon the assembled crowd and demanded from Ndabuko an explanation why he had issued instructions to his people to refuse payment of their taxes. It was obviously a trumped-up charge and coming at such a time and place deepened the feelings of resentment against the Resident. Ndabuko replied with commendable dignity that: 'No such orders had been given: at the present time they were engaged in burying their King but when these ceremonies were over they would inform the Resident and the people would no doubt pay all the taxes demanded.'[2] But following on the heels of the police came another message stating that unless taxes were paid forthwith police action would be taken.*

* Though officially denied it is clear from the following that such a demand *was* made at this time: 'The disorder in the Reserve has arisen from a rash and ill-judged attempt to collect taxes from dwellers on the soil who though they would not be unwilling to pay them under protest, are resolved not to forego their loyalty to their native and hereditary ruler.' (*Natal Witness*, 28 May 1884, leader.)

Meanwhile at Eshowe events moved fast. As soon as the Resident heard that the funeral party had gone to the Nkhandla he not only sent the above messages but proceeded to enforce his threats by assembling an armed force. Summoning the much-hated Hlubis* and the handful of chiefs in the Reserve who were loyal to him, he told them at a meeting on 12 April that they must arm and be prepared to march without delay against the Usutus in the Nkandhla. This was not enough, for by the use of threats he forced others in the vicinity to join him in his attack on their fellow-countrymen, 'Men whose only fault had been a persistent loyalty to the Chief whom the Queen had restored to rule over them.'[3]

News of these preparations soon reached Ndabuko and there can be no doubt whatsoever that this rash conduct of the Resident marked a definite turning-point in the attitude of the Usutus towards the authorities; henceforward they were in open rebellion. The spirit of opposition now stirred not only in Central Zululand but spread over almost the whole of the Reserve, its people stating with much truth that even when their taxes were fully paid they were hunted down like wild beasts just because they belonged to the King's party.†

In fairness to the Usutus it must be admitted that there was much justification for their attitude. They had been exasperated beyond measure by Osborn's vacillating policy, by his abominable treatment of their late King and his arbitrary conduct in the matter of his burial; by his construing their loyalty to the King's party as open rebellion; and by his marked favouritism towards Sibebu and his fellow-conspirator against Cetshwayo, John Dunn, who had been granted large tracts of Zulu territory under the impossible conditions of the King's restoration. They were bitter at his refusal to accept Dinuzulu's nomination as Cetshwayo's

* Certain Basutos who had been granted a portion of the country for their assistance in the war of 1879 and were loathed by all the Zulus.

† The state of this unhappy country was summed up as follows by the Editor of the *Natal Witness*: 'Zululand is now in an infinitely worse state than it was 6 months ago, than it was 12 months ago, than it was 2 years ago, than it has been at any time since Cetshwayo was first crowned by Sir Theophilus Shepstone in 1873.' (Leader, 17 May 1884.)

lawful successor; they deeply resented his failure to curb the constant raiding of their cattle, their only source of wealth, by the band of white filibusters who went unpunished. Last, but by no means least, they took the strongest exception to the enforced collection of the Hut Tax in direct opposition to Lord Derby's explicit instructions that 'such tax was only to be collected if no resistance was to be apprehended'.[4]

Thus the final rites in the burial of Cetshwayo, which took place on 23 April, were carried out in an increasing spirit of hostility towards the British authorities. The more the Resident attempted to enforce his decrees the stronger grew the feeling among the Usutus to defy the law and summon their people for the ceremony of the *ihlambo** in preparation for an act of open rebellion.

The interment had hardly taken place when other messengers arrived from Osborn warning the so-called 'loyals' of the Nkandhla against joining the Usutus, ordering them to remain where they were and not to cross the border into Central Zululand. His warning fell on deaf ears, for many had already gone to Mnyamana and others were preparing to follow at the first opportunity.

Meanwhile the Resident, sensing the rising tide of opposition, sent two messengers, Dhlaba and Lugede, to Mnyamana, ordering him to keep the peace. The message had about the same effect as that of Canute upon the waves of the sea. Scarcely had it been delivered before these two men were pounced upon by a band of Usutus and stabbed to death, their bodies later being thrown into a nearby gully.†

News of the murders soon reached Osborn along with the information that many of the 'loyals' had crossed into Central Zululand and joined forces with the National Party. He now realized that if any vestige of his authority was to be maintained immediate action was imperative. Instructions were therefore sent

---

* *Ihlambo :* the cleansing considered necessary after the death and burial of a King by the washing of their assegais in the blood of their enemies.

† This incident was confirmed by a white trader who was visiting Mnyamana at the time: he witnessed both the arrival and the murder of these men. (B.B. C4191, Encl. in 9, p. 11.)

to his sub-commissioner, Pretorius, to seize the cattle of all who had left the Reserve.[5] This only added fresh fuel to the flames, for nothing so angers the Zulu as to be robbed of his cattle. Retaliation followed swiftly; blood was spilled, the cattle recovered and by the time the Resident and his force reached the Nkandhla (5 May) the stage was fully set for a conflict which both sides now saw as inevitable.

Osborn's first act was to summon Ndabuko and other Usutu leaders to appear before him and give an account of their actions. The summons was disregarded, and to emphasise their defiance, a boldly impudent raid on some of his followers was carried out by two Usutu chiefs. The Resident struck back by seizing cattle, following this up by opening a heavy fire on a number of people who were hiding in the forest. Some lives were lost and the Usutus, now thoroughly roused, assembled their forces for an attack.

It came about 3 a.m. on 10 May. Shortly before that hour Osborn's scouts rushed in with the news that there was a Usutu *impi* about half a mile away under the command of Dabulamanzi, advancing rapidly on their position. Captain Mansell, who had been put in command, quickly formed his own men into two columns, placing them some yards in front of his native troops. Amongst the latter was a sprinkling of Europeans to give them the necessary support. All were on foot and as it was a calm and brilliant moonlight night, visibility was good.

The Usutus were allowed to approach to within 300 yards before Mansell's men opened fire, sending volley after volley into their closely packed ranks. Though they advanced bravely, shouting their blood-curdling war-cry '*Usutu*', this steady fire first halted and then sent them scattering for cover. The discipline of trained troops told and though the Usutus had some guns their bullets whistled harmlessly overhead. Mansell's casualties were one man killed and another slightly wounded, but the Usutus lost heavily.

Yet it was only a Pyrrhic victory for him. The Usutus not only recaptured all the cattle which had been seized but they struck such fear into Osborn's levies that nothing on earth would induce them to fight again. As a result he had to retreat, for he realised well enough that a much stronger attack would be made once Dabulamanzi could muster his reinforcements.

In this encounter the Usutus had been deceived by the rapid volley fire into believing that a strong body of white troops had suddenly arrived to help their comrades. Thus Dabulamanzi had ordered the retreat to bring up more men and alter his plan of attack. Mansell, anticipating this, and with Osborn's support, withdrew to Entumeni and later right back to Eshowe, which he reached on 13 May. The Usutus were left in full possession of the Nkandhla. Events now assumed a serious aspect and although Osborn attempted in every way to minimise the Usutu success it was obvious that his rash and uncalled-for attack had done incalculable harm. Yet had he even at this late hour, particularly in view of the threat of Boer intervention, made some serious attempt to settle without further resort to arms the many grave problems which were disturbing the Usutu leaders, there is little doubt that hundreds of lives might have been saved and Zululand spared from the disastrous events which followed. Instead, he made matters infinitely worse by wiring to Bulwer for reinforcements of *regular troops*. Bulwer, in turn, foolishly accepted Osborn's alarmist reports as accurate, and transmitted his appeal to London.*

The British Government can hardly be blamed for the action they took, dependent as they were on the reports of their officials on the spot. Unfortunately many of these reports were both inaccurate and misleading. Had the Government been supported

---

* On 28 January 1884 Bulwer had written to Osborn: 'It is no part of the duty of H.M. Government to send troops into the Reserve either to maintain order or to defend the territory; those duties devolving upon the Chiefs and headmen acting in concurrence with you' (B.B. C4037, Encl. 3 in 24, p. 27). Yet on 16 May he sent the following telegram to Lord Derby: 'Employment of troops now become absolutely necessary if Reserve is to be held' (*ibid.*, p. 27). According to the *Natal Witness* (26 May 1884), there was a leakage of official information which revealed that Bulwer had sent alarmist reports to London to this effect: 'Usutus invading Reserve killing and outraging on all hands: Osborn and officials in extreme danger; camp at Eshowe may be carried any day; possible Usutu attack on Natal.' It was in this way that official sanction was obtained for the right to use Imperial troops in the Nkandhla.

at this juncture by competent and unbiased men the situation might have been saved.*

The direct result of this series of blunders was not only to unite practically the whole Zulu nation in their opposition to the Natal officials but to drive them into the arms of the Boers who were eagerly watching for an opportunity to intervene. Here it was presented to them, and naturally they accepted it with alacrity.

On the other side of the Reserve more men were waiting to pounce on the Usutus and plunder their cattle. As soon as news reached John Dunn that Osborn was on the warpath he at once called out his forces, being joined by the filibuster Johan Colenbrander and his group of white followers known as the 'Stanger Disreputables'. This bunch of ruffians set off towards the Umhlatusi, hoping later to link up with Sibebu, to fall on the Usutus as a united force and annihilate them, leaving Osborn to deal with the other sections in the Nkandhla. However, it was discovered that a large and well-organised force of Usutu lay between them and Sibebu, and as their native contingent refused to advance, the project had to be abandoned. Determined not to return empty-handed, Dunn, Colenbrander and the Stanger Disreputables went on the rampage in and around the Reserve, burnt numerous kraals and carried off a large number of cattle.

At the time of these raids, events of great moment were taking place in the north of Zululand. Ostensibly with a view to bringing about a cessation of hostilities and the establishment of Dinuzulu on the throne, certain Boers on 1 May had crossed into Zululand, taking Dinuzulu with them, and set up camp near the Hlobane mountain. Here they formed themselves into what they termed 'The Committee of Dinuzulu's Volunteers'.†

---

* 'If through the mediumship of an independent, just and unprejudiced Commissioner the Imperial Government could at this critical juncture thus enlist itself on the side of peace and bring upon its own side the strongest forces existing in Zululand, a settlement of that country could be accomplished in 48 hours without a single drop of blood being shed.' (*Natal Witness*, 15 May 1884, leader.)

† This committee consisted of Coenraad Meyer, Andreas Laas, J. F. van Staden, H. J. Potgieter, A. J. Uys, Philip Spies and T. Steenkamp. (B.B. C4191, Encl. in 31, p. 55.)

As has been described, two of the Boer leaders, Meyer and van Staden, had previously conferred with Mnyamana and other Usutu chiefs. It had been decided that, if necessary, assistance would be given to the Usutus to compel both Sibebu and Uhamu to acknowledge Dinuzulu as King and to submit to his authority. Realising the bitter animosity of the Usutus towards these two chiefs, the Committee decided that before there could be any hope of a peaceful settlement immediate action must be taken against both. Accordingly the following letter was drawn up and sent by three trusted Zulu messengers to Sibebu and Uhamu:

We have the honour to inform you that Dinuzulu, the successor to the throne of Zululand, has in consequence of the continued bloodshed within his territory, and with the desire to see peace and tranquillity restored to his country, taken his refuge with us.

We have not come to wage war; our object is to restore and maintain peace throughout the whole of Zululand.

We do hereby inform you that Dinuzulu is at present with us and that we are on our way to Mahlabatini.

We have to request you to lay down your arms without further delay and to conduct yourself in a quiet and peaceable manner to enable us to consult and carry on negotiations with you.

We have further to request you to retire within your own territory and we promise you, on our part, to prevent any further bloodshed.[6]

The Committee's next step was to arrange their plan of campaign. It was decided:

1. To protect Dinuzulu as long as he was with them.
2. To endeavour to effect a settlement of the differences in Zululand without bloodshed.
3. To crown Dinuzulu when the proper time should offer.
4. To take land for their services.
5. To make a treaty with the Zulus.[7]

Two facts emerge from these moves. First, that the object of the Boers in persuading Mnyamana and Ndabuko to allow them to take Dinuzulu back with them to the Transvaal had not been merely to give him protection and later to make him King, but primarily to remove him from the influence of the Zulu leaders so

23

that they could exert pressure upon him to agree to the cession of a portion of his country in return for their services. No doubt Dinuzulu could easily be persuaded to accept their terms when there was dangled before his eyes the tempting bait of kingship over his people with the full backing of large numbers of heavily armed Boers. It must be remembered that he was only a boy of sixteen at this time and certainly would not grasp the full implications of the Committee's plans. Although they were in direct contradiction to the original promise made to Mnyamana and the other chiefs by Meyer and van Staden, who had sworn on oath that they did not require land in payment for their services, yet it is obvious that the Boers *did* manage to extract from Dinuzulu the promise of a grant of land; for almost immediately after the Committee was formed and their programme became known several hundred Boers from the Transvaal and the Free State flocked into Hlobane and Utrecht with no other object than that of pegging claims to farms in Zululand.

The official dispatches confirm this. As early as 27 April Sir Henry Bulwer received a telegram from Newcastle stating that 'A Committee of Boers had been formed to annex Zululand', and on 6 May he wrote to Lord Derby: 'A conference of some 800 Boers was being held at the Hlobane mountain in Zululand: that they had Dinuzulu with them and that they proposed to make him King of Zululand *in consideration of a cession of a tract of country* [author's italics].'[8]

Moreover, it was obvious that the majority of Boers who had rallied round the Committee were determined to enforce its decisions upon the Zulus, by force of arms if necessary. It should be noted that all had come *fully armed*; in fact, so great had been the demand for arms and ammunition in Newcastle that stocks of these had become completely exhausted.

Steps were now taken to put into effect the Committee's decisions, in spite of the fact that on 9 May the Acting President of the South African Republic, P. J. Joubert, had issued the following proclamation:

Whereas it is brought to the notice of the Government of the South African Republic that some persons of this Republic leave their wards for the purpose of connecting themselves with and giving help as volunteers to the Zulus in Zululand who are fighting among themselves. . . . The Government having regard to the evil involved therein, orders all Landdrosts, Commandants, Field-Cornets of the South African Republic strictly to see to it that no burger leaves his ward with the purpose of joining the fighting parties and enjoins them to warn all burgers that in case of transgression they will be severely punished according to law.[9]

No notice was taken of this injunction.

It was later followed up by a letter from the State Secretary of the Republic to the Resident in which the attitude of the British authorities towards the dead Cetshwayo was roundly condemned and their further dilatoriness in taking active steps to effect a settlement of the country was deeply regretted. Thus, it was pointed out: 'It is not surprising that the Boers now on their own authority and responsibility pass into Zululand to take control upon themselves or to establish and secure peace.'[10]

After the letters to Sibebu and Uhamu had been sent a party of about forty Boers now proceeded to Mnyamana's kraal at Shumayeleni. Having obtained Dinuzulu's consent to the cession of a portion of Zululand they hoped to persuade Mnyamana and the other Usutu chiefs with him to agree to this, with the proviso that should Sibebu also accept their terms there should be a peaceful settlement of all issues.

Undoubtedly, the Boers held the whip hand: they had won Dinuzulu over to their side; they promised their full support in making him King; they would crown him without delay; they would insist on the submission of Sibebu and Uhamu, by force of arms if necessary; and – the one thing that the vast majority of Zulus desired more than any other – they would effect a settlement of the country and bring peace to their land. Their terms – the cession of a portion of Zululand (the extent as yet undisclosed). To convince Mnyamana of their sincerity, three of their number, under the leadership of John Combrink, immediately set out for Sibebu's kraal to enforce his submission.

Mnyamana, full of hatred of Sibebu and determined on revenge, was in a dilemma. He remembered Cetshwayo's warning to have no dealings with the Boers; he deeply resented the cession of any portion of his country; he knew well the firm opposition of the British Resident to every move the Usutus had taken. What must be his decision? The astute Boers understood his dilemma and exerted every possible pressure upon him, even going so far as to suggest transferring their assistance to Sibebu should he not accept their terms. Grudgingly Mnyamana gave way but only on the condition that Sibebu should be crushed should he offer the slightest resistance.

Again the Boers had won the day by their clever manœuvring but, fearing an outbreak of violence should Mnyamana be left on his own with a large Usutu army only too eager to attack Sibebu, they took the precaution of forming a camp at Ngome, thus placing themselves between the Usutus and Sibebu's people, the Mandhlakazi.

Meanwhile the three Boers having confronted Sibebu informed him that it was their intention to make Dinuzulu King over the territory to which Cetshwayo had been restored; they would not interfere with Sibebu or his country but he, on his part, must not interfere with Dinuzulu or with any of the Usutus under his jurisdiction; they had come to see him in order to put a stop to the incessant strife which racked the country and would no longer tolerate the present state of affairs. Sibebu must also restore the women and cattle he had seized from the Usutus. Should he refuse to accept these terms then he must bear the consequences.

Sibebu feigned gratification at their intervention but stated that 'he had nothing to do with Dinuzulu or his territory. He himself held his appointment from the English and had no power to give the consent they desired without being told to do so by the English to whom he belonged.'[11] And with this reply the delegates had to be content; on their return Combrink reported the result of his mission to the Boer Committee.

Realising the dangers of his situation, the moment the Boer delegates had taken their departure Sibebu set about mobilising and arming every available man. Not only did he send urgent messages to Dunn and Colenbrander to come to his assistance but he also made a stirring appeal to the Resident to help him in his hour of need. His request was forwarded to Sir Henry Bulwer who sent it on to London, urging Lord Derby in the strongest possible terms to grant him authority to support Sibebu against Dinuzulu and the Boers. A further plea was added for the extension of British sovereignty over the whole of Zululand.

To these requests the following telegraphic reply was sent by Lord Derby on 16 May: 'After a full consideration of recent reports and recommendations H.M. Government adhere to the decision not to extend British sovereignty or protection over Zululand, but the integrity and peace of the Reserve must be maintained.'[12]

## CHAPTER 3

# The Battle of Tshaneni

Now that the Boers had succeeded in effecting a temporary peace between the main warring factions they proceeded with all haste in their preparations for the coronation of Dinuzulu, knowing that until this had taken place there could be no question of their obtaining any land cession.

Accordingly, the leaders of both parties, after considerable discussion, arranged that the ceremony should take place at Zalflaager where the Boers had already fixed their camp, consisting of about seventy tented wagons.*

On Tuesday, 20 May it was announced that Dinuzulu would be crowned the following day. The three brothers of Cetshwayo, Ndabuko, Usiwetu and Tshingana, were already there 'doctoring' the young Prince in preparation for the morrow. Mnyamana had absented himself on the grounds of illness but it was reported that a message had been received from him stating that he was in agreement with the arrangements made between the Boers and the Usutus, although at a later date this was emphatically denied.

A number of chiefs had arrived from Uhamu and through them it was learned that he had promised to acknowledge Dinuzulu as King and submit to his authority. More important still were the representatives of Sibebu who informed the Boer Committee that their chief was willing:

1. To give up all the women and children captured in the late disturbances.
2. To return all the late King's cattle.
3. To acknowledge Dinuzulu as the lawful successor to Cetshwayo provided the Boers and Usutus respected his

---

* Zalflaager is situated at no great distance from Cetshwayo's Refuge, in the Ngome Forest – the spot where Cetshwayo had been taken prisoner on Thursday, 28 August 1879.

territory and assured him that he would not be molested in any way.[1]

By dawn on the 21st a crowd of about 9,000 Zulus and 350 Boers had assembled. While some of the Boer Committee were interviewing Dinuzulu to see that all preparations were complete others were busy marshalling the Zulus into their appointed positions. About noon the *impi* escorting Dinuzulu was seen approaching and as they drew near a small commando of about fifty Boers met the young prince and led him to the two wagons which had been arranged to form a platform; on one of these an upturned empty liquor box had been placed to serve as a throne.

The Boers now formed up in two semi-circular lines in front of their laager while directly opposite them, but some distance away, the chiefs were seated in rows; behind them, in rough horse-shoe formation, were massed the main body of the Usutus. In the centre, in full view of all, were the two wagons on which the coronation was to take place; over these a large blue and white flag was flying.*

As Dinuzulu, accompanied by four members of the Boer Committee, climbed onto the platform it was obvious that he was impressed with his position and the importance of the occasion. At once his attention was arrested by the flag fluttering above him and, on asking one of the Boers what it meant, was told that it was under a similarly coloured flag that the Boers had long ago crowned Mpande and that as that King had reigned for forty years in peace, so it was hoped that this flag might have the same good fortune for him.

The ceremony began by one of the Boers reading out the terms of peace as laid down and accepted not only by the Usutus but also by Sibebu and Uhamu. They were as follows:

1. That all would acknowledge Dinuzulu as King.
2. That all women and children and all cattle taken during the war would be returned forthwith.
3. That all would keep within the boundaries as laid down by the British Government.
4. That all would keep the peace and bury their assegais.

* See a sketch plan in the *Natal Witness*, 28 May 1884.

The Boers for their part gave the Usutus their solemn promise that they would see to it that these conditions were fully carried out.

As the proclamation was translated into Zulu it was received with obvious signs of approval. The Installation now followed; Dinuzulu having been commanded to kneel, the four Boers, placing their hands on his head, swore to protect him against his enemies as long as he observed the terms of peace. Andreas Laas thereupon anointed the head of the newly appointed King by pouring over it a bottle of castor oil!

This completed the ceremony. Dinuzulu now stood up and read the following proclamations:

1. That as rightful heir to Cetshwayo he had that day taken possession of the throne and would henceforward take over the government of his people.

2. That he granted a full amnesty for all political offences committed against his late father or his family and promised protection to all; he wished all to return to their homes and commence their usual peaceful pursuits. All those who had committed any crimes would be brought to justice for he had entered into an agreement with the Boers to see that the government was properly carried on and they would assist him to give effect to these commands.[2]

With the intimation that all complaints would be considered on the following day the Boers dispersed and having handed Dinuzulu over to his people he was duly acclaimed in the time-honoured way by the whole crowd roaring out the royal salute, *'Bayete'*.

For that day, at any rate, old feuds were forgotten and the Boer Committee could undoubtedly congratulate themselves on the fact that the proceedings had passed off satisfactorily.

The whole of the next day was given over to a discussion with Dinuzulu and the leading Usutus on the question of the amount of land to be ceded, the Boers affirming that as they had carried out their part of the contract it was now the duty of the Usutus to honour theirs.

There can be little doubt that at this juncture the members of the Boer Committee expected and would have been satisfied with the area known as the Disputed Territory as a reward for the services they had rendered. But as the discussion ranged to and fro it became only too obvious that the Usutus desired further assistance to subdue Sibebu, for from the first they had disbelieved his promises and only that day a messenger had arrived from Mnyamana stating that some of his warriors had intercepted a couple of Sibebu's men carrying a letter written by Eckersley (Sibebu's white adviser) to Osborn in which the following passages occurred:

He [Sibebu] does not know what will become of him; if it was only the Zulus he would know what to do. He always depended on you for help. . . . Fighting against the whites he does not like but he will never give in to the Boers; he will be killed by them first.[3]

Whilst this letter was under discussion a further message arrived from Mnyamana stating that Sibebu had made other appeals to John Dunn and Colenbrander. Though Dunn had turned a deaf ear to his plea Colenbrander would undoubtedly have come to his assistance had he been able to do so, but he had got himself into serious trouble with the Government on account of an advertisement which he had placed in the *Times of Natal*.

This had read as follows:

Able-bodied men of good character who can ride and shoot well are required at once. Applicants must be prepared to find their own horse carbine, etc such as they may require for field service. Satisfactory remuneration offered. For further particulars apply by letter or personally.[4]

Twenty young men responded to the above. Colenbrander refers explicitly to his predicament in a letter to Grosvenor Darke, another of Sibebu's supporters:

If these messengers get through so much the better, though I greatly fear they will get killed. Sibebu wants to know why I don't come in. It is not because I am afraid, although I know he thinks so, nor is it John Dunn who is keeping me back but I have got into difficulty with the Government about guns and volunteers to help you poor fellows and since this has occurred I cannot proceed until I have made my peace with the Government. I had 20 well-armed and mounted men for service but the men have all been sent back to Natal and disbanded. . . . As soon as I see myself free from Government I'll lose no time in making for Mandhlakazi.[5]

The information about Sibebu was also placed by the Usutus before the Boer Committee who up to this point had firmly refused to proceed against him, stating explicitly that the main reason for their intervention had been to put an end to the incessant strife in the country; now, in view of these reports, they would have to reconsider the whole question. However, they would make one last effort to effect a peaceful settlement and would send another commission to Sibebu demanding the fulfilment of his promises.[6]

While this discussion was taking place reports of it spread throughout the Boer camp and as a result considerable pressure was brought to bear on the members of the Committee. Relatives and friends had been flocking into the laager, all anxious to share in the allocation of the farms, which they thought to be imminent. Their number was so great and their claims so insistent that so small an area as the Disputed Territory would never provide them with sufficient land. As it seemed certain that further help would have to be given to the Usutus here was a good excuse to press for more territory. To meet this demand it was therefore suggested that the Committee should, when drawing up the Treaty, make the amount of land indefinite so that more could be claimed at a later date.

On this suggestion being made to the Usutu leaders they, somewhat surprisingly, gave their assent, certainly not because they expected to have to give more land for Boer assistance against Sibebu, but simply because they could not agree amongst themselves as to where the new boundaries should be drawn.

Consequently, when they met again the next morning (23 May), Dinuzulu was persuaded to sign the following treaty:

The principal leaders of the Boers bind themselves and agree to assist with advice and deed to restore peace, law and order in the territory of the Zulu Nation and to carry out the lawful rule of the Zulu Nation; to settle all disputes to promote peace and when all measures for friendly settlement have failed then at the head of an army to assist and with the sword to fight for the subjection of all rebels.

Therefore I bind myself with the advice of my councillors and headmen to cede to the principal leaders of the Boers a tract of country from the north-western part of Zululand bordering on the South African Republic and *as large as above-mentioned principal leaders may consider necessary* [author's italics] for establishing an independent self-government according to agreement. . . . My people and subjects who may live within such land will have to remove to other parts of Zululand and will not be allowed to live and to enter with the object of annoyance that part of the country as now ceded to the Boers. . . . And I bind myself with the advice of my councillors and headmen to be ready at all times to assist the Boers in any way whatsoever and to live with them in everlasting peace. . . . And never to call in any other power or Government without the consent of their Government.[7]

With this treaty in their pockets the Boers now sent a further commission to Sibebu demanding his immediate compliance. To their astonishment they found his attitude completely changed, for instead of submission there was now open defiance and a flat refusal to recognise Dinuzulu as King. 'He is not a King,' he said, 'but a dog and when he is hungry he may come to me.'[8] Further, he refused to deliver up either women or cattle, affirming that he was a British subject and would look to the British Government for assistance.

This peremptory reply to the Boer commission was no surprise to the Usutus; Sibebu was more or less acting in keeping with his previous conduct. On numerous occasions he had received instructions from the British Government to restore plunder which he had unlawfully seized but those instructions had always been treated with contempt, for he had felt secure in the knowledge that Dunn and Colenbrander, assisted by their filibusters, would always come to his aid and he knew the Resident Commissioner would invariably turn a blind eye to such proceedings.*

* It should be noted that Sibebu was quite independent of the British Government which had refused to place a Resident with him. Further, he had again and again broken almost every condition under which he had been made an independent chief. 'The Blue Books are full of remonstrances addressed to him by or on behalf of the Special Commissioner to the greater part of which he has never condescended to give a moment's attention.' (*Natal Witness*, leader, 14 June 1884.)

It was obvious that once again he was temporising, hoping that in some way or another his former white supporters would assist him. In this he made a fatal mistake. He was now dealing with resolute men. The Boers were determined that, come what may, this question should be settled quickly so that they should have full justification in claiming the territory they were so eager to acquire.

The day following the signing of the Treaty the majority of the Boers left Zalflaager and retired to a spot near to the Transvaal border where they awaited the return of the second deputation to Sibebu. Within a couple of days their friends brought back not only the news of Sibebu's defiance but also an urgent message from Ndabuko informing them that they must either join the Usutus without delay and aid them in crushing Sibebu or else leave the country and forfeit all claims to their farms.

This firm stand of Ndabuko resulted in an immediate decision by the Committee to send a body of a hundred picked men; they were to be accompanied by a small number of Germans from Luneberg under the leadership of Adolph Schiel,* who were placed in charge of a contingent of Transvaal natives anxious to throw in their lot with the Usutus.

By the following afternoon they reached Ukwebezi – about a mile from Mnyamana's kraal – where they were welcomed by a Usutu army of approximately 10,000 men. Their arrival greatly cheered these warriors. Without this Boer assistance many of them doubted the outcome of their conflict with Sibebu, knowing from experience how often they had been outwitted and out-generalled by him. Now their confidence revived and they marched off full of hope.

* Adolph Schiel, a young German from Frankfurt-am-Main, had come out to the Transvaal and joined his fellow-countrymen who had settled in and around Luneberg. Before the Boer entry into Zululand he had been engaged as a tutor in a Boer family for a small salary out of which he had to maintain a wife and family. Leaving this employment he joined up with the Boers and in the fight at Tshaneni, along with several other Germans from Luneberg, was placed in command of a contingent of Transvaal natives. For these services he was entitled to a picked farm. He was never Secretary to the New Republic nor did he hold any office under it, but for a short period after Tshaneni he acted as Secretary to Dinuzulu.

Information had been received from their scouts that Sibebu had retreated towards the extreme north-east of his territory, so a four days' march along a route parallel to the course of the Mkusi river lay ahead. It was hard going owing to serious drought, no water was obtainable for two days and many of the Usutus suffered severely.

Sibebu had taken up a strong position near a deep gorge in the Lebombo mountains through which the Mkusi river flows. On

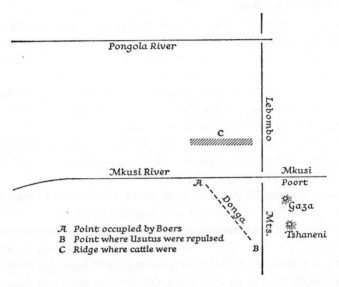

*The Battle of Tshaneni redrawn from* Natal Witness, *26 June 1884*

the southern side of this gap there are two lofty mountains, Gaza and Tshaneni, both covered with dense bush, the former culminating in a lofty peak, the latter in a dome of bald rock. Between the lower slopes of Tshaneni and the river, Sibebu had concealed the main body of his army; higher up and near the summit, also in hiding, were those who, through age or infirmity, were unable to bear arms. In front, running in a diagonal or south-eastern direction towards the mountain, was a deep, dry *donga* giving him protection from that quarter. Across the river, running westward, was a long ridge or spur behind which rose

D                    35

the great mass of the Ubombo mountain flanked by deep gorges of extremely dense bush. Here the wily general had hidden his great herds of cattle, his women and children; these were guarded by another section of his force. (See plan on previous page.)

His position had been carefully chosen; should he suffer defeat there was ample cover for any army in flight in the bush-clad mountains; should victory be his he could pursue his foes to destruction over the miles of dry, arid country which they would be compelled to cross.

As the Usutus approached (about 4 p.m., 5 June), supported by the mounted Boers, not a sign of the Mandhlakazi was to be seen, not the slightest indication of the fact that thousands of warriors were ready at a moment's notice to spring into action and hurl themselves with savage ferocity on their enemies. The Usutu were heading straight for the densely covered ambush where Sibebu had so cleverly concealed his army.

Suddenly a shot rang out. A Mandhlakazi traitor had given the warning to the advancing host and thus irretrievably shattered all Sibebu's carefully prepared plans.*

There can be little doubt that many of the Boers owed their lives to that shot, for Sibebu had instructed his men first to fire at the horses, thus bringing down their riders, and in the ensuing confusion to rush in with their death-dealing assegais. Once the Boers, his most formidable opponents, had been overcome he knew he had little to fear from the Usutus although they outnumbered him by nearly three to one.

That warning shot altered the whole course of the battle. Instantly the Usutus fell into formation – the usual chest and two horns†– only to find to their cost that the nature of this country was ill-suited for such tactics; no encircling movement was possible here owing to the limited space between mountain and river. As

---

* After the battle Sibebu dealt with this traitor. He was given a chopper and told to hack off one of his legs; whilst thus employed he was knocked on the head with a knobkerrie. (Told by one of Sibebu's old warriors to H. P. Braatvedt. See his *Roaming Zululand with a Native Commissioner*, p. 81.)

† The Zulu army was usually split into three groups: a large and compact central group forming what became known as the 'chest', with two smaller groups on each flank which were deployed into encircling 'horns'.

their right wing swept forward it met the full onslaught of Sibebu's army near the base of the hill. A fierce and bloody struggle ensued; no quarter was asked, none was given, but it was soon evident that the Mandhlakazi were gaining the upper hand. Cheered by the hope of victory they redoubled their efforts as they pushed back the enemy. Sensing defeat and seized with panic the Usutus suddenly turned tail and fled.

But the Mandhlakazi had yet to meet their most difficult task. Mounted on their horses, the Boers had taken up a position on some rising ground in the angle between the river and the *donga* and from this vantage point they had been quietly watching the struggle which had resulted in the rout of their allies. Realising that this was a critical moment they went into action. Taking their opportunity as the Mandhlakazi left the cover of the bush to pursue the fleeing Usutus across a clear open space, they poured a steady fire into them with such deadly effect that it soon became the turn of the Mandhlakazi to rush for cover. Their flight was the signal for the Usutus to rally and again they moved in to the attack, driving the enemy up the slopes of the mountain and thus cutting them off from all hope of retreat. The Mandhlakazi, greatly outnumbered, though fighting bravely to the last, were broken beyond recall.

Meanwhile, across the river, the AbaQulusi (another section of the Usutus) had stormed the ridge where the cattle and women and children were in hiding. Attacking with great ferocity they drove them headlong, scattering them in all directions, and thus gained an immense booty.

In an hour the battle was over and the rout complete. The remnants of the Mandhlakazi, attempting to escape across the river with its overgrown banks and deep pools, were either drowned or assegaied as they fled. The pursuit was unsparing and went on till night put an end to the carnage. Among the dead were no less than six of Sibebu's brothers beside many other members of his family.

In the closing stage of the battle three mounted men were sighted near a large rock on the slopes of the Ubombo mountain. They were Sibebu and two of his white advisers, Darke and

Eckersley. Immediately they were spotted an angry shout went up from the Usutus who raced up to kill them but by the time they reached the rock the men had vanished, lost in the dense bush which surrounded them.

Yet another glimpse of their hated enemy was granted to the Usutus. They saw him silhouetted against the sunset sky on the topmost peak of the mountain as he turned in grief to his companions and exclaimed, 'I have had my day: I wonder how I have lived so long, but Oh! my poor children.' With that he turned his horse and vanished in the gathering darkness.[9]

## CHAPTER 4

# The New Republic

THE pursuit of Sibebu's warriors continued for several days after the battle, but the main object of the Usutu search, Sibebu himself, managed to elude them. Disappointed, the Usutus turned on the trading stations of those white men who had assisted him and ruthlessly looted them, leaving them in ruins. Fortunately for themselves the owners had fled some days earlier, else they would certainly have been killed. However, the anger of the Usutus was in some measure assuaged by the rich booty they managed to capture – 60,000 head of cattle and a great number of women and children, some of whom were the womenfolk seized by Sibebu after his victory at Ulundi many months previously.

Meanwhile the Boer forces under Lucas Meyer had returned to their headquarters at Hlobane. News of the victory had preceded them with the result that great numbers of their fellow-countrymen had flocked in and the camp had now swelled to close on 1,000 people. Unfortunately a considerable rabble element had joined them, as often happens where a chance of loot appears, and still more unfortunately most of these were allowed to enrol as volunteers,[1] in spite of the fact that on 24 May the Boer Committee had passed a resolution to the effect that no more would be enlisted.[2] This rabble element now swept over Central Zululand and, intent on plunder, attacked many of the kraals, killed the occupants, seized their cattle, opened up their grain pits and loaded the contents onto their wagons irrespective of the fact that this meant starvation to an already impoverished people who had not been able to plant their crops for many months owing to the unsettled state of the country.[3] News of this vandalism quickly reached the ears of the Usutu leaders and it was with grave misgivings that they returned to Shumayeleni and reported it to

Mnyamana. Undoubtedly these acts by men who had taken no part in the subjugation of Sibebu roused very bitter feelings among the Usutus and stiffened their resistance to the Boer claims.

Meanwhile important developments had happened to Sibebu and the remnants of his defeated army. After vanishing in the dusk at the close of the battle he, together with Darke and Eckersley, had spent the night looking for a large cave where they could hide the remaining women and children who had gathered round them. It was the afternoon of the next day before one was found and there they all sought temporary refuge.[4] A number of Sibebu's followers arrived and an attempt was made to retreat toward the Pongola River. The move, however, was thwarted by Sambana, a Nywao chief* who had his men out on guard; thus Sibebu and those with him were compelled to retrace their steps.[5]

Two or three days later a small party was seen making its way to the Reserve and on the evening of 12 June three tired horsemen rode into Eshowe, Darke, Eckersley and Sibebu, the last reporting immediately to Osborn that he had been defeated by a combined force of Usutu and Boers. He had been attacked, he said, in his own territory without any cause; he had done nothing to provoke it. The Usutus, he continued, had gone over to the Boers; 'They belong to them and have helped them with an armed force against me.'[6]

Early the following morning Osborn wired to Sir Henry Bulwer: 'Sibebu arrived here at sunset on horseback accompanied by two white men. Reports he was attacked by Boers and Usutus 7 days ago; defeated with great loss; kraals burnt and cattle taken.'[7] To which the Governor replied, also by telegram: 'Am deeply concerned to hear of Sibebu's misfortune. Give him every hospitality in the Reserve.'[8] It is to be noted that no reference was made by Osborn to any duplicity by Sibebu.

On 21 June a second telegram was sent to the Governor: 'Sibebu extremely anxious to hear if you can render him assistance

---

* The Nywao tribe live in Northern Zululand, near the present Golela, on the borders of Swaziland. Sambana had taken a prominent part in the murder of Dingana many years earlier.

in recovering his territory; if you cannot do so he wishes to return at once.' Bulwer replied: 'Await letters. Sibebu could not get back to his country in safety.'[9]

In the meantime on 16 June Bulwer had forwarded to Lord Derby a garbled report extolling the virtues of Sibebu ('A Chief who has proved himself to possess as chivalrous and gallant a nature as the history of the Zulu nation can show') while considerably overstating the numbers of Boers employed in the attack (500–600) and roundly denouncing them for what he termed 'the first result of their declarations of peace and peaceful intentions'.[10] Again no mention was made of the intrigues of Sibebu.

This was followed by yet another dispatch dated 23 June in much the same vein ('an attack made without any provocation on the part of Sibebu' etc.) but to it was added a new element – that of alarm: 'There is nothing now to prevent the Usutus concentrating their whole strength against the Reserve and, even without aid from the Boers, carrying the work of destruction throughout the country.' It was the same old preliminary to an appeal for troops: 'The Usutus are free to attack the Reserve which will now require strong military assistance. If the Boers give active assistance this would be a declaration of hostilities against the British Government. The aim of the Usutus is the overthrow of the Reserve.'[11]

To these exaggerated and highly coloured reports Lord Derby sent the following sane and well-balanced reply:

Your communications assume that Sibebu is an ally to whom aid has been refused and that assistance has been withheld from a desire to avoid British loss of life and expense. This is not the view of H.M. Government. They do not consider that he was entitled to any assistance; if they had been under an obligation to him aid would not have been refused. In 1882 it was decided that Sibebu be left independent because he protested against being brought under Cetshwayo and represented that he could hold his own. . . . For some considerable period he has been at enmity with the Usutus and engaged in open hostilities against them. In 1883 these hostilities were revived, the King was attacked, defeated and driven into the Reserve as a fugitive.

In this invasion women were killed and the country of the Usutus was devastated. . . . In 1884 the war was renewed. At length the fortune of war was changed in favour of the Usutus with the assistance of certain Boer adventurers and Sibebu was defeated and obliged to fly into the Reserve. . . . You have striven to restore peace and your efforts have the approval of H.M. Government but beyond those endeavours, with the Reserve as a place of refuge for either party without distinction, H.M. Government does not perceive that it would have been right for them to intervene. . . . Sibebu has often acted on his own responsibility and his recent defeat was the consequence of his victory of 1883 and his ambitious projects of the present year and H.M. Government has never entered into any engagement to aid or defend him. All that he is entitled to is an asylum in the Reserve and it cannot be too clearly understood that his position of safety there must not be abused.[12]

Yet in spite of this clear directive no immediate steps were taken to put it into effect either by Bulwer or Osborn until 23 September when matters assumed such serious proportions that action *had* to be taken.

As soon as Sibebu had made his appeal for assistance he slipped out of the Reserve and made for the Umhlatusi River using this as a rallying point for his scattered forces, intending later to return with them to his territory. Here several Usutus were attacked and killed. On news of this reaching the Usutu leaders they quickly reassembled their *impis* and marched towards the Umhlatusi. But the Boers intervened and ordered them back to their kraals. They were determined not to allow a conflict in such close proximity to the Reserve, being well aware that should Sibebu be attacked he would retreat into that territory; it would then be impossible to restrain the Usutus and a violation of the Reserve would result; this they were desperately anxious to avoid in view of the complications that would then arise between them and the British Government.[13]

Events turned out as they anticipated. Sibebu, hearing of the approach of the Usutus and the Boers, fled precipitately with his people into the sanctuary of the Reserve to be welcomed once again by Osborn who settled him and his people at a spot between

Middledrift and the Nkandhla.* This time, however, Sibebu was given to understand, on Bulwer's instructions, that he must scrupulously respect the authority and hospitality of the territory and refrain from any hostile proceedings against the Usutus or others.[14]

As the Reserve figures so largely in the conflict between Osborn and the Usutus it will be well to consider the actual state of the territory at this time. The *official* view, which was continually being pressed on the Home Government was that it was 'a great success were it not for the Usutus who, encouraged by their Dutch allies, invade it and persecute the loyal inhabitants', whereas the *real* state of affairs appeared to be just the opposite for it had 'never been anything but a seething mass of discontent, the presence of which has been as far as possible concealed from public observation',[15] and although constantly depicted in official dispatches as being loyal to Osborn was in truth 'almost wholly on the side of the King's party'.[16] It must also be remembered that the whole of the Nkandhla (an area which split the Reserve in half) after Osborn's defeat was entirely in the possession of the Usutus.

The Boers for their part, whilst scrupulously observing the boundaries of this territory, nevertheless criticised its administration in the most scathing terms, stating emphatically that it could not be left in its present anomalous condition but should without delay be replaced by a strong, firm government; otherwise it would become the refuge of all the disaffected spirits of Zululand and form a rallying point for those who lived by plotting and disturbance. That the Boers were right in their forecast is only too obvious from official dispatches which record numerous raids from various gangs of freebooters who acknowledged no authority, not even that of the Usutu leaders. In most cases these forays were motivated by sheer necessity and were carried out by men driven

---

* It is interesting to note that the area allotted to Sibebu was near the spot where Osborn wished to establish a strong military post, Fort Yolland or Esungulweni (near Entumeni, about fourteen miles from Eshowe). The district was occupied by the relatively small group of people who were loyal to Osborn. Thus, with this area as a base the Usutus who held Nkandhla could be attacked.

desperate by the pangs of hunger, for, owing to the shocking condition of the country, they had been unable to plant any crops and most of their cattle had been plundered.

At about this time the Boers, through the Sub-Commissioner in Zululand, attempted to make approaches 'not unfriendly' to the British Government with a view to the settlement of the Usutu question. They were fully prepared not only to guarantee the integrity of the Reserve but to enter into negotiations regarding the settlement of Central Zululand. Bulwer also urged upon Great Britain the necessity of recognising Boer intervention, but all attempts at reconciliation were shattered, first, by the uncompromising attitude of Osborn who resented any interference with his authority and cold-shouldered all efforts towards a peaceful settlement that did not coincide with his own personal views, and secondly, by the callous indifference of the Home Government to the tragic state of Central Zululand and their emphatic refusal to intervene. As a result the Boers naturally came to the conclusion that the Government did not care and left them to do as they pleased. This was exactly what they wanted, to be left with a free hand, and, up to a point, they cannot be blamed for acting as they did. Unfortunately, after the defeat of Sibebu, the rabble element under the leadership of Swart Dirk Uys gained the upper hand (owing to further enrolments being allowed after Tshaneni) and these men by sheer force of numbers overrode the more moderate counsels of Lucas Meyer with the result that many excesses took place, discipline became non-existent and all ideas of bringing peace and order to the land were forgotten in the mad desire of everyone to seize a farm and stock it with cattle plundered from the Usutus. It was a time of unparalleled vandalism and grave suffering.

In the midst of this chaos another figure returned to the scene to help make the confusion worse. William Grant re-emerged from his obscurity in Durban to take up the post of adviser to the Usutu leaders. This man had first entered Zulu affairs during the closing months of Cetshwayo's life when he held a similar post under that unfortunate king. Soon, however, he became *persona non grata* to

Osborn and was ordered out of Zululand. His name reappears on 9 February 1884, the day after Cetshwayo's death, when Ndabuko applied to Osborn for a pass to send two messengers to Grant to inform him of the circumstances of the King's death. This request was refused but a month later, on 3 March, we are told 'Mtokwan arrived from Zululand', having been sent by Mnyamana and Ndabuko with the message: 'Go to our father Grant and tell him ever since we have been at Eshowe we have been in trouble. . . . Cetshwayo's last words were "Take Dinuzulu and give him to my father Grant to present him to the authorities." '*

This messenger on his return reported to Mnyamana that it was impossible for Grant 'to present Dinuzulu to the authorities' owing to the ban on his re-entering Zululand and he also added the startling news that at Grant's in Durban on 4 March he had seen two Boers, one of whom was Wilhelm.† An account of this interview is given us by Grant himself in a letter dated 4 August 1885 which he wrote to Sir Henry Bulwer. In it he says, *inter alia*:

During the early part of last year two gentlemen deputed by the Boer leaders waited upon me in Durban. After the interview I wrote the following minute, copy of which I handed to the deputation. A body of Boers are about to organise for the purpose of establishing peace and order in Zululand. . . . Failing any immediate action on the part of the English Government this force will subdue all turbulent chiefs and inaugurate a fixed government in Zululand under the hereditary Chief and rightful heir to the Zulu throne. . . . That in consideration of the services which it is thus proposed to render they, through their rightful Chief, agree to allow such Boers the peaceful occupation of certain farms known as the Disputed Territory. . . . That in virtue of the position I held under the late King and under the belief that my advice and counsel would be followed by the heir and chiefs, I have been called upon to advise and if practicable to aid by my recommendations the carrying into effect the foregoing proposals. In reply to a pressing request that I should visit the Boers in the capacity of adviser to the Zulus I stated that in the month of October 1883 I was peremptorily ordered to leave the country and I should not attempt to return without

---

* The following particulars, except where otherwise stated, are taken from Grant's Diary.

† An accredited agent of the Boers.

the permission of the Government. I declined to express any opinion in regard to the Boer movement without conference with the heads of the Zulu nation.*[17]

On 15 April other messengers from Ndabuko reached Grant with the report that 'They were removing the remains of the King and wished very much that I would go up', but again he had to reply (on 26 April) that it was impossible as 'he had been ordered out of the Reserve and could not see an open door to pass over the Umhlatuze.' However, on the same day he wrote a letter to the Governor, Sir Henry Bulwer, in which he asked 'whether he was at liberty to pass through the Zulu Native Reserve in order to comply with the request of the leading men in Zululand.' To this appeal the Colonial Secretary, on instructions from Bulwer, replied (on 5 May) 'You must be aware that His Excellency cannot prevent you from going where you choose and that you

* This is a startling document for the following reasons:

1. It reveals that certain of the Boers must have drawn up their plan of campaign for the occupation of the Disputed Territory, by force of arms if necessary, *before Meyer and van Staden had set out to interview Mnyamana and Ndabuko*, for Grant explicitly gives us the date of this Durban interview with Wilhelm as *4 March 1884* (B.B. C4645, Encl. 3 in No. 21, p. 34). On this date Wilhelm stated that the Usutus 'through their rightful Chief' *had already agreed* to grant them the Disputed Territory. This was utterly impossible, for no agreement was reached with Mnyamana and Ndabuko until considerably later, but it indicates only too clearly the cleverly conceived plan of Meyer and van Staden to get Dinuzulu away from Mnyamana so that they could exert pressure on him to promise them the Disputed Territory in return for their making him King.

2. It is stated that Grant was called upon 'to advise and aid by his recommendations the carrying into effect of the foregoing proposals': that it was 'a pressing request' that he should visit the Boers. In actual fact when Grant reached Zululand and attempted to act as mediator between the Zulus and the Boers the latter mistrusted him and would have nothing to do with him for several days. It was only later after being backed by Krogh and Wilhelm that he was accepted by them.

3. Grant explicitly states that 'he declined to express any opinion in regard to the Boer movement' without consultation with the Zulu leaders. Yet the Dispatch Book of Melmoth Osborn, under the date 4 Sept. 1885, states that when Wilhelm told Grant 'That the Boers would use forceful means to subdue Sibebu for which services they would claim a cession of Zululand', *Grant agreed to this* and 'undertook to report favourably to the Aborigines Society, thus influencing the House of Commons, and gave Wilhelm a signed Memorandum.'

therefore require no permission.'[18] Within a couple of days of the receipt of this letter (on 8 May) two messengers (Magoff and Koliwe) again came from Ndabuko and his brothers giving an account of the burial of Cetshwayo and urging Grant:

To come and look after us for we have no one to direct us, to see all that transpires and report for we know that a great many lies are told of us. Mnyamana wants you to take charge of Dinuzulu who has been left in his care by the King: he says 'I have taken Dinuzulu because he was sleeping in the bush but I shall give him to Grant as soon as he arrives.'[19]

Grant now decided to move to Zululand at the earliest opportunity and on 26 June he left Durban, arriving on 23 July at the Ceza mountain in the Bhekamusi valley where he found Mnyamana, Ndabuko and several chiefs. In the meantime he had sent a message to Dabulamanzi, who was at his kraal in the Reserve, telling him 'to sit perfectly still in the Nkandhla and to send word to Osborn that they had no intention of defying the Queen and would pay all their taxes if allowed time'; under no circumstances were they to make any further attacks on those loyal to the Commissioner.

On the day that Grant left Durban an approach was made to Osborn on Dinuzulu's behalf for the restoration of the Reserve to the Usutus. Schiel, as Secretary to Dinuzulu, accompanied by Frederik Meyer, his interpreter, and two Zulu headmen, Zeizi and Sibamu, presented a formal document to the Commissioner requesting this transfer of land, which, stated Dinuzulu, 'was promised my father the late Cetshwayo'. Should the delegates fail in their petition to Osborn they were instructed to proceed to the Governor 'and in my name to represent my interests to H.M. Government through His Excellency'.[20] The request was made 'in a friendly manner, not as a demand', but it is obvious from the way in which it was presented that little hope was entertained of its success. As was to be expected the Commissioner bluntly refused to consider it and so definite was its rejection that Schiel realised the uselessness of attempting to take the matter further.

Meanwhile trouble had broken out in the Boer camp, for the number of claimants for farms had now risen to over 1,000. Thus the handful of men who had actually taken part in the defeat of Sibebu was completely swamped by this freebooting element who were making the most outrageous demands, even though not one of them had rendered the slightest assistance to the Usutu cause.

News of their demands in due course reached the ears of the Usutu leaders and this naturally aroused feelings of bitter resentment; Mnyamana was particularly forthright in his opposition and, to prevent Dinuzulu from being unduly influenced by this old warrior, Conrad Meyer again took him to his farm on the Bevaan River, ostensibly to protect him from possible injury, but in reality to get him away from the Usutu opposition.

Daily the situation deteriorated, demanding more than ever before the immediate intervention of Britain, an intervention which would undoubtedly have been welcomed by the more moderate section of the Boers, but the British Government refused to move, leaving the stricken Zulus to their fate. A writer commented bitterly: 'The Boers in the Orange Free State and the Transvaal hate us for our cowardice and policy. The people of the Cape detest us and the natives of Zululand mistrust us.'[21]

The day after Grant's arrival thirty Boers headed by Lucas Meyer arrived at Ceza and the following morning (25 July) ten of their number held an interview with Mnyamana, Ndabuko and Siwetu during which they demanded an immediate settlement of the question of the land they were to receive in return for the services rendered. To this the Usutus replied: 'The country is still unsettled, the people are still in the bush and those who remain in Sibebu's country continue to kill. . . . What sort of friends are you that while the country is as it is you come and talk as you do?'[22]

The wrangling continued for many hours, the Boers exerting every effort to reach a settlement, arguing, cajoling, threatening, yet always with the same result – an unqualified rejection of all their claims. At last, realising the futility of further discussion, they returned to their laager near Mkuzi, thirty-five miles away.

It is important to note that Grant, though camped near by and readily available, was excluded from these proceedings by the Boers who regarded him with suspicion, considering him as a sort of British spy.[23]

Three days later Mnyamana and Ndabuko called on Grant in his tent and it was at this interview that he heard of the document signed by the Boers and Usutus on 23 May by which the Usutus had ceded to the Boers as much land 'as they considered necessary' to form a New Republic.

Meanwhile the Boers, although temporarily thwarted by the refusal of the Usutus, became more determined than ever to insist on their claims. Pressure had already been exerted on Dinuzulu, then at Conrad Meyer's farm, and he had been persuaded to accept the Boer terms. Probably this had not been too difficult a task, for owing to youthful ignorance (as already stated, he was only sixteen) he certainly did not at the time realise the far-reaching implications of his consent.

It was now decided by some of the Boer leaders to try to get Grant on their side. If they could achieve this they felt certain that a settlement could be forced on the Usutus. To this end Krogh and Wilhelm exerted all their powers of persuasion to overcome the prejudice felt by some of their countrymen against him.[24] Their efforts met with a measure of success, and a few days later several of the Boers called on Grant 'in a friendly way'[25] and had a long private talk with him. In course of this interview the Boers revealed: 'That they thought that the committee would be satisfied if they secured 3 million acres of land, a right of road to the coast and the appointment of a Boer Resident.'[26] It is evident that the extremists had won the day, for from this point onwards even Lucas Meyer and his more moderate followers were at one with the majority in their rapacious demands.

Grant's reply was:

That the late King Cetshwayo was restored under conditions which prevented the sale or alienation of land and that the sea-coast rights were also reserved by the British Government and that as the Zulus were a conquered people without any sovereign rights in the land the sanction of the British Government was necessary before they could obtain a valid title.[27]

To this the Boers, whilst admitting that Cetshwayo was restored under certain conditions, one of which was that he should not alienate any portion of the land, argued that 'As he had been overthrown by Sibebu and the country had been in a state of anarchy without any interference whatever by the English Government, that Government had thereby forfeited all claim to it and had practically abandoned it.'[28]

Undoubtedly Grant, in Zululand expressly to act as adviser to the Usutus, was placed in a most difficult situation. On the one hand he realised that lacking real leadership and utterly demoralised, they had in their ignorance and folly attached their signatures to what amounted to a blank cheque on the alienation of their country. On the other hand, here were 800 to 1,000 Boers, the great majority of whom had done nothing to assist the Usutus, all well armed, already in virtual possession of the land, determined to crush any opposition – by force of arms if necessary – and compel these almost defenceless people to submit to their unjust and exorbitant claims. Worst of all, England, to whom the Zulus looked for guidance and help, stood by in callous indifference, ignoring the fate of a fine nation that she had brought to the verge of ruin. All that Grant could say in reply was that possibly England might agree to the alienation of a portion of the country if some satisfactory arrangement could be concluded with the Usutus.

Whilst these negotiations were being carried on numerous official dispatches were passing to and fro between Bulwer and England, and in one of them, dated 4 August 1884,[29] he reported that, according to Osborn, numerous raids had again taken place on the Reserve. This is a somewhat revealing document in which Bulwer complains that 'there is no properly established authority across the Umhlatuzi'; for though the Boers state that 'they would neither attack the Reserve themselves nor allow the Usutus to do so', yet raids were being carried out at frequent intervals, indicating that they had little or no control over the land. Thus the Usutu complaint that the whole country was still in a state of upheaval and their refusal to consider Boer demands were more than justified.

On the day that Bulwer wrote this dispatch Dinuzulu was

Dinuzulu at the age of
nineteen

Ndabuko, Dinuzulu's uncle

General Lucas Meyer

Melmoth Osborn

allowed to return to his own people at Ceza with instructions to summon all the Usutu leaders to another meeting to be held at Mkuzi on 9 August, when the question of the land cession would have to be settled.

Accordingly the Usutu leaders, along with Grant, made their way to the Boer laager where several interviews were held before the actual meeting took place, with a view to paving the way towards a settlement. At 2 p.m. on 9 August Lucas Meyer taking the chair opened the proceedings.*

Then Mnyamana, speaking through Hemulana on account of his infirmity, recapitulated the course of events from the first interview of van Staden and C. F. Meyer with the Usutu leaders. It was at this point that Landdrost Krogh challenged van Staden, stating emphatically that he never gave the order to take Dinuzulu to Wakkerstroom. After an acrimonious dispute during which Meyer rejected the Zulu offer of land as being insufficient for their needs, the Usutus asserted, 'We did not invite all these men; why should we give farms to old men and little children in the laager? Only a small number fought. Uhamu is still troublesome and the King's cattle have not been returned. . . . Now we see that we are being forced by the Boers. We never knew that wages were taken by force but always given.'[30] To which Meyer replied, 'We can't protect the country against foreign enemies with the 100 men who fought against Sibebu',[31] but the Usutus remained adamant in their rejection of the Boer claims and the meeting closed with a decision as far away as ever.

Two days later (11 August) the whole company reassembled and Meyer stated that he and his people wanted an answer that day. Mnyamana answered that they were prepared to concede a slightly larger area of territory but no more, adding, 'We can't give land to all those people who came after the rout of Sibebu. The understanding was that we should simply pay those who

---

* There are several records of these proceedings in B.B. C4645: there is Grant's version (Grant's letter to Bulwer, No. 21, pp. 30–3); Report of Schiel (Secretary to Dinuzulu) to the Sub-Commissioner Cardew (Encl. 1 in 56, pp. 80–4); Schiel's Minutes of the meetings, approved by Dinuzulu (Encl. 2 in 56). Reference is also made in the Memorandum of Esselen (Secretary to Boer Committee) to the Colonial Office (Encl. 1 in 30, pp. 45–8).

fought with us on that day and we think that their services have been sufficiently paid; we stick to this.'[32]

Further argument was useless; the Usutus were inflexible. The Boers then became clamorous and threatened to enforce their demands, Esselen* saying, 'If the Kaffirs will not give up the farms willingly we must take them by force and bring the Kaffirs to their duty.'[33] It was all to no purpose, the Usutus would not yield and the meeting ended in confusion.

Careful note must be made of the fact that right up to this point the Boers had still refused to allow Grant to be present at any of the interviews in spite of the repeated requests of the Usutus.[34]

It was now decided to adopt sterner measures: the Boers would return to their headquarters at Hlobane where they knew their numbers would be greatly augmented by many of their countrymen, all with one aim – the acquisition of a farm in Zululand.

The Usutu leaders, along with Grant, followed and it is significant that now, instead of rebuffs, Grant met with every courtesy from the Boers. On arrival he was requested to pitch his tent alongside that of Lucas Meyer himself;[35] he was supplied with a copy of the Agreement of 23 May; he was informed that the contents of this document had been fully explained to the Usutus; he was treated with marked friendliness and hospitality. All this had its effect as future events show, for from that day a complete transformation took place in all the negotiations. Henceforward the Usutu leaders were ignored and proceedings were conducted through Grant and Dinuzulu alone, the former being publicly proclaimed as 'the representative and adviser of the Zulu nation'. (Up to this point 'strong influence had been used, even from official circles in Natal, to induce the Boer Executive not to receive Mr Grant or to recognise him in any way and for some time there was great opposition to him on the Boer Executive. . . . This opposition was eventually overcome because it was found that the Zulus would consent to no final settlement unless Mr Grant was present.'[36] As soon as his recognition by the Executive was

---

* At this time Esselen was secretary to Meyer; later he became Secretary to the New Republic.

acknowledged Grant supported the Boer claims and agreed to the seizure of the territory.)*

The Boers were now in an immensely strong position; behind their leaders stood at least 800 armed men whom they would not hesitate to use should the Usutu leaders refuse to agree to their terms, and Grant and Dinuzulu were clay in their hands.

Events moved swiftly. The Usutu leaders were summoned and presented with the following ultimatum by Lucas Meyer:

Whereas every endeavour has been made on the part of the Government of the New Republic to obtain from you the lands required by it as per Treaty to enable it to attain the restoration of peace and quietness, and whereas you have hitherto still refused to comply with the Treaty entered into with it:

NOW THEREFORE it is compelled to take the government of Zululand in its own hands and thereby to promote the peace, welfare and happiness of the Zulu nation and to secure the safety of the neighbouring states.[37]

Next, Grant was summoned to a meeting of the Boer Executive presided over by Lucas Meyer. No Usutus were permitted to attend. A carefully prepared Proclamation was read out and Grant was informed that the Usutu leaders had already been asked to signify their acceptance of this document but, being ignorant of its contents, they had steadfastly refused to do so until an opportunity had been given them to consult their so-called adviser (in whom, unfortunately for themselves, they still put their trust). At Grant's request the meeting adjourned for two hours to enable him to consult his clients and a copy of the Proclamation was handed to him.

What happened in those momentous two hours can readily be surmised. The Usutus were completely ignorant as to the amount of land demanded of them; cowed and defenceless in the face of overwhelming odds, knowing that refusal would bring upon them the wrath of over 800 armed men; led by a cowardly and treacherous 'adviser' who was 'afraid the Boers would fire upon him', as he later admitted to one of their number[38]– what loophole

* See Appendix III, 'Grant's support of Boer claims'.

of escape was there for them? Distrust in their adviser was already stirring and their resentment against the dishonest and unjust claims of the Boers roused them to make one last stand in defence of their rights – Grant and Dinuzulu could sign but not a single one of them would signify his acceptance of that Proclamation.

So, angry and exasperated, they watched Grant disappear into the tent where he and Dinuzulu appended their signatures to the following document which took from the Usutus so much of the land for which they and many of their countrymen had bravely fought and nobly died:

Be it hereby made known that I, Dinuzulu, King of the Zulu nation and of Zululand, with advice and consultation of William Grant, Representative and Adviser of the Zulu nation, and of my principal Counsellors and Chiefs, proclaim and make known that I, in conjunction with my said Counsellors and Chiefs, have granted to a certain number of South African farmers in Zululand, for their free use and as their property, a certain portion of Zululand, bounding on the South African Republic and the Reserve Territory, in extent more or less 1,355,000 (One million three hundred and fifty five thousand) morgen, with the right to establish there an independent republic, called the New Republic, and I further proclaim that from this date the remaining portion of Zululand and the Zulu Nation shall be subject to the supervision of the said New Republic.

Given under my hand at Hlobane in the New Republic on this 16th day of August, 1884.

(Signed)  DINUZULU<br>WILLIAM GRANT

*WITNESSES*
S. C. KROGH
D. J. ESSELEN[39]

❧

## CHAPTER 5

# The Rape of Zululand

A CAREFUL survey of the question of the land cession will make the reason for the Usutu intransigence more readily understood. To begin with it is essential to have a clear picture of the amount of territory the Usutus were willing to concede in return for Boer aid in the subjugation of Sibebu. The *original* territory offered was bounded by the line of Nkande, the Zungeni mountain, Celebantu to the Pemvane River. This offer was flatly rejected by the Boers as being totally insufficient and on their adopting a threatening attitude against the Usutus, the line was altered, on Krogh's recommendation, from the Pemvane to the Bivane River, thus making the area to be ceded considerably greater.

When the Usutus signified their assent to this increased grant Krogh told Mnyamana, 'Stick to this line and give no more land.' This is vouched for by Martin Lutuli who overheard Krogh making this remark.[1] It is to this line that the Usutus adhered with the greatest persistence and when the Proclamation was signed there can be little doubt that this was the line, with possible slight variations, that was understood by the Usutus to have been accepted by the Boers.

Looking at the question from the Boer standpoint it is of paramount importance to note that no clear indication was given by them as to how far the acquired territory would extend, for *no definite boundaries were laid down*, the Proclamation merely stating: 'A certain portion of Zululand bounding on the South African Republic and the Reserve Territory, in extent more or less 1,355,000 morgen [approx. 2,720,000 acres].'

This area had been calculated by the Boers on the basis of 240 farms of 1,000 *morgen* each and 560 farms of 2,000 *morgen* each, a total of 800 farms in all. This fact that all 800 Boers were to receive farms was carefully concealed in the Proclamation, the total acreage only being stated, yet it was the granting of farms to any but the 100 odd men who helped them in their conflict with Sibebu which the Usutus contested. This undoubtedly accounts for their refusal to sign the document, for the fact that no definite boundary line was indicated caused them serious misgivings and it is obvious that they had no idea as to the amount of territory involved.

Further, though Grant states emphatically that he made a full explanation to the Usutus it was an utter impossibility for him to have done so when *he himself had no idea that the territory claimed by the Boers would comprise practically the whole of Zululand.* This is confirmed by a remark he made later to the German missionary Stalbom that:

He was not aware that the 1,350,000 morgen, more or less, mentioned in the Proclamation would extend further east than a line drawn from the lowest Bivane Drift to the Umnyati Mission Station, thence through Tabankulu to the Reserve.[2]

Thus Grant signed not only in total ignorance of the extent of territory involved, but also from the fear of armed intervention by the Boers. This he admitted in his letter to Sir H. Bulwer; he signed because 'The Boers asserted their determination to enforce, by arms if necessary, what they deemed their just claims.'[3]

It is a startling fact, and one that is not generally recognised, that not a single person who was in any way connected with the signing of this document had the slightest idea as to how far the territory claimed would extend. This is made obvious by a careful study of later reports and events.

The Boers themselves had no conception that the area claimed would necessitate the occupation of so large a portion of Zululand; they originally believed that the boundary of the ceded territory would extend roughly along the line Babanango, Inhlazatye, Ngome and thence to the Bivane River. This is confirmed by Sir H. Bulwer in his dispatch to Lord Derby in which he states *inter alia*:

It was supposed at one time that this territory would come down to a line drawn from the Babanango Hill to the Inhlazatye, thence to the Ngome and thence to some point on the Bivana River. *That was the extent of territory originally contemplated by the Boers* [author's italics].[4]

Indirect corroboration comes from an interesting little sketch map indicating the suggested sub-division of the country by the signing of the Proclamation. It is reproduced below:

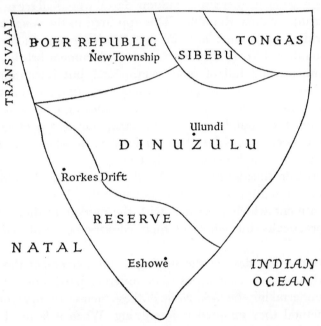

*Zululand as affected by the new arrangement between the Boers and the Zulus,*
Natal Witness, *26 August, 1884*

Moreover, Ndabuko in his statement to Sir Arthur Havelock, Bulwer's successor as Governor of Natal, on 7 May 1886 stated that:

The boundary discussed between the Boers and Grant was from the Nkande, along the western end of Inhlazatye mountain to the eastern end of Uhamu's country, taking in all his district, *leaving the whole eastern portion of Zululand free.*\*[5]

\* Author's italics. See also B.B. C4214, Encl. 1 in 53, where it is stated by Sub-Commissioner Pretorius to Sir Henry Bulwer: 'The Usutus will retain possession of the remainder of Central Zululand.'

Dinuzulu also 'Was not acquainted with anything but that in holding the feather [pen] he was giving the boundary we have described', and Ndabuko summed up the firm belief of every Usutu leader by stating, 'All thought it [the Proclamation] referred to the boundaries they had given.'[6]

On the very day the agreement was signed (16 August) Lucas Meyer issued a further Proclamation 'To all who shall see or hear', setting up the New Republic. This appeared in the *Natal Witness* on Friday 29 August and in the *Natal Mercury* on Tuesday 2 September 1884. It is an extraordinary document bristling with inaccuracies and full of pious sentiment,* but it contains the following sentence in parenthesis, which is of supreme importance to the question under consideration: 'Lines and beacons to be fixed after the ground has been inspected.' This is a positive proof that the Boers themselves had no idea as to where the boundaries of the New Republic would be.

There can thus be little wonder that the Usutus showed deep and bitter resentment at the way in which they had been tricked, a resentment which increased with the passage of time as they saw practically the whole of their country being filched from them.

Within a few days of the signing of the agreement the Boers started to survey their farms, four different parties of four men each undertaking the task. None of these men were surveyors and the method they adopted is interesting. When a farm of 4,000 acres had to be surveyed, one of these men, on horseback, would ride at a walking pace for forty-nine minutes on each side of a square and land so enclosed was marked with the appropriate beacons. Each farm so surveyed was numbered and when the whole 800 had been marked out a lottery was to be held. Each man eligible would draw a ticket with the number of a farm on it and the farm would be his.[7]

For a few weeks the country was quiet as the Usutu leaders returned to their kraals; it was the lull before the storm, for as more and more land was seized so resentment increased and by the end of November feelings were at boiling point as the Usutus

* See Appendix IV for the text.

began to realise the vast extent of territory claimed in the cession and the stranglehold placed upon them by 800 Boers with rifles in their hands.

As the survey was continued the Boers soon discovered that the territory bounded by the line Babanango, Inhlazatye, Ngome was totally insufficient for their needs; so a meeting was summoned for 8 January 1885 at which it was resolved to go right ahead with the work, irrespective of all previously suggested boundaries and without any further consultation with the Usutus, until the whole 800 farms had been beaconed off.

The Usutus, deeply resenting this, decided to appeal to the Boer leaders at Hlobane, only to be told that nothing could be done. Ndabuko was then sent on to Wakkerstroom where he was instructed to put their case before the Government of the South African Republic. He was informed that 'It was not a matter of the Transvaal Government, it was the Boers of Lucas Meyer, not the Boers of the Transvaal Government who had taken the country.'[8]

Tension increased daily as the tactics adopted by the Boers were callous in the extreme. When they were asked what the Usutus would do for land they replied bluntly, 'It was no business of theirs; they can live on our farms as tenants subject to servitudes of rent or labour.'[9]

Meanwhile resentment against the Natal officials was also growing, once again owing to the foolish behaviour of the Resident Commissioner in his dealings with the Nkandhla situation. During the month of August Dinuzulu had sent a present of five oxen to him with the request that certain selected men be allowed to remain in that area as guardians of Cetshwayo's grave. The request was rejected on the grounds of Usutu hostility to British administration and the Usutus were informed that Osborn himself would shortly be proceeding to the Nkandhla to receive the submission of all the chiefs. Meanwhile he made the most elaborate preparations, gathering together a small army as if for a military expedition; a force of 200 cavalry, 200 infantry, a large body of loyal natives plus another force to join them from the north, together with 100 mounted Hlubis. Undoubtedly it was Osborn's intention to use this large force against the Usutus should they show the slightest opposition.

Fortunately, sanction for this military move had first to be obtained from the Governor, Sir Henry Bulwer, and this was not merely refused but Osborn was severely rebuked:

It is most to be desired that a settlement of this question should be effected in a peaceful and quiet manner. . . . No effort should be spared to this end. As the employment of troops is a measure to which resort should not be had without the strongest necessity I think it will be well that the Lt-General should have the opportunity of entering into direct communication with any of the native chiefs in respect of whose attitude the advance is necessitated.[10]

It would be well at this point to consider Osborn's attitude to the many Usutus who were living in the Reserve whom he chose to regard as rebels to British authority; the resentment of these people can then be more readily understood.

First, hostility was shown to any Usutu residing in the Reserve who acknowledged Dinuzulu as the rightful successor to Cetshwayo and professed allegiance to him. All such, the Resident decided, should be driven out to seek new homes beyond the Umhlatuzi. This attitude was not only unjust but one that inflicted great hardship on many, for though the Reserve was established in the first instance for those who disagreed with the restoration of Cetshwayo, it must never be forgotten that many who were loyal to the late King and who now transferred that same allegiance to his heir Dinuzulu, had their kraals in that territory long before it was declared a Reserve. These were their homes, the homes of their forbears, lands which had been granted to them by their kings for loyal service to their country, lands to which they had a right and lawful claim. Dabulamanzi, one of Cetshwayo's bravest warriors, was a case in point; Sigananda was another and there were many more.

To drive these people out and to regard them as rebels because of their continued loyalty to the Zulu Royal House was iniquitous. They were certainly *not* disloyal to the Queen; as a matter of fact they made frequent attempts to petition her and present their grievances before the British Government in England, but every attempt was crushed by the man who knew only too well that should any impartial inquiry be held he would lose his job.

Another reason why many were attached to the Reserve was to see that the grave of Cetshwayo was guarded from desecration, for that grave was – and still is – regarded as one of the most sacred spots in Zululand. The graves of their Kings were very hallowed places, closely associated with their religious beliefs, and they did not wish to see Cetshwayo's grave desecrated as had been done by certain unscrupulous British treasure-seekers in the case of Mpande, a disgraceful blot on the name of Britain.* Rather than see such a thing happen again they were willing to fight and die.

Fortunately Osborn's rebuke by Bulwer bore fruit and no military action was taken, for the time being at any rate, but the bitterness remained and Usutu resentment was exacerbated by the refusal to allow their accredited representatives to be recognised as guardians of Cetshwayo's grave.

Meanwhile the Boers were proceeding with their seizure of the country, even taking possession of old-established mission stations such as KwaMagwaza and St Paul's, driving out the occupants and disregarding all the missionaries' appeals. At the former station they had placed Wilhelm to act as one of their commissioners. All along the borders of the Reserve the surveyors were busy and before long had reached the coast, an objective which they were very anxious to attain, for one of the cherished ideas of the Transvaal Boers had always been to secure a port.

As news of these proceedings reached the ears of Sir Henry Bulwer he sent an impassioned appeal to London for British intervention, pointing out the serious repercussions the Boer occupation would have on the people of Natal: not only would it mean the closing of all outlets between Natal and the native territories to the north but it would prevent the many Zulus living in the towns from returning to their homes as they often wished to do; this seizure of their homelands was causing grave unrest. The Governor concluded by saying: 'On behalf of the interests of the Zulu people and on behalf of the interests of Natal I would urge that such an

* See B.B. C4274, p. 49: 'The chair on which he [Mpande] sat was seen in Pietermaritzburg' – one of the personal possessions which was buried with him.

occupation of the Zulu country as is now threatened may be prevented.'[11]

The Natal colonists also took up the cudgels on behalf of the Zulus:

Emphatically and unhesitatingly asserting that humanity demands that something should be done to mitigate the great evil now present amongst the unhappy Zulu people and to avert the still greater evil impending, the annihilation of the race. The protecting hand of H.M.'s Government is urgently required by the Zulus and nothing short of the government of their country by British magistrates will save them from becoming the prey, on the plea of friendship, of the present Boer occupants of Zululand.[12]

This petition was signed by over 2,000 of the leading citizens of Natal and forwarded to London on 30 March 1885.

It was followed in July of the same year by a resolution of the Legislative Council that 'In the opinion of the Legislative Council it is desirable that H.M.'s rule should be at once extended over the whole of Zululand.'[13]

Britain again disregarded these appeals, taking notice only of the small area around St Lucia Bay. In October 1843 King Mpande had made a grant to Britain of this bay and the land immediately surrounding it, and now that it was threatened by the Boers Commander Moore of H.M.S. *Goshawk* was ordered to proceed there, erect flagstaffs, hoist the Union Jack and leave signboards on which were posted the words 'British Territory'. This was carried out on 18 December 1884.

There ensued a lengthy dispute with the Boers on this question and although they attempted to inveigle Germany to take their part she would have nothing to do with it since she had about this time concluded an agreement with Britain defining the respective spheres of action of the two countries on the coasts of Africa. Britain therefore sent a strongly worded note to the Boers, declaring her title to St Lucia and the adjacent territory as valid and informing them that Boer occupancy would not be permitted.[14]

Lucas Meyer, as President of the New Republic, 'most solemnly protested against the aforesaid acts of Commander Moore'[15] and ordered his men to carry on with the survey of plots for a township and with the sub-division of farms in that area. This was typical of Boer arrogance at this period, yet how they anticipated being able to substantiate their claims is beyond comprehension: the Treasury of the New Republic was empty and at a meeting on 5 April 1885 summoning the burghers for commando purposes although 250 were called out only seventy turned up.[16]

Others at this time were casting longing eyes on the rich and fertile native areas of South Africa and one morning in the early winter of 1885 there appeared at the kraal of Dinuzulu a certain Emil Nagel, a German, who suavely introduced himself to the Usutu leaders, telling them that he was the representative of the German Land Colonization Company of Berlin and had an important business proposition to put before them – no less than the purchase of the whole of Zululand from the Pongola to the ocean for a sum of £2,500. Payment would be made in twenty-five yearly instalments of £100 or the equivalent value in weapons. In return the German Company would allow the Zulus to live on the land free of hut taxes with the exception of a grant of 100,000 German *morgen* and sundry smaller areas for townships, railways, etc. The farms given by Dinuzulu to the hundred Boers who had supported him in his fight with Sibebu would be given over to them but all other grants would be subject to the decision of the German Government in Berlin. The Company in the meantime would take over the government of Zululand and people of any and every nationality living there would be under the control of this government. They would recognise Dinuzulu as King but reserved the unquestionable right to instal all future heirs to the throne. Dinuzulu was to encourage the work of Christian missionaries and to confirm the grant of 6,000 acres to each of the six Hermansburg Mission Stations. In the event of war every Zulu would give armed support to the German Company and they on their part would guard the Zulu nation from outside aggression. The Company would hold the concession from the Zulus under the German Government and both parties would subject themselves to the German Imperial Government.

This amazing document was actually signed by Nagel on behalf of the Land Colonization Co. of Berlin and by Dinuzulu for the

Zulus on 1 June 1885.* Fortunately for all parties Nagel was looked upon by both Germany and England as a mere adventurer and nothing came of this wild scheme.

Anger against the Boer usurpation was steadily mounting. As the Usutus realised that they had considerable support in Natal and elsewhere so their opposition stiffened and when the Boers made attempts to graze their cattle on Usutu lands it was not uncommon for skirmishes to take place and cattle to be driven off or killed. Thus, though the Boers had the whip hand by reason of their being well armed, yet it was precarious in the extreme for them to attempt to build houses or to settle on their farms.

On 14 April a Government notice was issued by the New Republic summoning all burghers who were eligible for farms to be at Vryheid on Monday 27 April as it was hoped that the final lottery would take place on or around 11 May.

To secure a satisfactory lottery it was necessary that some sort of a settlement should be arrived at with the Usutus before the day of the draw and in an effort to achieve this the Boer officials called on Dinuzulu and the Usutu leaders, 'Giving them notice that the allotment would take place on May 11 and desiring them to inform them [the Boers] what land they had taken in excess of that agreed upon.'[17] The Boers had been urged to do this by Piet Joubert, an influential Boer from the Transvaal Republic who had been staying in Vryheid a few weeks previously. He had advocated a policy of conciliation and had suggested that the authorities of the New Republic give way to some extent to the Usutu demands, for, as he pointed out, they were in any case gaining an immense tract of country at no expense to themselves.

Accordingly when the meeting took place the Boers adopted a more conciliatory attitude towards the Usutus than they had shown on any previous occasion, even going so far as to suggest a reduction of 300 *morgen* (600 acres) in the size of each farm. This would enable them to hand back a block of territory some 400,000 acres in extent which would include the whole of Ulundi and its surroundings. Dinuzulu was prepared to accept this concession but Ndabuko and the others would have nothing to do

* See Appendix V for the text of this document.

with it and insisted upon the original Babanango, Inhlazatye, Ngome line as the only basis on which a satisfactory settlement could be effected. Argument lasted from ten in the morning till seven in the evening but as neither side would give way the meeting ended in a complete failure to come to terms.

On 11 May the town was full of burghers all eagerly anticipating the lottery, yet many of them filled with misgivings by the rumours circulating about corruption among the officials. At the head of the malcontents was a man called Liversage and shortly after the meeting started he launched a devastating attack on both Meyer and Esselen, even going so far as to address the former as 'Kaiser Meyer', and accused them both not only of misappropriating the £2,000 received from the sale of plots in Vryheid but also of seizing the best and largest farms for themselves without taking their chance in the lottery as all others were compelled to do. He further charged them with bringing the New Republic to the verge of bankruptcy, stating that if the misgovernment was not checked the existence of the Republic itself as an independent country would be impossible.

His attack caused an uproar and when the President, Meyer, could make himself heard he refused to proceed with the business of the meeting unless Liversage was immediately prosecuted for slander. Consequently an adjournment was agreed upon and the Executive Council assembled to try the case. Liversage immediately raised an objection on the grounds that it was the members of this very Council whom he had accused and it was therefore impossible for them to sit as his judges. His argument was supported by the burghers who proposed that he should be examined by the Land Court. Liversage again objected, stating that the members of this court had all been appointed by the officials whom he accused. This objection, however, was overruled and the trial took place. It resulted in a verdict against him and a fine of £50 which he paid immediately, stating at the same time that he would reserve his defence for another day when he would make some startling revelations. The whole case caused grave dissatisfaction among the Boers and the direct result was the postponement of the lottery to 21 May.

Accordingly another meeting was summoned for that day and when the burghers assembled the suggestion was put to them that in view of the Usutu claims and their persistent opposition to the present arrangement the size of each farm should be reduced by 300 *morgen*. To this the burghers gave their consent and in due course the lottery took place, but it was impossible for them to take immediate possession of their farms as a new survey had now to be made in order to demarcate the reduced acreage.[18]

A report of these proceedings later reached the Governor and once again he made urgent representations to Britain for intervention, emphasising the fact that owing to discontent amongst the rank and file of the burghers the bulk of them would welcome annexation and the stability that would result from such a procedure.

As soon as lots had been drawn by the burghers many of them dispersed throughout Zululand to make an inspection of the farm which had fallen to their lot, and some of them, in spite of the official warning that no definite boundaries could be fixed until the new survey had been completed, at once began to settle on the land, driving off any Usutus who had their kraals in the area. In one case it was reported that a Boer had seized and destroyed a native garden, chased off its owner and then replanted it with his own wheat. In another, a man had constructed a dam from which he led a channel to irrigate his lands. Long before the final survey was completed farmers had driven their stock onto lands they expected to possess: some had even begun to build. The Usutus, driven from their ancient homelands, sought refuge in the hills and caves or on such areas as were not yet occupied by the Boers where they watched and waited with growing anger. Then they struck, regardless of the consequences.

In the first case, when the wheat was well established they swooped down and hoed it all up; in the other they allowed the dam and channel to be made, then invaded and broke everything down. Where attempts to erect buildings were made they were destroyed and the owners informed that no buildings or occupation of the land would be allowed. Then Dinuzulu himself issued a notice to the Boers that in spite of their measuring off farms he

The site of the Battle of Tshaneni (left, Gaza Mountain; right, Tshaneni Mountain)

Chief Sibebu and his *indunas*

The destruction of Dinuzulu's Usutu kraal after his exile

Dinuzulu (second from left) *en route* for Eshowe after his return from
St Helena

would not recognise their right to a single inch of ground in Zululand.[19]

The Boers retaliated by burning any Usutu kraals situated on their farms, seizing their goats and cattle and resorting to the use of firearms.[20] In other cases the Usutus were told that they now belonged to the farm and would have to work for its new owner if they wished to live there.[21] All over the country Boers were turning their cattle into Usutu cornfields and leaving them there to graze. Should resistance be offered the natives were seized and thrashed mercilessly.[22] It was war, each side equally determined, with the advantage of course on the side of the well-armed Boers.

Famine now raised its head among the Usutus, caused by the destruction of their crops by the invaders. Unscrupulous traders, taking advantage of the situation, came in with mealies purchased cheaply in Durban and charged exorbitant prices to the half-starved people who were forced to sell their few remaining cattle in order to keep alive.[23] Zululand was in chaos; law and order were non-existent, for every man was a law to himself. Cardew, the sub-commissioner at Rorke's Drift, who was daily in close touch with the true state of affairs, in desperation and ignoring Osborn, his immediate superior, wrote direct to the Acting Governor, Sir Charles Mitchell, saying: 'If England's intentions are not to interfere it will not be long before the Zulus as a nation are wiped out.'[24]

## CHAPTER 6

# The Intervention of Britain

IT WOULD be a grave injustice to blame only the Boers for the state of anarchy which prevailed in Zululand; other factors also largely contributed towards the general upheaval.

Sharp traders from Durban not only became rich through the sale of food but also, knowing the great demand for arms and ammunition among Boer and Zulu alike, peddled huge stocks surreptitiously over the border (for such trade was illegal), retailing near useless guns costing ten shillings apiece at fantastic prices, guns which generally were more dangerous to the holder than his assailant.

Another factor which caused much bitterness was the perfidy of British politicians who were willing to barter the lives and welfare of a countless number of Zulus in order to retain a parliamentary majority. True, they were in some measure misled by dispatches sent to them by their officials in Natal and Zululand, but they had ample opportunities for ascertaining the real facts from reports sent by residents in South Africa. A brief analysis of a few of Sir Henry Bulwer's dispatches is enlightening and indicates the false impression that was often created in the minds of those in authority in London.

In the first place it must be remembered that Bulwer had been bitterly opposed to the return of Cetshwayo and had made his existence as King intolerable. This resentment had coloured all his dispatches to London and when the King died and Dinuzulu was nominated as heir the Governor continued to display the same spirit of hostility, repeatedly refusing the son recognition, yet all the while blaming Cetshwayo's brothers for not having made any official nomination: 'Dinuzulu . . . who has not even gone through the form of asking our recognition and approval of his succession.'[1]

Naturally this was a source of grave irritation not only to the royal brothers but to the whole Usutu people.

Again, Bulwer's infatuation with Sibebu and constant support of him, even when his rebellious raids and treachery were proved beyond the shadow of doubt; his repeated comparisons of the loyalty of this man with the rebellious spirit of the Usutus angered the latter beyond endurance. Grant aptly expressed their feelings in a report to the *Natal Witness* (2 August 1884) in which he wrote: 'To talk of Sibebu as "loyal" is about as anomalous as citing Potiphar's wife as an emblem of chastity.'

Further, Bulwer's references to the trouble in the Reserve were grossly inaccurate, influenced largely by Osborn's erroneous dispatches. ('The leaders stirred up rebellion in the Reserve and organised an armed resistance against the Government.')[2]

As has already been pointed out (see chapter 2) it was Osborn in the first place who sent an armed force into the Reserve to enforce payment of taxes at a most inappropriate time and it was his force that made the first assault. Also it must not be forgotten that many of the Reserve natives, the so-called 'loyal' element, constantly crossed the Umfolosi and raided Usutu cattle in Central Zululand, but no action was taken against them nor were they ever held up to condemnation.

Moreover, whenever Bulwer reported on the land cession he invariably blamed Grant and the Usutu leaders for all the trouble, stating that 'they knew well enough what they were doing',[3] when *no one* knew the extent of territory involved; in two cases Bulwer explicitly speaks of the cession of 800 farms when this figure never appeared in the Proclamation and in fact had been purposely omitted in order to trap the Usutu leaders.*

These are the *facts*, facts which aroused a deep resentment against the people who were supposed to be the Usutus' friends and protectors, and instead maligned and abandoned them. No wonder this proud nation rebelled.

As the months passed by the Boers, accustomed by now to British

---

* 'The written document of cession of 800 farms' (B.B. C4274, No. 45, p. 55) and 'The Usutu leaders have agreed to cede to the Boers 800 farms' (B.B. C4214, No. 42, p. 60). The *Natal Witness* of 3 March 1886 also confirms this.

dilatoriness, continued with their expansionist programme in spite of protests and numerous dispatches from London. In the *Natal Witness* of 5 September a notice appeared advertising the sale by public auction, in the township of Vryheid, on Friday 2 October 1885, of 304 *erven* near St Lucia Bay. In Bulwer's last dispatch as Governor* to Lord Stanley, the Colonial Secretary, he reported that this sale had actually taken place, 'some of the lots fetching as much as £60, the prices ranging from £15 to £60'.[4]

The Boers had two reasons for conducting this sale. They were determined to stake their claim to a port and at the same time they were anxious to raise money to replenish the republican treasury, which was empty, mainly owing to official squandering of its resources. In one instance alone the State Secretary, Esselen, had been granted £700 out of a meagre total of approximately £5,000 to take a trip to Europe in order to try to persuade Germany to support them in their claims to Zululand and St Lucia.

The sale of these plots was followed by a Proclamation dated 26 October defining the new boundaries of the Republic, which now embodied about five-sixths of Zululand, including the territory around St Lucia Bay.[5] To add insult to injury Lucas Meyer at about the same time sent a messenger, Cala, to Mnyamana: 'To ask for his share of cattle as he had not received any of the cattle taken from Sibebu . . . though he was the Great Commandant and head of the Boer forces.'[6]

Commenting on the above Cardew, the Sub-Commissioner, noted: 'The grasping meanness of these Boers passes all comprehension: Lucas Meyer has already got a thumping farm (6,000 acres) out of the Zulus and now he must needs cajole them out of their cattle.'[7]

Esselen's trip to Germany proved a failure, for that country had already come to an agreement with Britain not to interfere in any of the affairs of Zululand or St Lucia. He then proceeded to England to urge the claims of his countrymen and sought, as representative of the New Republic, an interview with the Colonial Secretary. This being refused, he left behind a lengthy document setting out the grounds for Boer intervention and their

* His Governorship came to an end in October 1885.

seizure of the country. The following extracts from this 'Memorandum of Facts' reveal the type of document it was and some of its inaccuracies, many of them subtly worded to cover up the numerous misdeeds of his fellow-countrymen:

Many appeals had been made by the Usutu people to the Boers that they should establish peace in the country. [It was the Boers who made the first approach, and this and later offers of intervention were rejected. See Chapter 1.]
After careful inquiry the Boers were satisfied that the only way to settle the country would be by establishing Dinuzulu on the throne. This required a large Boer force and on 23 May the Boers promised to support them to maintain law and order in return for an undefined piece of land which was ceded to them to establish a Republic. . . . Sibebu prepared to resist with outside help so the number of volunteers was increased to 800. [The number of volunteers was not increased till *after* Sibebu's defeat at Tshaneni.]

Agreements were entered into with Dinuzulu without the use of any threat or pressure on the part of the Boers. . . . No force was exercised and *no threat was used* to induce Dinuzulu to accept these terms. [True, no threat was used to induce Dinuzulu to accept, as far as is known, but very definite threats were used against the Usutu leaders. Esselen himself said, 'If the Kafirs don't want to give the land we must take it and bring them to their senses'.[8]]

There can be no doubt that ample room has been left for the Zulus to exist comfortably. [See map 2, p. xiii, which shows the extent of territory claimed by the Boers.]

Grants have been made to the missionaries at such places where mission stations formerly existed. . . . Many of these farmers have spent large sums in the purchase of their farms. . . . It is estimated that the expenditure incurred in establishing the Republic to the date of the Proclamation was not less than £25,000 sterling. . . . The only danger which they fear is that the natives may be incited by those who do not wish well of the Republic to violate the agreement into which they have entered in the hope of recovering a portion of the territory *which they voluntarily ceded*. . . . The Boers would deeply regret the necessity for any exercise of force which would probably involve loss of life. . . . They take great pride in the fact that hitherto *their relations with the Zulus have been of the most friendly character.*[9] [Author's italics.]

London. 19 October 1885

The final paragraph must have somewhat failed to carry conviction to the Secretary of State, for only a few days previously (on 13 October) Bulwer had written to Lord Stanley that: 'The Zulus are in a very unsettled state and the Boers are so uneasy that they have warned all the burghers who have farms in Zululand to be ready to turn out armed at any time.'[10]

As the Boer occupation of the greater part of Zululand went steadily forward, increased pressure was brought to bear on the British Government to intervene before it was too late and requests urging this began to pour in from all quarters.

In the first place the Usutus themselves had again approached Osborn:

Mnyamana and other chiefs anxiously pray that the British Government will protect them against the aggressive proceedings of the Boers. They ask that the Zulu people be taken, with the country they inhabit, under the protection of the British Government and beg that this may be done soon. . . . The chiefs dread the vengeance of the Boers should it become known to them that they have applied to the British Government for protection.[11]

Even Osborn himself had come to realize the terrible state of the country and was compelled by sheer force of circumstances to support this appeal:

I feel convinced that it is of the last importance to the natives and in the interests of humanity that if it be the intention of H.M. Government to take steps to bring about a settlement of the urgent and grave questions now pending between the natives and the Boers that they should be taken immediately for reasons that are obvious.[12]

A few days previously he had sent the following dispatch to Sir Charles Mitchell, the Acting Governor, which was immediately transmitted to London:

The land left to the Zulus is beyond question entirely too small for their occupation; it will not suffice for even one third of the native population and unless something can be done to secure for them a very much

72

larger area it is clear that the people will be compelled to seek refuge outside the borders of Zululand.[13]

As has already been pointed out the Natal Legislative Council had pressed for British intervention and this was followed up by a resolution from the Durban Chamber of Commerce stating: 'That in the opinion of this Chamber it is necessary that British authority be extended over the whole of Zululand.'[14]

The Anglican Church also lent its voice and the following letter from the Bishop of Zululand (Bishop McKenzie) to the Colonial Secretary berated the British Government in the strongest terms:

For God's sake, my lord, in common justice and mercy take the whole land and RULE IT. . . . Not a sixpence nor a soldier would have been needed in Zululand if only England had taken what all Zulus acknowledged to be her proper position after the Zulu war and had done what most people considered her plain duty. How much British money, how many thousand lives of Zulu men, women and children have been sacrificed by British weakness since the return of Cetshwayo.[15]

At long last the British Government began to awaken to a sense of their responsibilities, stung into action not only by the pressure brought to bear from Zululand and Natal but by the fact that their behaviour was now being criticised in several European capitals. Bismarck and the German Chancellery were watching events closely and though some sort of agreement with Britain had been concluded there was no saying what a man like the Iron Chancellor might do in the future should Britain continue to show such indifference in the affairs of Zululand. There is no doubt that the Boer seizure of St Lucia Bay had startled her and the anger of Natal was rising as was that of the British public. Sir Henry Bulwer had been recalled as Governor and on his arrival in England (he left South Africa on 23 October 1885) a full account of the happenings in Zululand was presented to the British Cabinet. Whatever his faults and failures may have been, Bulwer is to be credited with his emphatic insistence on effective British intervention.

Under these pressures the British politicians were forced to remember their obligations and tried – albeit very late in the day – to retrieve their honour. As a first step Lord Stanley on 4 January 1886 sent the following telegram to the Acting Governor in Natal:

Intimate to persons in chief authority among Boers in Zululand that H.M. Government have been informed as to extent of land which they have surveyed for farms and these allotments would severely and injuriously encroach on territory of Dinuzulu and his people. Warn them that H.M. Government could not recognise the survey and occupation of these lands. . . . Repeat protest to Lucas Meyer with reference to St Lucia Bay and adjacent territories.[16]

Acting on these instructions Mitchell (on 8 January) wrote to Lucas Meyer:

I have to warn you that H.M. Government can neither recognise the survey nor the occupation of the land in question as conferring on the occupants of it any valid title or as in any way affecting the existing rights either of H.M. the Queen or of the Zulu tribes. . . . I have to repeat the warning to all concerned that St Lucia Bay with the adjacent territory to the north and west of it is British territory and that the occupation thereof will not be permitted.[17]

Important new appointments were now made: a new Colonial Secretary, Earl Granville, replaced Lord Stanley and Sir Arthur Havelock had taken over as Governor of Natal on 13 February 1886. Immediately there was a marked change in the policy adopted towards Zululand and a firmer stand was taken on the question of Boer aggression. It was obvious that Lord Granville had made a careful study of the problems affecting the country, had a thorough grasp of the situation and was determined to act with as little delay as possible to bring about British intervention. With this in view he sent the following important dispatch to Havelock on 11 March 1886:

This country has at no time surrendered its rights and the obligations of its position as the paramount power in that portion of South Africa. On the right of H.M. Government to interfere when they think it necessary to do so in the affairs of the Zulu country there can be no question. . . . Apart from the question of the validity of the grant which the Boers obtained from Dinuzulu in August 1884 a new proclamation has been issued by them under which a far larger extent of territory is declared to be annexed than could possibly be claimed under that grant even if it were a valid one. It is based on no title. This claim would cause the most serious inconvenience to the Zulus and to the people of Natal and the Reserve. . . . The Government are satisfied that the Zulus did not know how much of their country they were giving away and cannot be held bound by the treaties. The recent action of the Boers in taking far more country than was agreed upon in August 1884 renders it even less necessary to consider the value of these agreements. It is admitted however that the Zulus agreed to alienate a portion of their country and though not bound to admit the validity of this agreement it is proposed to recognise the occupation of a part of Zululand by the Boers on reasonable conditions. It is therefore desirable that you should enter into communication with the Boer leaders. . . . It will be advisable to bring under British rule all the Zulu country beyond the Reserve, including that portion which will be occupied by the Boers. If the Boers wish to retain their present political organisation it may be possible provided satisfactory territorial settlement is effected.[18]

At long last it was indicated that England was being aroused from years of apathetic and callous policy towards Zululand. At the same time the Boers were adopting an even more aggressive attitude. Esselen had returned from his futile European trip, embittered by the snubs he had received both in Berlin and London, with the result that hatred of Britain became intensified, showing itself in a more fixed determination to consolidate the seizure of Zululand by adopting even harsher and more high-handed methods against the Usutus. Armed bodies of Boers were now sent out to collect taxes from them, non-payment being punished by heavy fines of cattle and in some cases by merciless floggings.

The Usutus were not the only victims. The Boers, determined to keep all trading in their own hands, arrested a number of British traders, confiscated their wagons, oxen and goods and sent them off to Vryheid under armed escort where their possessions were sold by auction, the proceeds being used to swell the coffers of the New Republic.[19]

Regulations were passed compelling occupation of the farms by

75

the men who had been successful in the lottery; non-compliance meant forfeiture of the land which then reverted to the state.

The stretch of the country which had been promised to the Usutus when the farms were reduced in size was also appropriated by the state, thus curtailing even further the area allotted to them.[20] In order to enforce this latest act of oppression a Boer commando rode out to Inhlazatye and from there sent a message to the Usutu leaders demanding their immediate presence. Mnyamana refused to go but several others, led by Ndabuko, answered the summons. Angered by Mnyamana's non-appearance the Boers moved nearer to his kraal and rounded him up, after which the Usutus were ordered to accompany them on a tour of inspection of the new boundary line; it was also demanded of them that they agree to the finality of the settlement by signing yet another document.[21] The Usutus refused point blank either to accompany them or to sign any agreement. Angered by this resolute stand, which the Boers attributed to the Usutu leaders' reliance on help from Britain, they straight away inflicted a fine of 300 head of cattle on them, ordering them to accompany the animals to Vryheid. As the cattle were being collected Mnyamana managed to escape, so four of his men were seized as hostages. On arrival at their destination the Usutus were compelled to sign a paper promising to find Mnyamana and hand him over to the Boers – only on this condition were they allowed to return to their homes.[22]

Mnyamana himself, having summoned Umfunzi and Martin Lutuli, two of his trusted messengers, to his hiding place in the Ngome Forest, now ordered them to make their way as quickly as possible to Maritzburg where they were to seek an interview with the new Governor. Leaving immediately they reached the capital on 4 March and an interview was arranged for the following day before Mr Justice J. W. Shepstone and Mr S. O. Samuelson, who acted as interpreter. After giving an account of all the latest events in Central Zululand they concluded by making the following appeal:

That Dinuzulu may take the place of his father. All the people of

Zululand agree to this and request that it may be announced to Zululand and the surrounding countries. We ask that Dinuzulu may be taken under the wing of the Queen and we wish to return to the British and live under them. We ask that the Boers may be removed from and go out of our country; we cannot live in peace with them.[23]

This message, which not only requested assistance and protection but constituted a definite act of submission to Britain on the part of the Usutu leaders, undoubtedly created a deep impression on the mind of the new Governor. The all-important dispatch from Lord Granville had not yet been received; consequently the reply to the two messengers, though holding out some hope to the sorely stricken Usutus, was largely non-committal. After rebuking them for their foolish conduct in having called in Boer assistance for the conquest of Sibebu he told them:

The utmost that the British Government may be induced to do is to bring about an agreement with the Boers by which a portion of land may be secured for the Zulus; this I will be prepared to recommend. If Government consent to do this the Zulus should be thankful. With regard to the request that Government would recognise Dinuzulu as successor to Cetshwayo and install him when he comes to full age it appears that Dinuzulu is recognised by the principal Zulu chiefs to be heir and successor of Cetshwayo. Formal recognition by the British Government must yet be considered.[24]

A few weeks later Granville's dispatch reached Maritzburg and the Governor, anxious to get the Zulu question settled as expeditiously as possible, took immediate steps to carry out the instructions it contained. On 6 April he sent the following letter to Lucas Meyer:

. . . Actuated by a desire to see a settled state of affairs established in that portion of Zululand lying beyond the Reserve H.M. Government have decided to intervene with the object of effecting an arrangement by which, while the occupation by the Boers of a portion of Zululand will, under reasonable conditions, be recognised, the interests of Her Majesty, of the Zulu nation and of others concerned will be secured. In my capacity of H.M.'s Special Commissioner for Zulu affairs, I am authorised to open up communications for this purpose with you and your colleagues. As the most convenient way of initiating such communications I would suggest that you should depute representatives to come to Maritzburg with authority to confer with me. . . . I shall be prepared to enter with them into a consideration of the present situation generally and of the views as set forth in D. J. Esselen's letter to the Secretary of State dated Oct. 20 1885. I shall also be able to express the conclusions arrived at by H.M. Government. Pending the communications which you are now invited to enter upon, I would strongly urge on you the expediency of using your authority among the members of the Boer community in Zululand to suspend the further occupation by them of lands or farms.          HAVELOCK.[25]

Some days later (on 11 April) Sir Arthur forwarded his reply to Granville's dispatch in which he stated:

. . . The Boers while steadily persisting in the occupation of a large portion of the country are fully aware of the weak points of their position and are quite prepared to accept the intervention of H.M. Government in hopes of thereby obtaining, in exchange for the abandonment of a portion of their present claims, valid titles and a secure position. The power of the Zulus is utterly broken; they have neither the heart nor the strength to resist the Boers. They would submit to a great sacrifice of what they profess to claim in order to obtain a settlement which would secure to them some portion of their country and protect them from the Boers. The present moment is a favourable one for the negotiation of a settlement. The first step is to communicate with the Boer leaders and I have accordingly sent a letter to Lucas Meyer informing him of the course of action proposed and inviting him and his colleagues to confer with me in Maritzburg.[26]

In due course the Governor received Lucas Meyer's answer:

The Executive Council after due consideration of the contents of your letter have decided to depute Mr D. J. Esselen to confer with Your Excellency and to acquaint you with the views of the council upon the different matters contained therein.

Mr Esselen will leave Vryheid on Monday and may be expected to arrive in Maritzburg on the Thursday following.[27]

Accordingly on 26 April Esselen presented himself before the Governor and it was arranged that a full discussion of all the questions under consideration should take place the following day.

At this preliminary discussion three men only were present, the Governor, his Private Secretary Gerald Browne, and Esselen. The talks ran on for two days (27 and 29 April) and during them Sir Arthur demonstrated the invalidity of the Boer claims by stressing the following points:

1.  The Zulus are precluded by a treaty engagement contracted with the British Government from alienating any portion of their territory.
2.  The Zulus are under an engagement *not* to make any treaty or agreement with any people without the consent and approval of H.M. Government.
3.  Nomination of any successor to Cetshwayo is subject to the approval of H.M. Government.
4.  H.M. Government, though it has not interfered in the affairs of Zululand, have never surrendered their rights as the paramount power acquired as a result of the Zulu War of 1879. This had been reasserted on the restoration of Cetshwayo.
5.  All Boer claims for the establishment of a republic are consequently invalid for they have not received the sanction or approval of the British Government.
6.  Boer claims as at present constituted are injurious to the interests of the Zulu people and prejudicial to the interests of both British and foreign subjects. Zulus and Germans alike have complained to the British Government regarding certain actions of the Boers.

Nonetheless, the Governor pointed out, H.M. Government were willing to admit the existence of an agreement between the Zulus and the Boers to alienate a portion of their country, and would be prepared to consider Boer occupation of a certain portion of Zululand on reasonable conditions.

As a basis of agreement he suggested the following terms:

1.  The area left to the Zulu people under the Boer proclamation of 26 October 1885 was manifestly inadequate for their needs and required drastic alteration.
2.  It was suggested that the boundary of the New Republic

79

should be formed by a line running from Babanango to Inhlazatye and thence in a northerly direction to the Pongola River.

3. All claims to a Protectorate over Zululand must be abandoned by the Boers.

4. The rights of all mission stations, no matter of what nationality, must be guaranteed.

5. Further occupation of any farms to the east of the suggested boundary line must be suspended forthwith.

On Esselen promising to submit the above to Meyer and the Executive Council the interview terminated.

The Usutus, learning of Esselen's visit to Government House, felt that it was necessary that they too should send a delegation of their leaders to interview the new Governor and an approach was made to Osborn to make the necessary arrangements. Their request was granted and the Resident was instructed to facilitate their journey to Maritzburg.

On 7 May Ndabuko and Tshingana, accompanied by five of their *indunas* and twelve followers presented themselves at Government House. There were also present, in addition to the Governor and his Private Secretary, H. C. Shepstone (Secretary for Native Affairs), F. W. Watson, F. B. Fynney, W. Windham and William Grant, the last-named being summoned by the Governor to obtain some enlightenment on the questions so hotly disputed by the Usutus.

The very lengthy talks lasted throughout 7, 10 and 17 May. During them the chiefs recapitulated a history of the whole course of events in Zululand which related to the Boer occupation. Their statements for the most part were a repetition of those previously made from time to time by various messengers from the Usutu chiefs. One of the main points of interest was the emphatic and repeated denial by the chiefs of the correctness of Grant's statement, Grant just as stubbornly maintaining its accuracy. In this connection stress was laid by Ndabuko on the fact that when Dinuzulu signed he was a minor and had no authority to cede any land without the leaders of the nation being acquainted with his actions; further, Grant had no power to sign at that time as he had not then been appointed by the Zulu people as their agent.* 'Grant,' he said, 'was a thief; he robbed us of our land.' The chiefs frankly admitted that they and their colleagues, with the exception of Mnyamana, had consented to a limited cession of territory but certainly not that described in the proclamations of 16 August 1884 and 26 October 1885. What they did, declared Ndabuko, 'was done with death staring us in the face. It was done to save our lives and was not a voluntary act.'[28]

This exhaustive discussion was eventually brought to a close by the Governor stating that though the Queen was sorry for the sad state in which the Usutus found themselves the utmost that he thought his Government would be able to do would be to restore a portion of their country.

At this juncture Sibebu reappeared on the scene. As deputations to the Governor on the subject of land cessions seemed to be the order of the day he too determined to be in at the final distribution and sent six of his leading men to the Secretary for Native Affairs with an appeal to the Governor for the restoration of his territory on the grounds that it was only his loyalty to the Queen that had made him an outcast. His case was quickly dealt with by his being told that this was impossible while Zululand was in such an unsettled state but his representations would 'receive careful attention', and with that he had to be content for the time being.

Meanwhile the stipulation that there should be no further occupation of farms to the east of the border, suggested in the interview with Esselen, was being flagrantly disregarded, so much so that the Governor wrote a strong protest to Lucas Meyer on the matter, pointing out that since their discussion no fewer than sixty-three farmers had occupied land in that area.

Some days later a letter was received from Meyer informing the Governor that Esselen had presented his report of the interview of 27–29 April to the Volksraad and they had decided to send a

* The agreement was signed on 16 August; Grant's appointment as Adviser to the Zulu people was not signed till 11 September. (B.B. C4274, Encl. in 14, p. 21.)

deputation to Maritzburg for further discussion at a time convenient to the authorities; the question of certain Boers occupying farms in the proscribed area would also be dealt with on that occasion.

To this communication the Governor sent an immediate reply suggesting 1 July or thereabouts as a suitable date.

Accordingly Meyer, Esselen and four members of the Volksraad arrived at Government House on the 3rd and an interview was arranged for the morning of the 5th. With the Governor were the Secretary for Native Affairs, the magistrate of Newcastle (G. M. Rudolph) and the Clerk of the Legislative Council who took shorthand notes of the proceedings.

After Sir Arthur had given a résumé of the proposals he had submitted to Esselen at the earlier interview he invited the deputation to let him have their reply and also to give him further information about the occupation by the Boers of lands beyond the suggested boundary.

Meyer, acting as spokesman, answered bluntly:

1. That the deputation could not agree to any of the proposals.
2. That the lands beyond the Babanango Inhlazatye line were the private property of the burghers who held title to them and they were not prepared to give them up.

Although the Governor reiterated the claims of the British Government to Zululand, Meyer persisted in asserting that the land in question was settled and the boundaries finally defined by the proclamation of 26 October 1885.

As the deputation refused to yield and were not prepared to discuss the Governor's proposals as a basis for consideration, Sir Arthur closed the meeting and the delegates left in high dudgeon, later making their way to Harry Escombe, a Durban lawyer whom they asked to draw up a statement for publication in the Press.

## CHAPTER 7

# Protection Imposed

THE statement giving a report of the interview duly appeared in the *Natal Mercantile Advertiser*; it was anything but a correct record, for it laid the blame for the breakdown of the negotiations on the inflexible attitude of the Governor, asserting that whilst the Boer delegates were willing to grant certain concessions he had remained adamant that no other basis for discussion would be considered than that which he had submitted to Esselen in April.

On the publication of the report the Governor immediately telegraphed Meyer requesting further information on the concessions referred to, pointing out that none had been indicated during the interview.

Meyer replied that the Boer claims were threefold:

1. Recognition of their independence.
2. The granting of 800 farms totalling 2,269,600 acres.
3. Suzerain rights over the whole of Zululand exclusive of the Reserve.

These claims, he said, were founded on:

1. The agreement signed by Dinuzulu and Grant.
2. The statement in the House of Commons to the effect that England was not concerned with Zululand, outside the Reserve.
3. Their successful establishment of peace and order in Zululand in lieu of anarchy and bloodshed [*sic*].

The terms offered had been rejected because the Governor had insisted that no negotiations could be entered upon unless they were willing:

1. To renounce 250 of the 800 farms.
2. To renounce all pretensions to the suzerainty.

In view of this reply one cannot blame the Governor for stating in his dispatch to Granville that he was unable to understand why Meyer and his colleagues should ever have agreed to attend this conference after he had so clearly indicated to Esselen the basis on which negotiations were to rest.[1]

Thus for the time being an impasse had been reached and the Boers returned to Vryheid. But the breakdown was only temporary for on 4 September the Governor received the following dispatch from London:

H.M. Government attach great importance to a settlement of Zululand without avoidable delay and that, subject to retention of sufficient land for the Zulus, they consider the establishment of some boundary as of more importance than the precise limits of the territory reserved. . . . Give the Boers to understand that if the negotiations were not resumed it might be necessary for H.M. Government to send a Commission to fix the boundary at once, after local enquiry.[2]

On receipt of this the Governor immediately reopened negotiations (on 6 September) with Meyer, for his hand was now strengthened by the threat of a boundary commission should the Boers refuse to come to terms. In his letter he indicated clearly that:

1. All claims to a Protectorate over Zululand must be abandoned.
2. The rights of missionaries must be fully guaranteed.

These two points, he stated, would admit of no discussion. He was, however, prepared to reconsider the vexed question of the boundaries of the New Republic but he must warn the Boers that should they be unable to arrive at a satisfactory decision on this matter then H.M. Government would send a commission to fix a line 'in such a manner as may appear expedient to them after enquiry on the spot'.[3]

Meyer, no doubt somewhat taken aback by the strong line now being taken by the British Government and evidently playing for time, replied on 16 September, '. . . To prevent avoidable costs and misinterpretation I beg that Your Excellency will be good enough to let me know your proposals on which Your Excellency intends to negotiate, upon receipt of which I will be prepared to answer Your Excellency's letter of the 6th more fully.'[4]

The Governor (on 24 September) sent a detailed reply reiterating the terms for the reopening of negotiations which he had already stated quite clearly in his earlier letter, and again repeated the warning that unless a prompt settlement was reached H.M. Government would send a commission to fix a line of demarcation without further delay.[5]

Another appeal had meanwhile come to the Governor from the Usutu leaders (its accuracy vouched for by Shepstone, Secretary for Native Affairs):

The planting season has arrived but we cannot sow because the Boers have taken possession of all our fields. They turn their stock into the people's gardens and destroy them. We lived through last year as we still had cattle with which we bought sacks of mealies. This year we have no cattle, they have been taken by the Boers. We shall die and the country will be desolate.

We report the desecrating of the burial places of our Chiefs, the trees of which they cut down and the graves of which they open and when they are remonstrated with they say they do not care. They have already desecrated the burial places of Undaba and Jama. One Boer opened the grave of Senzangakhona, our originator and root, and took out the pots which were buried with him and left the grave wide open. We appeal to you for our people are tied up and beaten, men, women and children. The Boers have devastated the country.

With regard to Grant we were deluded; he beguiled us with good words saying that he would help us to get out of our trouble; we were in great trouble and were beguiled, fatally injuring ourselves. We took up a torpid snake and put it in our bosom and behold! when it became warm it woke up and bit us. We now declare that he must go and never again be named in connexion with the Zulu nation. Today we are about to wipe him out by letter.[6]

This the Usutu leaders carried into effect by a Proclamation dated 4 August 1886: 'Today we wipe out Grant's name. . . . His name is not wiped out by us; he has wiped it out himself by his own conduct of misrepresenting us.'

The next development was a shocking act of violence. Within a couple of days of the Governor's last dispatch to Meyer an urgent message arrived from Lt-Col. Cardew, the Sub-Commissioner at Nqutu, with the news that Dabulamanzi, the half-brother of the late King Cetshwayo, had on 22 September been murdered in cold blood by a Boer known to the natives as Peula, and to make matters worse, this crime had taken place within the Reserve Territory.

The facts of the case were as follows. Dabulamanzi and his son Umzingeli had been arrested by Field-Cornet Vermaak on a charge of cattle theft which they hotly disputed. Vermaak refused to allow them to plead and arbitrarily fined them £3. The fine was paid but as the two were walking away Vermaak called them back and asked Dabulamanzi what he meant by saying to another Boer that the land on which he lived belonged to him as he had been settled there by Dinuzulu. 'What right have you to say,' demanded Vermaak, 'that the land is Dinuzulu's; it belongs to the Boers. I arrest you and make you a prisoner and will send you to Vryheid.'[7] That night they were kept in custody and the following morning were sent on to Vryheid in charge of two Boers, Wilhelm Joubert and Paul van der Berg (Peula).

Dabulamanzi and his son decided that when they drew near to the Nondweni River they would try to make good their escape over the border (which was close at hand) into the Reserve, so that if a case was then preferred against them they would be brought before the Sub-Commissioner where they knew they would be allowed to plead and would receive a fair trial. Here they were lucky, for as they approached their goal the two Boers, who were riding a little way behind, were engrossed in reading a letter. Grasping the opportunity father and son put their horses to a gallop and crossed the Nondweni. Riding hard they reached the kraal of Mankentshane and ascertaining that they were now well within the Reserve, dismounted and entered one of the huts, Dabulamanzi remarking, 'We are now in the Reserve and the Boers can't do us any harm.' Umzingeli remonstrated with him, saying, 'We had better go on as we don't know these people.'

Shortly after the Boers arrived and ordered Dabulamanzi to come outside, adding, 'If you don't come out we will shoot you inside the hut.' Van der Berg advanced to the door with his rifle at the ready. Dabulamanzi replied, 'I am in the Reserve and you have no right to touch me nor to take me to Vryheid; I have stolen no man's cattle nor done any harm; if you take me any-where take me to the Colonel [Cardew].'

The rest of the story can be told in Umzingeli's own words as taken down by Col. Cardew:

The Boers replied, 'All right, come out, we will take you to the Colonel.' My father said, 'Will you swear that you will do me no harm if I come out?' to which Peula replied, 'I swear.' My father then came out and after we had proceeded a short way towards the Colonel's office Peula, who had handed his rifle to Wilhelm, caught hold of my father and attempted to tie him up with reims saying, 'Now I will take you to Vryheid.' My father resisted saying, 'No, if you take me anywhere you must take me to the Colonel as I am.' Peula and my father then struggled together, my father seizing hold of Peula's bandolier. After a bit they separated, my father having possession of the bandolier and Peula of my father's knobkerrie. I was prevented from assisting my father by the other Boer who threatened to shoot me. Peula said, 'Give me back my bandolier.' My father replied, 'Return me my knobkerrie.' My father threw the bandolier to Peula who then seized the gun from Wilhelm and said he would shoot my father if he wouldn't go to Vryheid. My father replied, 'You won't shoot me on Government ground.' Peula said he would and after some more words he shot my father who was standing within two or three yards of him, through the body, the bullet entering his stomach below the left side and coming out above his right hip. My father ran away and as he was doing so Peula shot at him again twice, the first shot struck him above the left hip, the second passed through his right elbow and left wrist. Peula then fired two shots at me as I was riding away on which the horse bucked me off and I sprained my knee. My father, after receiving the second shot, fell close to me; he had only run about 200 yards. After this I saw the Boers seize our horses and ride away and presently the people from a nearby kraal came up and carried us to their huts. It was dark by the time we arrived at the kraal. My father was then in a very weak state. This morning about sunrise he died. His last words were 'I don't know why they killed me on Government ground.'[8]

On the afternoon of the day that Dabulamanzi died a report of the murder reached Col. Cardew who set out immediately, along with Lt. Addison of the Zulu Native Reserve Contingent, to visit the scene of the crime. After making a careful examination of the body and taking possession of two empty Martini Henry cartridge cases found on the spot, he took a detailed statement from Umzingeli and discovered on questioning him further that not only had the Boers stolen the victims' horses and left the two of them to their fate but also that Peula had even promised to let Dabulamanzi go free if he handed back his bandolier; yet immediately this was done he deliberately shot him in the stomach, inflicting the wound which caused his death. The reason why no one had come to their assistance was simply that all the men-folk from the adjoining kraal were away at a dance but after the two Boers had ridden away some women came to the wounded men's aid and carried them into a nearby hut.

Commenting on the murder Col. Cardew stated, 'The act appears to have been done deliberately and determinedly for the struggle had ceased some moments before and a parley had been going on about the restoration of the bandolier.'

A full account of the crime was immediately forwarded by the Sub-Commissioner directly to the Governor and also to Lucas Meyer. Havelock took a very serious view of the incident and wrote to Meyer asking for full information on both the murder and the violation of Reserve territory; he also wished to know what proceedings were being taken against the accused.

Meyer's reply, though expressing extreme regret at the occurrence, nonetheless differed in certain material respects from the facts as related by Cardew. Meyer inferred that it was during the struggle with van der Berg that the fatal shots were fired. The culprits, he stated, had then returned to Vermaak telling him that Dabulamanzi had fled into the Reserve. Vermaak had sent them on to Vryheid to report the incident but only Joubert had turned up and made a statement. A warrant was immediately issued for the arrest of van der Berg; Joubert had been released on bail of £1,500.[9] There the matter rested for the time being.

Meanwhile Meyer had also been taking steps to enter into further negotiations on the question of Zululand and on 9 October had informed the Governor that a deputation consisting of Spies, Esselen and himself would wait upon him to make another attempt to arrive at a settlement which would be mutually acceptable. Realising the urgency of the matter, they intended to set out for Maritzburg without delay and Monday the 18th was suggested as a suitable date for the interview.

On the appointed day the delegates presented themselves before the Governor who at once opened the discussion with a brief outline of the course which the proceedings were to take. Sir Arthur Havelock was accompanied by the following: his Private Secretary, the Secretary for Native Affairs (H. C. Shepstone), Capt. Yardley, A.D.C., Mr Hugo, Government Dutch translator who acted as interpreter, and Mr Watson, Clerk of the Legislative Council who once again took shorthand notes of the proceedings.

It was a lengthy series of meetings and lasted for five days. There was much hard bargaining. At times it appeared that negotiations would break down but common sense prevailed, both sides realising that considerable concessions were necessary before agreement could be reached. On the last day, to the relief of all, a draft treaty was signed by both parties and it was decided that a Commission, consisting of representatives of H.M. Government, the Zulus and the Boers, should be appointed without delay to carry this into effect.*[10] The conference closed with expressions of goodwill on both sides.

Numerous telegrams now passed between the Governor, Meyer and the Colonial Secretary (Edward Stanhope) as a result of which the agreement was ratified by all parties and the following Commissioners were appointed to carry out the task of marking the new boundaries: Melmoth Osborn, Lt-Col. Cardew and a chief appointed by the Zulus; P. F. Henderson, I. J. Vermaak and J. W. Andrews representing the Boers; Major McKean of the 6th Inniskilling Dragoons to act as Surveyor.

* For the text of the draft treaty see Appendix VI.

Whilst these negotiations had been taking place the members of the Natal Legislative Council had been making approaches to the Governor for a consideration of their opinion regarding the settlement of Zululand. It was felt, with considerable justification, that they had not only not been consulted in any of the negotiations but the whole of the proceedings with the Boers had been conducted in secret and all reports of these had purposely been withheld. This attitude they strongly resented, for the Zululand settlement was of vital concern to the people of Natal as a neighbouring state. Feelings were running high, so much so that J. Liege Hulett, an elected member of the Legislative Assembly, had given notice of his intention to move a series of resolutions on the affairs of Zululand. The import of these can be judged from a couple of extracts:

That the peace and order of south-east Africa, including this Colony demands a settled form of government in Zululand under British rule and in union with Natal.

The Council feels keenly that the blood shed by the Colonists in the Zulu War and the heavy contribution paid by Natal in aid of the expenses of that war entitled the Colony to greater consideration than has been paid to its former resolutions.

When these came before the Council the Colonial Secretary, acting on instructions from the Governor, rose and stated that 'This was an inconvenient moment for such discussion' and debate on the motion was accordingly adjourned. Later the Governor sent for Hulett and his seconder and told them in the course of the interview that as negotiations with the Boers were about to be renewed discussion on these resolutions might jeopardise a settlement and he would be glad if they could be withdrawn. Hulett replied that he could make no promise of such withdrawal till he had consulted his friends in the Council.

Following this, on 12 October, twenty-two of the elected members sent a letter to the Private Secretary requesting an interview with the Governor on the Zululand question. This was refused on the grounds that the present was a particularly unfavourable time for any discussion as the Boer delegates were then on their way to Maritzburg to enter upon the difficult and delicate task of negotiating a settlement. Naturally, this further incensed the members of the Council with the result that on 21 October Hulett reintroduced his resolutions and the following amendment was passed by twenty-two votes to six, the only opposing votes being cast by the official members: 'That the Legislative Council is prepared to accept the responsibilities of the government of Zululand and the Reserve and requests the Governor to send down a Bill during the present session to give effect to this.'[11] The Governor was requested to telegraph this resolution to the Secretary of State and was informed that the Council would adjourn until 27 October, pending an answer from London.

It was now the Governor's turn to be annoyed, for this action by the Council clearly implied direct disapproval of the policy of the Imperial Government. However, he forwarded the resolution but could not resist adding the phrase 'notwithstanding strong remonstrance of Government', and to justify his authority over the Legislative Council he concluded by stating: 'Do not consider myself at liberty to publish result of negotiations with Boers without permission.'[12]

The British Government, true to the folly of a long tradition in Africa of overriding important resolutions of the local legislature, wired back almost immediately: 'Resolution of Legislative Council cannot be entertained by H.M. Government. You will soon be in position to communicate to Council result of negotiations.'[13]

No doubt the Governor took great delight in transmitting the contents of this telegram to the Council where it created a stormy scene. Determined to carry on the fight and to bring their views before the British Cabinet, the Council now (29 October) passed a much more strongly worded resolution, also telegraphed to London, to the effect that:

This Council claims a voice in any settlement of question so vital to interests as are future disposal of Zululand and the Reserve and control of trade route to the north and Swaziland. This Council protests against its persistent exclusion from any definite information on the subject of negotiations that are going on between Special Commissioner, Boers and Zulus; it respectfully asks that provisions of arrangement under consideration be communicated to Council prior to any decision arrived at: this Council reiterates urgency of immediate extension of British jurisdiction over that portion of Zululand other than that already alienated to Boers in terms of offer made in March last.[14]

In order to give time for a reply the Council adjourned until 2 November.

The very next day the answer came: 'Inform Legislative Council representations received and will be carefully considered by H.M. Government.'[15] And on 2 November a further telegram reached the Governor: 'You have authority to give details of Agreement to Legislative Council, adding that we shall be glad to act in concert with Council in consideration of future relations of Natal with Reserve and both portions of Zululand.'[16]

This in some measure poured oil upon the troubled waters but the anger of the members of the Council had been thoroughly aroused. Thus when the Agreement was submitted to them, together with a map illustrating the line of demarcation, their immediate reaction was to pass what amounted to a vote of censure on the Governor; pointing out:

This Council is of opinion that the interests of Natal have not been duly considered by Your Excellency in the negotiations which preceded the Agreement of Oct. 22 in disregard of the resolution passed by the House on the previous day and it feels keenly that it was not frankly treated in regard to this question. It also expresses the opinion that the terms of Agreement make it doubly necessary that the Territory should now come under H.M. rule and is prepared to pass a Bill extending the laws of Natal over Eastern Zululand and the Reserve.[17]

The Governor, commenting on the above when transmitting it to London, stated that he did not recommend that Zululand come under Natal for the following reasons:

1. Natal is poor and financially embarrassed, therefore could not assume this new responsibility.
2. The Zulus would not agree to the introduction of Natal's Native laws. This view, he added, was supported both by Shepstone and Osborn.[18]

To this the Secretary of State replied that the representations of the Council would be fully considered 'when further information was received' and in order to supply this the Legislative Council presented the Governor with a lengthy Address which was to be forwarded to London.

This Address consisted of a résumé of all the former proceedings, once again stressing that: 'Though anxious to express itself in regard to the affairs of Zululand and eager to obtain information in regard to the course of policy there, it [the Council] was effectually shut out from knowledge and precluded from action until the time for action was past.' Further that:

Although the Agreement has been drawn up and ratified the Council desires to emphasise its conviction that the extension of British rule over both the Reserve and Eastern Zululand under the Government of Natal offers the only sound solution of the Zulu problem and it advances these grounds for this conviction:

1. For years past Natal has borne a charge of £15,000 p.a. as interest on Zulu War expenditure and for administrative charges in connection with Zululand and the Reserve.
2. The Zulus, whether in Natal or Zululand are one people.
3. The uninterrupted good government in peace and order of the Native people in Natal affords a moral guarantee for the good government of Zululand.
4. The administrative experience of Natal offers the best field of selection for the requisite official machinery.
5. The Zulus, if left in tribal isolation, will assuredly come into collision with the Dutch or fall out among themselves.
6. The cost of government would ere long altogether relieve the Imperial Exchequer from any expenditure on account of Zululand and the Imperial Government from any responsibility of administration in that country.[19]

On 3 February 1887 the Colonial Secretary sent the considered reply of the British Government to this Address:

H.M. Government are not prepared to entertain the proposal that Eastern Zululand and the Reserve should be annexed to Natal. There is no evidence that the Zulus are willing to be brought under the laws and administration of Natal, nor would these be applicable to the present condition of Zululand. Moreover the finances of Natal appear to be quite unable to bear these costs. . . . The Reserve must continue to be administered on its present footing, the control over it being extended to Eastern Zululand.

H.M. Government do not object to consider whether it may be possible to bring these territories under the control of the Governor of Natal, giving him power to legislate by Proclamation: and further whether there would be advantage in the appointment of a small number of elected members of Council to be a committee to consult with the Governor and Executive Council on the administration of the Reserve and Eastern Zululand in order that the Council may have a due voice in the expenditure of any funds which may be provided from the Colonial Revenue for advancing the interests of Natal and Zululand in such ways as H.M. Government may approve.[20]

The members of the Legislative Council were not the only people who were dissatisfied with the manner in which this settlement had been determined. The Zulus themselves were loud in their complaints at the way in which they too had been excluded from all discussion of the terms of the Agreement. Consequently Tshingana with a following of headmen representing the principal chiefs of Zululand set out for Maritzburg to request yet another interview with the Governor. This request was granted and on 10 and 11 November 1886 they presented their case. Not only did they object to the new boundaries but they strongly resented not having taken part in all the discussions as they wished to meet the Boers face to face and argue matters out with them in the presence of the Governor. They desired the expulsion of every Boer from Zululand except from that small portion which they had originally been prepared to grant.

After pointing out the futility of a meeting with the Boers in his presence the Governor again stressed the fact that much of the trouble in which they now found themselves had been brought about by their own foolish behaviour and they should be grateful that British intervention had saved a considerable portion of Zululand for their exclusive occupation. He then emphatically reaffirmed that the decisions arrived at were final and the Zulus must submit to them without further equivocation.

Realising that further argument on the question of the Agreement was useless the Zulus requested that consideration be given to the inclusion of the Emakosini Valley in the area allotted to them. This was the most sacred part of their country as it was the burial ground of their early kings and a number of the graves had already been desecrated by the Boers; this had not only given great offence to their people but had resulted in much ill-feeling.

The Governor, realising the reasonableness of this request and the sincerity with which it was made, agreed and promised that every endeavour would be made to readjust the boundary in order to include this area in their portion of the country. To this end he would communicate with Lucas Meyer without delay.[21]

Shortly after this interview the Governor issued explicit instructions to the Commissioners regarding their duties in determining the demarcation of the new boundaries; he also added a special note to Osborn as President of the Commission requesting him to inform the Zulus that the present Agreement was final but H.M. Government were prepared to assume a Protectorate over Eastern Zululand should this be acceptable to them. Further, it was for them to decide as to whether they preferred to come under the laws of Natal or a system of administration similar to that operating in the Reserve.

Accordingly Dinuzulu, Mnyamana, Ndabuko and all the leading chiefs, together with about a thousand of their followers, arrived on 2 January 1887 at Osborn's camp where once again they reaffirmed their strong resentment of the present partition of their country and their exclusion from all deliberations on its settlement. Further, they expressed their desire to send a deputation to England to be confronted with a Boer deputation before H.M. the Queen and her Ministers, and until the result of such an appeal was made known to them they declined to discuss the question of a British Protectorate, for they could not believe that the existing arrangements were final. On being asked by the Commissioner whether they wished to come under the government of Natal the chiefs stated that neither they nor the Zulu people had ever entertained or expressed such a desire.[22]

On 8 January the Governor telegraphed a report of this meeting to London to which he added the postscript: 'Minds of chiefs probably influenced by pernicious advice [referring of course to Miss Harriette Colenso's influence]. Repetition of finality of settlement in Queen's name and decisive answer as to reception of deputation by the Queen might be useful.'[23] The anticipated reply came back on 12 January: 'Send message to Chiefs that settlement is final and deputation will not be received.'[24]

The Zulu chiefs were informed of this decision without delay and for the next few weeks nothing of any moment happened except that the Boundary Commissioners proceeded steadily with the work of demarcation.

Then on 12 February a telegram from London put the question: 'What is present attitude of Zulus? Do you think there is now any more favourable feeling towards British Protection?'[25] To which the Governor replied:

Views as to general favourable feelings of Zulus strengthened by subsequent information received. Cardew expresses opinion that people are prepared to accept British government. Osborn said on Feb. 1 only obstacle is opposition of Ndabuko. Thinks majority will gladly accede. People will be specially glad of British rule.[26]

In the meantime Osborn, feeling the necessity for immediate action, had taken the bit between his teeth and before official sanction had been granted sent a message at noon on 5 February by his *indunas* to Mnyamana and the principal chiefs stating that he deemed it his duty to notify them that owing to the urgency of the situation British Protection, carrying with it the supreme authority of H.M. Government, was extended over Eastern Zululand and the chiefs and people therein from and after that date.[27]

Within a couple of days the *indunas* returned bearing the news that this announcement had been favourably received by Mnyamana, Dinuzulu, Ndabuko and the various headmen. This information was immediately telegraphed to the Governor with a strong recommendation that Zululand be annexed to the Empire rather than made a British Protectorate.[28]

In a lengthy dispatch to the Governor dated 8 February Osborn stated that the reasons for his having taken such action were twofold:

1. Zulu tradition and law prevented any Chief, under any circumstances, from voluntarily consenting to the transfer of any portion of their country to any power or person. Consequently, even in self-preservation, they could not make any offer to be taken over by any friendly power, nor could they openly consent to any measure involving such a condition. On the other hand, they would cheerfully submit to any act, even to total absorption by the British Government who had conquered them and to whom they still admit they belong. But *they could only submit on the initiative of that power* as they would then be relieved of all responsibilities imposed upon them by their own tradition and law.

2. The bitter hostility existing, in spite of the October Agreement, between the Zulus and the Boers, an hostility which might at any moment flare up into an open conflict unless the strong hand of Britain intervened to establish order and confidence.*[29]

With these considerations in mind and having been convinced that further delay would result in 'most serious and irretrievable mischief', the Commissioner had taken action and so averted, as he firmly believed, 'all risk of disorder and its mischievous consequences'. It now remained for his action to be confirmed by the British Government.

On 18 February the reply came from London, stating tersely: 'Osborn's action is approved.'[30]

---

* Author's italics.

## CHAPTER 8

# The Causes of Unrest

THE Boundary Commission had been advancing as quickly as possible with the survey of the new line, for the urgency of a speedy settlement was realised by both British and Boers. It was a most arduous task as anyone acquainted with the broken and mountainous type of country that had to be covered must know. Further, the hardships which the Commissioners had to face almost daily were accentuated by the fact that their work had to be carried out at the worst possible time of the year for surveying. It was summer when drenching rains and tremendous thunderstorms were all too frequent an occurrence. Roads were non-existent, tracks became quagmires, mountainous paths were slippery and dangerous. It was also the season of heavy mists when visibility was reduced to a minimum and surveys rendered impossible. It was greatly to the credit of the Commissioners that their task was completed in so short a time; it was commenced on 4 December 1886 and the last beacon was set up on 25 January 1887. No small measure of this credit must go to the surveyor, Major McKean.

In the midst of this heavy work Osborn received an urgent deputation from the Zulus resident in Proviso B complaining of their treatment by the Boers who were demanding their labour, refusing to permit them to cultivate their gardens, threatening to seize their few remaining cattle and, in some cases, evicting them from their lands.*

* It should be noted that according to Osborn's report this area was generally regarded as one of the finest of Central Zululand, 'very healthy, extremely good for stock and fairly so for agriculture.' It had been divided into about sixty-five farms for the Boers and included two old-established mission stations, Umfule and KwaMagwaza. The kraals of no less than eight Zulu chiefs, embracing a population of approximately 5000 people, were also situated in Proviso B and here they had lived for many years. This area is still (1966) largely in European hands. (B.B. C5143, Encl. 1 in 7, pp. 10 ff.)

These were serious and justifiable complaints, for in this territory although the Boers were granted occupation and possession they had not been given freehold title by the British Government. The tenure on which their allotments were held was that sanctioned by Zulu law and practice, which did not give them jurisdiction over the natives. Consequently the Zulus were entitled to enjoy undisturbed the lands upon which they had lived for many years and they had every right to cultivate their gardens and fields. It was this state of affairs which induced the Governor to urge the bringing of Zululand under the direct control of Britain rather than under the administration of a Protectorate.

After his interview with the Zulus Osborn took immediate steps to remedy the situation before it got out of hand, and on 26 December 1886 the following notice was issued from his camp at Emtonjaneni:

This is to notify all whom it may concern:

1. That the Boers have no right to exercise any jurisdiction over the Natives now residing within the said district [Proviso B].
2. That pending definite arrangements by H.M. Government all persons residing within the limits thereof are entitled to continue to enjoy full and undisturbed occupation of the lands upon which they have hitherto dwelt and to proceed with the cultivation of their gardens and fields unhindered by anyone.[1]

This in some measure pacified the Zulu inhabitants and enabled them to carry out their planting without risk of eviction and to tend their cattle without fear of seizure.

Instructions were also forwarded to Osborn that where the natives were unable to come to terms with the Boers, land was to be provided for their occupation in the parts of this territory which still remained unallotted; otherwise provision was to be made for them in some other part of Zululand.[2]

Once the Boundary Commission had completed its task (see map 3, p. xiii) the question of the future administration of the country had to be tackled and the first step was to obtain a definite decision from the Home Government as to whether it was to be administered as a Protectorate or whether it was to come directly under the Crown. In view of the fact that the Governor and all local officials strongly urged the latter course London, on 11 May, telegraphed: 'H.M. is pleased to approve of Zululand becoming part of the British Dominions. You are authorised to issue Proclamation declaring that the whole of Zululand, including Native Reserve, will become a British Possession under the name of Zululand.'[3]

Accordingly, on 14 May, the Governor issued the following Proclamation:

In the interests of peace, order and good government it has been deemed expedient that H.M.'s sovereignty should be proclaimed over Zululand as is hereinafter defined:

Now therefore I do hereby proclaim, declare and make known that from and after the nineteenth day of May next the whole of Zululand, including the territory known as the Zulu Reserve Territory but excluding the territory known as the New Republic . . . shall be and shall be taken to be a British Possession under the name of Zululand. And I hereby require all H.M.'s subjects in South Africa to take notice of this my Proclamation and to guide themselves accordingly.

GOD SAVE THE QUEEN![4]

Commenting on the annexation the Editor of the *Natal Witness* in a leader dated 21 May 1887 wrote: 'The best thing for the Zulus is to accept with as good a grace as possible the final termination of what must surely be one of the most disgraceful episodes of British administration and diplomacy in any part of the world.'

In order fully to bring the new status of their country to the notice of the Zulus they were summoned through their respective chiefs to attend a ceremony on 21 June at Eshowe where Sir Arthur Havelock would be proclaimed Governor of Zululand.

On the appointed day Government officials, local troops and about 9,000 Zulus duly assembled and after the reading of the Proclamation the Union Jack was ceremonially hoisted. This was greeted with a roar of approval by the Zulus and hailed with the royal salute '*Bayete!*' The various tribes then marched past, each company repeating the salute as it reached the flagstaff. After a military parade the Zulus entered with gusto upon a series of tribal dances. It was a lengthy ceremony and continued till sunset when Osborn presented the chiefs with fifty-two head of cattle for a feast in honour of the occasion. Great enthusiasm was shown – especially in the feasting – and everything passed off satisfactorily, good order prevailing throughout the whole proceedings. Many of the leading chiefs were present, including Tshingwayo, Sibebu, Sigananda and John Dunn, but there were two noticeable absentees, Dinuzulu and Ndabuko.

This day also marked the occasion when Melmoth Osborn was appointed Resident Commissioner and Chief Magistrate of Zululand. He was now entrusted with authority 'To take all such measures and to do all such matters and things as are lawful and may appear to you expedient for promoting peace, order and good government within the said territory.'[5]

Laws and regulations for the future government of the country were also drawn up and made public. Those which most closely affected the Royal House and the power of the chiefs may be briefly summarised as follows:

1. The Supreme Chief over Zululand and its native population would in future be the Governor of Zululand.
2. The Court of the Chief Magistrate would be constituted as a Court of Appeal.
3. Resident magistrates were to be established at Eshowe, Nkandhla, Nqutu, Emtonjaneni, Ndwandwe (Nongoma) and Lower Umfolosi.
4. The crime of murder would be punishable by death.
5. The trial of every person charged with a crime punishable by death would be held before a Court consisting of the Chief Magistrate and any two of the Resident Magistrates, the Chief Magistrate being the President of such a Court. No sentence of death would be carried into effect except upon the warrant of the Governor.
6. Resident Magistrates, except in civil cases reserved to Native Chiefs, would have jurisdiction in all civil suits and proceedings. All such suits would be dealt with according to the law in force in the Colony of Natal except in cases where all parties

to the suit were Natives; such cases would then be dealt with according to Native Law. Magistrates would also have jurisdiction in all criminal cases, save only in respect of crimes punishable by death.

7.  Native Chiefs would have jurisdiction according to Native Law in all civil cases between natives of their own tribe. They would also have jurisdiction according to Native Laws in all criminal cases arising exclusively between Natives of their respective tribes other than in cases of rape, murder, culpable homicide, witchcraft, assaults arising from faction fights and theft from other tribes. No Chief would be permitted to inflict any punishment involving death, mutilation or grievous bodily harm. The infliction of any such punishment would entail deprivation of all criminal jurisdiction. Any person would have the right of appeal from the decision of his Chief, first to the Court of the Resident Magistrate and in the event of dissatisfaction with such judgment, to the Chief Magistrate.

8.  Every person practising witchcraft would, on conviction, be deemed guilty of an offence punishable by fine or imprisonment, or by both fine and imprisonment.[6]

From these regulations it will be seen that an entirely new order was introduced: the despotic rule of the old kingdom was now a thing of the past; no longer could men be put to death at the whim of a ruler or at the behest of a witch-doctor; a stable government was set up and every man in the land could now claim the protection of the law.

Although many Zulus accepted these laws without demur there were some – notably Dinuzulu, Ndabuko and others connected by ties of blood with the royal household – who took the change ill and tried by all means in their power to upset it. Thus the freshly appointed magistrates faced a difficult task. The country was in a chaotic state owing to years of misrule; its people had been ruined by the rapacious Boers who had not only seized their land but dispersed their herds of cattle; Britain herself, though claiming possession of the country, had hitherto turned a deaf ear to all appeals for assistance. To build up a stable government on such foundations and to transform a warlike and barbaric people into a state approaching civilisation was a work that would take many years of wise guidance and patient administration. Troubles were bound to arise but had the Resident Commissioner and some of his subordinates shown a better grasp of the situation, much suffering could have been averted and many lives saved. The result of some of these blunders is with us even today, for there still exists in the minds of many thinking Zulus a feeling of deep resentment at the wrongs perpetrated at this time.

Although *all* the chiefs had been informed of the Proclamation by special messengers and had been summoned to Eshowe, yet, as has been seen, several of them had failed to attend; the Resident Commissioner therefore felt that it was advisable to repeat the procedure in order that there could be no possible excuse for anyone not being fully acquainted with its contents. Accordingly, a second summons was issued calling the chiefs to meet him at Nkonjeni* on 25 June when the Proclamation would again be read, translated into their own language and fully explained to all present.

On the appointed day when Osborn reached his destination he was met with the news that neither Dinuzulu nor Ndabuko could come, the former stating that he was ill and the latter excusing himself on the grounds that one of his wives had recently died. Mnyamana reported that as none of the chiefs of Cetshwayo's family would come he was reluctant to do so himself. Sensing the emptiness of these excuses the Commissioner sent yet again to these chiefs pointing out that their conduct, if persisted in, could not fail to bring disgrace upon themselves and warning them that if they continued to disregard his summons he would report their conduct to the Governor.

This had the desired effect on all except Dinuzulu who still affirmed that he was ill, and on Thursday 7 July the chiefs, head-men and about six hundred of their followers assembled in a semi-circle near the flagstaff at Nkonjeni where Osborn again read

---

* Nkonjeni is situated between the White and Black Umfolosi Rivers, about eight miles to the north of Ulundi and within fairly easy distance of the kraals of Dinuzulu, Ndabuko and Mnyamana.

the Proclamation. The Union Jack was hoisted and 'the Chiefs and people saluted it heartily by shouting simultaneously the Royal Salute, *Bayete*.'[7] Mounted infantry and a 75-man detachment of the Zululand Police also gave the Royal Salute, fired three volleys and the ceremony concluded by all present giving three cheers for H.M. the Queen.

The Commissioner then proceeded to explain to the gathering the new political position of Zululand, urging upon all obedience to the laws and respect for the newly-appointed magistrates, for only in this way, he stated, would they obtain for themselves and their families absolute security and good order. Two of the magistrates were introduced to them, Addison for Ndwandwe and Arthur Shepstone for Lower Umfolosi.

In the course of the discussion that followed the chiefs pointed out that owing to the new delimitation a considerable number of their people were now included in the New Republic. The Commissioner promised to convey this information to the Governor and at the same time told them that if these people did not wish to remain in the New Republic they were at perfect liberty to move into Zululand where there was ample room for all.

Before leaving Osborn was careful to forward to Dinuzulu by his own special messengers copies in both English and Zulu of the Proclamation and Commission which he had read to the people that day.

Within a few days of Osborn's return to Eshowe disquieting news reached him about the conduct of Dinuzulu; not only had he purposely absented himself from the reading of the Proclamation but he was now acting in open defiance of British authority. It was reported that one of his people, Mfokozana, accused of witchcraft, had been sentenced to death according to old Zulu custom; fortunately, before sentence could be carried out Mfokozana had escaped but Dinuzulu had seized all his cattle. News of this soon reached the ears of Addison, the magistrate at Nkonjeni, and a message was sent ordering their immediate return. The injunction was ignored and the men who conveyed it reported back that a large gathering of chiefs, headmen and their followers, all fully armed, had been seen at the Usutu kraal. They further reported that these men had assembled for the purpose of escorting Dinuzulu to Vryheid where it was his intention to interview the Boer authorities. On hearing this news Osborn instructed Addison not only to warn Dinuzulu of the serious consequences of any breach of the peace but also to tell him that if he wished to leave Zululand in a peaceful manner, no obstacle would be placed in his way.[8] Osborn's action was supported by the Governor who stated in his dispatch to London: 'Dinuzulu's departure would relieve us of one of the chief sources of embarrassment in our efforts to establish quiet and contentment in Zululand.'[9]

The official attitude of the Boers to the Usutus had meanwhile changed considerably, for since the delimitation they were anxious to keep as many as possible of them in the New Republic for the following two reasons:

1. The Republic was desperately short of cash and they anticipated collecting a considerable revenue from them by way of hut tax.
2. They wished them to remain in the country as a source of supply of cheap labour for their farms.[10]

Dinuzulu and some of his chiefs, sensing this changed attitude, set off for Vryheid on 26 August in high hopes of gaining their assistance against the British authorities. Thus on meeting the Boer officials they attempted to pave the way for this by claiming Boer protection, stating that they refused to consent to the withdrawal of their guardianship over them. Much as the Boers desired to have many of them settle in their country they would have nothing to do with Dinuzulu's suggestions and bluntly told him that the boundaries of the New Republic and Zululand had been agreed upon and finally settled and under no circumstances would they countenance rebellion against Britain; consequently Dinuzulu and Ndabuko had to return to their kraals without having gained anything but the distrust of the Boer officials who immediately sent a letter to the Governor informing him of Dinuzulu's visit and the purpose of his mission.

Dinuzulu and Ndabuko were back at Usutu by 31 August.

There messengers were awaiting them from Osborn summoning *all* chiefs and headmen to meet him at Nkonjeni on 3 September. Old Mnyamana, Tshingana, Siwetu and the principal headmen duly turned up but once again neither Dinuzulu nor Ndabuko put in an appearance. The Resident, after explaining the position and powers of the chiefs under the new administration, urged all present to loyalty and obedience.

After a quiet and orderly meeting Osborn spoke of Dinuzulu's misconduct and his illegal seizure of Mfokozana's cattle. These, he said, must be returned forthwith to the magistrate, Addison, who would then hand them back to their owner. For his violation of the law Dinuzulu would be fined thirty head of cattle and the Commissioner hoped that this would serve as a salutary lesson to him and to all others, indicating that the new regulations must be obeyed.

When the chiefs returned to Usutu and told Dinuzulu of the fine and the order to return the cattle he was furious and refused either to pay the fine or return the cattle, stating that he had only acted within his rights. On this being reported to Addison, he decided that steps must be taken to enforce the law and accompanied by an escort of sixty police he rode over to Usutu. As Mfokozana's cattle could not be found he ordered the seizure of an equal number from the herds of Dinuzulu.

The letter from the Secretary of the New Republic had now reached the Governor who forwarded its contents to the Resident with instructions to take action. Accordingly Osborn sent three messengers to Dinuzulu informing him that he had heard of his claim to Boer protection and would interview him at Nkonjeni on 16 September to obtain from him an explanation of his conduct.

When the messengers arrived at Usutu Dinuzulu refused to meet them and they were compelled to deliver their message to an *induna*. A curt reply was sent to them stating that Dinuzulu would meet the Commissioner as ordered but the moment they had left, sensing trouble, Dinuzulu issued instructions that his women, children and cattle were to make at once for the Pongola where they were to hide. He then sent his own messenger to Osborn telling him that he would be unable to be at Nkonjeni on the 16th but would come later.

On receipt of this message Osborn, justifiably angry at Dinuzulu's insubordination, sent another messenger demanding compliance with his orders. This man on reaching Usutu was attacked with a knobkerrie, some of the bystanders going so far as to shout, 'Split his head.' Fortunately others, remembering the sanctity of an envoy, intervened and saved him from serious harm but the incident indicated the antagonism felt against the new regime.

Some days later Dinuzulu, realising the need of some excuse for his intransigence, sent word to Osborn that he was afraid to come to Nkonjeni because he feared the military escort.

Meanwhile a series of telegrams had been passing between Osborn and the Governor in which the former had again urged the use of a strong military force to smash this incipient insubordination. This request was refused but in its place the Governor sanctioned an increase of one hundred native recruits for the police whom Osborn immediately enlisted from the Hlubis, a most indiscreet move under the circumstances, knowing how bitterly these people were hated by the Zulus.

But the crowning act of folly was yet to come.

In his messages to the Governor Osborn had persistently been pressing for the return of his old favourite, Sibebu, to his former territory.

It will be remembered that this restless warrior had made numerous applications to be allowed to return to his former home but on each occasion had been refused on the grounds that the time was inopportune. Now, however, he was fully supported by the Resident, who took the view that conditions had so changed that his return could be effected without causing any upheaval, in fact it would rather assist the British to maintain order and discipline throughout the land. 'I consider,' he stated in his dispatch to the Governor, 'it will be an act of great prudence to permit him and the people of his tribe to return to their old district.'[11] 'There would be no difficulty,' he continued, 'in preventing any collision between Dinuzulu's followers and those of

Sibebu.'[12] In support of this he affirmed that a number of Sibebu's people were back in their old territory under a headman by the name of Hlomuza who, although professing loyalty to Dinuzulu, was in reality a strong adherent of Sibebu's and was constantly carrying on secret negotiations with him for his return; unless such a return was officially sanctioned 'It will not be possible without resorting to forcible measures to prevent him.' Further to bolster up his support of Sibebu he persuaded the Secretary for Native Affairs to present a report which was also forwarded to the Governor. In this the Secretary stated:

As a matter of policy I would suggest the return of Sibebu and his people to their own country. We know their loyalty and can depend upon them in case of any disturbance there. By sending them back we would have a strong loyal body at the extreme end of the country and the Zulus would thus be between it and us and would feel the danger of their position should they contemplate any rising. . . . Circumstances are changed. The whole country is to be under British rule with white magistrates and *I apprehend no danger of a disturbance from the fact of Sibebu being allowed to go back* [author's italics].[13]

This was the *official* view; unfortunately it did not reflect the true state of affairs as is obvious from the following report in the *Natal Witness* of 1 July 1886: 'The feeling of animosity that existed between the Usutu and the Mandhlakazi has in nowise abated. . . . Sibebu is so hated that if he were put back in his old district the Usutu would rise against him to a man and could he be found now by any one of them alone in the veld his life would not be worth much.' But Osborn, obsessed with the idea of Sibebu's restoration and impervious to all criticism, unwisely pursued his course and brought about a blunder of the first magnitude, as later events proved.

During the last months much of Sibebu's territory had been occupied by the Usutus, for it was the one part of the country where they felt more or less secure from Boer rapacity; consequently kraals had been built, lands tilled and gardens established, and many of these people were truly settled in the area from which they had driven their former enemy; they realised only too well that his return would mean that once again they would be hounded out of their kraals and chased off the lands which they had cultivated and from which they were expecting to reap crops which would feed them and their children during the hard months of winter. It was futile for the Commissioner to suggest that as Britain had now taken over the country both Usutu and Mandhlakazi would have to obey the law and refrain from fighting. The gunpowder was there and it needed only a spark to cause an explosion.

The danger was further increased when it was brought to the Usutus' ears that Sibebu was refusing to pay his taxes until he was returned to his old lands, yet in spite of this the Commissioner had refrained from taking action against him. The Usutus remembered their own experiences at the Nkandhla when they were burying their King; because they delayed payment till the completion of the ceremony Osborn had sent troops against them and they were shot down.

The situation was daily deteriorating throughout the country and reports came in from all quarters of growing unrest. In a last attempt at pacification the Commissioner sent his chief *induna*, Yamela, to Usutu with 'a friendly message' urging Dinuzulu to return Mfokozana's cattle and pay the fine imposed upon him; thus he could regain possession of the beasts taken from his own herds. 'His only desire,' he stated, 'was to uphold the law and if Dinuzulu would but comply with these requests every leniency would be shown to him.'

His appeal was unsuccessful and Dinuzulu was not even allowed to meet Yamela, for Ndabuko had assumed full authority. The cattle would not be returned and neither Dinuzulu nor Ndabuko would appear before the Commissioner; they were afraid to do so for they mistrusted him.

In an attempt to circumvent Osborn messengers were sent direct to the Governor complaining that the Proclamation had left Dinuzulu naked, for his chieftainship had been taken from him, his country given to the Boers, he was being persecuted by Mali-mata (Osborn) and he could not understand the workings of the new order.

To these excuses the Governor replied that it was simply because the Zulus had proved unable to rule their country and had been foolish enough to call in Boer assistance that they had landed themselves in such trouble; the Queen had stepped in and saved a large portion of the country for them; if Dinuzulu did not like the Queen's rule he was at perfect liberty to leave the country but once he left he would not be allowed to return; if he remained, he and his chiefs would have to obey the law or take the consequences; if he submitted as a loyal subject he would be left in charge of his tribe and would receive a monthly allowance of twenty-five pounds.[14]

Some days later the Governor received a dispatch from Osborn reporting the disloyal conduct of Dinuzulu and Ndabuko in refusing to appear when summoned. An immediate reply was sent in which the two chiefs were ordered to appear before him at Eshowe on or before 1 November to explain their conduct: 'If they show a disposition to submit to legitimate authority by obeying this summons I will take as lenient a view as possible of any offence that may have been committed by them.'[15]

Before recording the details of this interview the various grievances of the Usutus need to be recapitulated, for undoubtedly there were real grounds for complaint.

In the first place grave dissatisfaction was felt at the way in which the murder of Dabulamanzi was being handled. It will be remembered that the man who fired the fatal shots, van der Berg, had not been brought to justice. The other culprit, Joubert, had been charged, let out on bail and then released on the grounds of insufficient evidence. The last news of van der Berg was that he had fled to Swaziland but a grave suspicion existed that his whereabouts were known well enough but no serious effort had been made to bring him to justice. There was also a strong feeling of resentment against the British officials for the half-hearted manner in which they had pressed for the arrest and prosecution of the murderer. Seemingly the whole affair had now been dropped.

Another sore point was the question of the royal graves in the Emakosini Valley. Repeated requests had been submitted for this area to be included in Central Zululand but no satisfactory answer had been received. It was known that Sir Theophilus Shepstone had stated that it was a matter that only concerned the members of the royal family; this may have been the *official* view but it certainly did not reflect the attitude of the Zulu nation.*

Another matter that caused much ill feeling was the question of tenure in the area known as Proviso B. The Usutus felt that until some definite ruling was decided upon their position as tenants was full of uncertainty.†

An event that had considerable bearing on the future of the Usutus was the union of the New Republic with the Transvaal under the name of the South African Republic. This took place only a couple of weeks after Dinuzulu's abortive visit to Lucas Meyer and his colleagues, seeking their assistance against the British authorities. For some time secret negotiations had been taking place, for the officials of the New Republic realised that it was impossible for them to stand on their own, both from a financial and a political point of view, and as the two states had much in common it was felt by all parties that union was desirable.

Accordingly a Treaty of Union was signed on 14 September 1887 and Stephanus Johannes Paulus Kruger became the first President.[16] Intimation of this Union was sent to the British High Commissioner at Capetown.

* See Appendix VII.
† This question was not finally settled till 17 March 1888 (B.B. C5522, No. 4, p. 7). On 9 August 1887 a Government notice appeared (B.B. C5331, No. 47, p. 80) ordering all persons who claimed ownership of land in this area to submit their claims in writing to the magistrate of Emtonjaneni before 9 Nov., after which date no claim would be considered. Eventually it was decided that farms would be held under the system of quit rent tenure. It would be compulsory for the tenant to occupy his farm for a minimum of nine months in each year, a substantial dwelling house must be erected to the value of not less than £100 and the land must be used for pasture or for cultivation. The penalty for a breach of any of these conditions would be forfeiture of the farm. Government reserved to itself the right of making public roads through the land and of taking, without compensation, materials for the construction and repair of such roads. Most of the persons to whom farms had been allotted lodged their claims and obtained possession but until these regulations were promulgated great uneasiness prevailed amongst the Usutu.

## CHAPTER 9

# 'The House of Shaka is Dead'

ON 4 November 1887 the Governor sent the following telegram to the Secretary of State in London:

Ndabuko arrived yesterday; he is coming before me today. Reasonable grounds for hoping Dinuzulu will follow; if he does not, warrant will be issued for his apprehension on charge of treason-felony.... Country quiet and people, with exception of few followers of Dinuzulu and Ndabuko, loyal to Government.[1]

When this interview took place Ndabuko was immediately questioned as to the reason for Dinuzulu's absence; his reply was:

He did not think it of any importance that Dinuzulu should be present as he was a child and if he had come he would not be able to say anything; he thought that if *he* came it would be sufficient, but as it had been impressed upon him on his way down that it was imperative that Dinuzulu should appear he had sent a message informing him that he must follow without delay.[2]

It was not merely the words which were spoken but the defiant manner in which they were uttered that brought a reprimand from the Governor:

It was not for Ndabuko to consider whether it was necessary or not for Dinuzulu to appear when he had been summoned; Ndabuko must do as he is told; his conduct of late had been shameful; he had plotted against the Queen's authority, sought Boer protection against the English Government and, when summoned to explain his acts before the Resident, had not only neglected to appear but had assaulted one of his messengers. He must now give an account of himself and of his doings.

It was a heavy indictment but Ndabuko, unabashed, attempted

to exonerate himself with a series of excuses, some of which were obviously untrue. The Governor was clearly annoyed and showed this by terminating the meeting abruptly and informing Ndabuko that he could go and would be sent for when wanted.

It was 14 November before Dinuzulu arrived; he was accompanied by Ndabuko, Tshingana and twenty-two other chiefs and headmen. At the interview to which they were summoned the Governor had with him not only the Resident Commissioner but various magistrates, Government officials, military and police officers.

Proceedings were opened by the Governor who stated that he had long wished to see Dinuzulu whom he had always desired to treat as a friend; unfortunately, on this their first meeting he had to censure him for delay, disloyalty and misconduct. Some time ago Dinuzulu had sent a message to him which was both disloyal and foolish: it was disloyal because he sought to set aside the Queen's sovereignty; it was foolish because it spoke of his succession to Shaka, Dingana, Mpande and Cetshwayo –

Such a thing is now impossible. Dinuzulu must know and all the Zulus must know that the rule of the House of Shaka is a thing of the past. It is dead. It is like water spilt on the ground. The Queen now rules in Zululand and no one else.[3]

He, the Governor, now represented the Queen and was determined to maintain her authority in Zululand; if the Zulus were left alone they would fight among themselves and others would come and take their country and cut it up into farms; to save them from this misery the Queen had stepped in. It was largely due to the ill-advised acts of Dinuzulu and some Zulu chiefs that a portion of their land had fallen into the hands of the Boers, so the Queen, fearing the loss of the whole country, had resolved to prevent this by assuming the government of it herself.

Five months ago her Proclamation and Commission were read, first at Eshowe and later at Nkonjeni, and the new laws were fully explained to the chiefs and people. Although Dinuzulu was not there most of the great chiefs attended and many of them understood that those laws were to be obeyed. The Government also expected Dinuzulu, as a chief holding high rank, to obey them and set an example to others and so aid the Government in the administration of law and order. Instead of doing this, three months ago Ndabuko and he had held a large meeting of armed followers at the Usutu kraal for the purpose of plotting against the Queen's authority. Later they had gone to the leaders of the New Republic and asked them to extend their protection over them. The Governor had received intimation of this by letter from the Boer authorities. Then, when summoned by the Commissioner, not once but several times, to explain their conduct both had made vain excuses and neglected to appear. Finally, Ndabuko had sent a message which was both insolent and disloyal and when later the Commissioner had sent his chief *induna*, a man of rank, Dinuzulu had refused to see him and, to add insult to injury, one of Osborn's messengers – and the person of a messenger is always regarded as sacred – had been publicly assaulted at the Usutu kraal and no apology had as yet been received for such a disgraceful act.

Dinuzulu must now explain his conduct and answer these charges.

As question and answer followed each other, it soon became obvious that Dinuzulu had been carefully coached by Ndabuko in the replies he must give.

The meeting at the Usutu kraal, he said, was called to explain the Proclamation to the people; there was no sinister purpose whatever in it and his refusal to receive a copy of this document from Osborn was simply because he could not read.

When he visited the Boers at Vryheid it was to see his people, many of whom were living in the New Republic, and he was unaware of the fact that it was necessary for him to have a pass. He did *not* go to ask for the protection of the Boers.

His neglect to obey the summons of the Commissioner was because he was ill and others were busy collecting the cattle which had been demanded of them; they were afraid to appear without them lest they should be imprisoned.

Regarding the attack on Osborn's messenger he felt that he could not give an apology till this man had been found, for he had disappeared and they had no idea as to his whereabouts. As far as his refusing to meet Yamela, the Commissioner's *induna*, was concerned, this was simply because he felt he was too young to speak to him on any matters of importance and for this reason 'his fathers spoke in his place'.

It was a lengthy inquiry and though every opportunity was afforded Dinuzulu and Ndabuko, no satisfactory explanation could be given for their misconduct and many of their excuses were patently false. The Governor closed the discussion with instructions to the chiefs to present themselves again before him on the following morning.

On their reassembling, after again reminding them of their obligations to the Queen and the necessity of obedience to her laws the Governor introduced the question of Sibebu and told the chiefs that he had that day granted him permission to return to his old territory. 'Sibebu,' he said, 'was loyal to the Queen and would obey her laws and it was his wish to have loyal Chiefs and people throughout Zululand who would help the Government.'[4]

He desired now to speak particularly to Dinuzulu and Ndabuko. He had summoned them to appear before him to explain certain acts of disloyalty and misconduct which they had committed. If after today they obeyed the Queen's laws they would continue to enjoy their privileges as chiefs, but he warned them that if they broke those laws they would not come before him as today but would be brought as prisoners before the magistrate's court and would be dealt with as the law prescribed.

Continuing, the Governor said he had thought over what Dinuzulu and Ndabuko had stated in reply to the charges made against them and he was not satisfied with their excuses. The first and second charges were of a very serious nature but in view of their denials and his wish to treat them leniently he would not take action against them on these counts, but for neglecting to obey the Resident's summons to appear before him he found them guilty and must punish them for their disobedience; each of them must pay a fine of fifty head of cattle.

In conclusion, he wanted to say once again to Dinuzulu that he wished to regard him as a friend and treat him kindly but he must remember that it would depend entirely upon his future conduct as to whether he would be able to do so. The same applied to Ndabuko. He would hear through the Commissioner of their behaviour and if those reports were satisfactory then he would be pleased to see them in Maritzburg whenever they wished to interview him.[5]

A further meeting took place the following morning, this time between the Commissioner and the chiefs, the latter stating quite frankly that 'they thoroughly understood everything the Governor had said to them' (according to Osborn's report to the Governor). There was one matter, however, which caused them great dissatisfaction and that was the return of Sibebu, for they all felt that 'it would have been better to keep him and them wide apart so as to prevent disputes and troubles arising', but as the Governor had ordered it they trusted that he would see that they were not molested by him. The Resident explained that Sibebu would no longer be an independent chief but would reoccupy his lands *as a British subject* and would have to obey the laws in exactly the same way as every other person in Zululand. He would be under the authority of the magistrate whose duty it would be to see that he caused no trouble. This explanation in some measure poured oil upon the troubled waters and the meeting appeared to close in a satisfactory manner.[6]

Earlier that day (15 November) the Governor had held an interview with Sibebu during which the chief had been told that permission was now granted him to return to his former lands on condition that he understood quite clearly that henceforward he was no longer an independent chief but would have to obey the Queen's laws just like every other person living in Zululand. If he accepted these conditions he could return to his old country as soon as he wished. If difficulties should arise, under no circumstances was he to take the law into his own hands; he must refer them to the magistrate, Mr Addison, who had been appointed to represent the Government in his district. If he assisted the Government, kept his people in order and saw that the hut tax was paid by all he would receive a salary of £20 a month, but should he misconduct himself this payment would be stopped and he would be charged in court like any other law-breaker. These conditions being readily accepted by Sibebu, the Governor dismissed him with the hope that he would behave himself and so enable the Government to look upon him as a friend.[7]

On 24 November Sibebu and the menfolk of his tribe commenced their move from near Bond's Drift on the Tugela, where they had been living for some time, and made their way to the Ndwandwe district. They were accompanied by Mr Galloway, the Superintendent of Roads, and four police messengers who were to assist in maintaining order en route and to assure a peaceful return to their former home. On 5 December they reached their destination where they were received with considerable hostility by the Usutus living in that area.

In the meantime Addison had moved from Njonjeni to his new quarters near the Ivuna River, close to the Mandhlakazi. One of his first acts on arrival was to dispatch a message to Dinuzulu and Ndabuko demanding the cattle in payment of the fine imposed upon them by the Governor. They replied that they had no cattle – an obvious lie, for it was well known that each possessed large herds.

It was a critical time, for the arrival of Sibebu had inflamed old passions and rumours were afoot of the Usutus arming themselves for an attack upon him. On 8 December Dinuzulu and some five hundred of his men protested to Addison against the way in which some Usutu were being forcibly ejected from their homes in order to allow Sibebu's people to occupy them. They had tilled the ground, their crops were ripening, but they had been chased away without compensation and left with the prospect of no food for the winter months.

There can be no doubt whatever that the officials, particularly Osborn and Addison, had gravely underestimated the depth of feeling against Sibebu and this animosity was greatly intensified by the behaviour of the latter and the contradictory reports which Osborn sent forward to the Governor, as the following will show: 'It is certain that Dinuzulu sent a deputation of Indunas to solicit the active assistance of the Government of the New Republic in resisting the re-occupation of the Mandhlakazi by Sibebu.'[8]

On making investigations the Governor stated: 'I communicated what I had heard on the subject to Lucas Meyer and was assured by him that the statement made to me was a fabrication from beginning to end. His assurance in this matter has been corroborated by evidence obtained from other sources.'[9]

Later Osborn sent in a further report contradicting his earlier dispatch: 'When Dinuzulu appeared to have gone to the New Republic he was really at Ceza constructing a round kraal of stone to be used by him as a laager where it is his intention to muster the Usutu in order to raid Mnyamana and Siwetu and armed men are collecting there.'[10]

The Governor states that he learnt from the Assistant Commissioner at Ceza on 20 December that:

An official messenger sent to ascertain the nature and size of the fortification said to have been erected by Dinuzulu, having searched Ceza for two days could find no stone kraal whatever or fortification of any description. Further, the messenger did not meet any natives at Ceza or its neighbourhood except people going about their ordinary occupation.[11]

In support of his accusations Osborn wrote:

There is much disquiet and unrest prevailing in the Ndwandwe district. This is attributable to two causes (1) Dinuzulu and Ndabuko fear the Government will punish them for negotiating with the New Republic again and for asking their assistance in an attack upon Sibebu which there can be no doubt they fully intend to make if they can get such assistance. This assistance being refused they fear the consequences. Thus Dinuzulu is fortifying Ceza out of fear of punishment. Without Boer assistance he will not dare to attack Sibebu. (2) Dinuzulu, disappointed at not being allowed to succeed his father, is resorting to such proceedings as will annoy the British Government to such an extent as to induce it to withdraw as it did in the case of the Transvaal.[12]

Commenting on these disturbing statements the Governor reported to London:

After carefully sifting all the information and considering all the circumstances of the situation I am disposed to believe that fear and suspicion are the motives of Dinuzulu's present attitude and that such preparations as he may have made are intended only for defence against a suspected combination of the forces of Sibebu and of the Government. . . . The right course to adopt seems to be to try to reassure Dinuzulu and his adherents. I have accordingly addressed a despatch to Osborn instructing him in that sense. Meanwhile Dinuzulu and his headmen have been emphatically warned of the consequences of attempting any acts of violence and have been told that they will be held personally responsible for any disorderly proceedings.[13]

It is time to see what had actually been happening at Dinuzulu's kraal.\* After Dinuzulu had been officially informed that Sibebu was to return to his old kraal at Bangonomo he was very angry and later when he met his aged Prime Minister, Mnyamana, said: 'This dog who killed my father cannot stay near me. I do not wish to see him at all nor to have anything to do with him', to which Mnyamana replied: 'My child, I advise you against fighting because if a man approached us here leading a dog on a chain and you hit that dog, you would really be attacking its owner. Sibebu is the dog but the British are the owners and they will attack you with their soldiers against whom you cannot fight, else you will suffer defeat.'

Unfortunately Dinuzulu, dominated by the recalcitrant Ndabuko, did not take this wise advice and from that day Mnyamana broke with him and though his sons and his *impis* fought with Dinuzulu he himself henceforward withdrew completely from all political activity.

The Governor followed his despatch to London with a note to Osborn requesting him to urge Addison to visit Dinuzulu with as little delay as possible; the visit was to be made in a friendly spirit not only with a view to acquiring trustworthy information but also to gain Dinuzulu's confidence and so obtain a measure of influence over him.

Addison ignored these instructions and replied that 'his going would be of no use'; and instead of making personal contact sent three of his messengers. Thus the Governor's wish to try and foster

\* The following information was given to the author by Dinuzulu's daughter, the Princess Magogo, and confirmed by her son, Chief Gatsha Buthelezi.

a measure of confidence was completely thwarted. In due course the messengers returned with a reply from Ndabuko stating that 'he had made no preparations nor given any orders to any of his people to assemble for the purpose of attacking Sibebu.'[14]

Some days later (on 2 January 1888) the ever-provocative Sibebu turned up at Addison's station at Ivuna with a thousand armed men at his heels, insisting on the immediate removal of the Usutus from his area. As the seat of the magistracy was situated ten miles from Dinuzulu's kraal and only five from that of Ndabuko the stir this created can well be imagined. As Dinuzulu reported later,[15] 'When Sibebu came to the magistrate's office with his army we were terrified', and to counter this menace he himself mustered two thousand of his warriors as quickly as possible. Addison was now in a fright and wired for troops. Accordingly the Government ordered a detachment to move up from Nkonjeni to stand between the opposing forces and prevent a clash; both sides were ordered to disarm and disperse and for the time being the storm blew over and the troops were allowed to return to their quarters.

This is where Addison so failed in his task, for although repeatedly instructed to make every effort to reconcile the opposing parties by frequent visits to the respective kraals he neglected to do so until it was too late. When these visits were insisted upon by both Governor and Commissioner, Addison found that Dinuzulu and Ndabuko had some very real grievances against Sibebu who, with his usual aggressiveness, had not only been taking possession of his old lands but was driving the Usutus from areas to which he had no claim; in addition, he had been opening up their grain pits and seizing the contents.

When these facts reached the ears of the Governor he issued instructions that Sibebu must be severely reprimanded for seizing lands which did not belong to him and the Usutu must be resettled there; full compensation was to be paid without delay, either in cash or kind, for all corn which had been illegally seized. Further, Addison was instructed to promise Dinuzulu that a full inquiry would be made into all his complaints and the boundaries of Sibebu's territory would be carefully adjusted. For this task he had appointed the Commissioner and the magistrate of Emton-janeni (Knight) and had instructed them to proceed to the site as soon as possible.

It is obvious not only from Government dispatches but from outside sources at this period that the Governor apparently was the only official who had a real grasp of the situation. Even the Secretary for Native Affairs (H. C. Shepstone) was anything but impartial in his outlook. Reporting to London the Governor said:

From the whole tenour of the information that reached me I was reluctantly compelled to think that more care and greater consideration and discretion might have been exercised in arranging Sibebu's resettlement. It has been made clear to me that the risks attending his return were underrated. Great vigilance, discretion and forbearance are needed to avert trouble. . . . The animosity of the Usutu party and such designs as they may have are directed against Sibebu personally and not against the Government except in so far as they believe Government to be supporters against them of Sibebu. It is difficult to persuade Dinuzulu and his friends that we are impartial and it will take time to disarm his suspicions that we are combining with Sibebu for his destruction.[16]

By 5 February the state of tension had apparently eased and the warriors had quietly dispersed, no doubt owing to the Governor's insistence on Addison making several visits to the kraals of both Dinuzulu and Sibebu, for on this date Addison reports that though Ndabuko was still defiant and yet owed forty-three head of cattle in payment of his fine, Dinuzulu had settled up in full.

Towards the end of March trouble broke out in another part of the country, undoubtedly because of the tactlessness of the magistrate (Arthur Shepstone). Two old chiefs who had procrastinated in their response to an order had been summarily arrested and sentenced to work as hard labour convicts on the roads. This was a shocking indignity to impose on any chief for so trivial an offence and in this case it was heightened by reason of their age. Naturally the anger of their followers was roused and when news of this reached Ndabuko there can be little doubt that it aided him in his tireless efforts to stir up trouble.

Dinuzulu, chafing at the loss of his regal status, filled with bitterness at the restoration of Sibebu and constantly egged on by his uncle Ndabuko, set off for the Transvaal to try once more to gain the sympathy and assistance of the Boers. His pleadings were in vain as far as Lucas Meyer was concerned and although a few adventurers, contrary to orders, offered their help against Sibebu, his quest was unsuccessful. Thwarted in this quarter he turned to the Swazi King only to be met by yet another Shepstone (T. Shepstone, Adviser to the Swazi King) who persuaded that monarch to refuse Dinuzulu permission either to reside in Swaziland or to use his country as a base of operations. Disheartened and angry he turned his footsteps towards home to find that a few days before his return Addison, on Osborn's instructions, had ordered a raid on his kraal by two sub-inspectors (one of whom was Osborn's son) and eighty men. These had seized twenty-five cattle from Ndabuko towards his fine, a further twenty-two head from Dinuzulu as reparation for those he had taken months before from Mfokozana, plus another thirty as his fine for this offence. In addition, Ndabuko had been accused of harbouring certain culprits and an attempt had been made to seize four men wanted for contempt of court.[17] Ndabuko, supported by a large number of armed followers, had refused to give them up and as the police were greatly outnumbered they had had to make a hasty retreat. On news of this reaching Osborn he sent a telegraphic request for permission to call out the troops and although the Governor gave his assent he coupled it with a censure for this hasty and severe action by stating that 'the time for this arrest might have been deferred', and once again urged the Commissioner 'To do all in his power to encourage any desire that may be shown to submit to authority. Am strongly opposed to any measure that involves general punishment of Usutu people. Try to reassure them and induce them to return to their homes.'[18]

Little attempt was made at a reconciliation, Osborn had gained his point, the calling out of the troops, and both Dinuzulu and Ndabuko felt that they could not now withdraw from an armed clash without serious loss of face in the eyes of their supporters.

Ndabuko, greatly cheered by the thought that he had caused

the retreat of the police, now summoned every available man to arms and ordered them to assemble at the Ceza Mountain; he also sent Dinuzulu on a mission to Mnyamana to urge him once again to throw the weight of his great influence on their side. But Mnyamana resolutely refused to change his attitude; in retaliation Dinuzulu warned him that his life would be in danger as would that of Siwetu who stood loyally by his aged leader.

On the arrival of the troops they were marched up to Ivuna and from there on to Usutu and to Ndabuko's kraals only to find both places deserted. However, news quickly filtered through of rebel activity: trader Louw's house, near the Ceza Mountain, had been plundered and his horse and rifle taken; Dinuzulu's *impi* had seized 103 cattle and a large quantity of mealies from five of Mnyamana's kraals; scouts also brought the information that the rebel force consisted of at least 1,500 men and Ndabuko had sent a summons to Tshingana at the White Umfolosi ordering him to call up his warriors.

When Osborn arrived at Nkonjeni on 21 May he was met by both Mnyamana and Siwetu who had moved to that spot with a number of their followers for protection; the former reported that the cattle stolen from his kraals had all been killed immediately by order of Dinuzulu and fed to the *impis* which had assembled at Ceza. Being informed of these events the Governor telegraphed an order for the arrest of Dinuzulu and Ndabuko for cattle theft; when this was effected the two were to be taken to Eshowe under a strong escort and lodged in gaol.

The rebels, now faced with the serious problem of feeding so large a number of men, proceeded to raid the kraals of all who opposed them. Siwetu was the next victim, his kraals were looted and his cattle seized. To terrify the people into submission Ndabuko spread reports that the Boers were coming to their aid, that the British were about to abandon Zululand and Dinuzulu would be reinstated as King and when this took place all who had failed to support him would be put to death.

The flames of rebellion were spreading. Chief Qetuko of Emtonjaneni signified his support and prepared to collect his warriors but before this could be accomplished Knight, the magistrate, had him arrested and though an attempt was made at rescue it was repulsed with some loss of life and Qetuko was sent to Eshowe under a heavy guard. Further afield, at the Nkandhla, Sigananda had openly espoused Dinuzulu's cause and had sent a number of his warriors to support him.

On 2 June the first real clash occurred. Acting on the instructions of the Governor sixty-six police, under Commandant Mansel, supported by a detachment of about 140 men of the 6th Dragoons under Captain Pennefather, proceeded to Ceza to execute the warrants of arrest on Dinuzulu and Ndabuko. They were accompanied by a contingent of about four hundred of Mnyamana's men. Osborn had also instructed Sibebu to take up a position near the magistrate's post at Ivuna with about 750 of his warriors. Pennefather was ordered to support the police who were to go ahead and make the arrest; should they get into difficulty he was to extricate them, avoiding as far as was possible any collision between troops and natives.

The force reached Ceza about noon and found that the Usutus had taken up a position in the bush near the top of the mountain but when the troops had been sighted they moved out onto a triangular plateau jutting out from the forest. As Mnyamana's men refused to proceed unless accompanied by the troops the whole body advanced along a rough track to the left of the Usutus. The approach was very bad, the ground steep and full of ravines, with large boulders scattered around which fortunately afforded good cover for the men. The police advanced to make the arrests and rode to a point about 300 yards from the plateau but as they did so the Usutus threw out the right and left horns of their army in an attempt to surround them. To check this movement the police dismounted and opened fire only to be met by a heavy fusillade from the Usutus who now attacked in full force, with their horns doubling out at a great pace and the main body charging swiftly down the hillside. The troops, realising the dangerous situation of their comrades, rushed to the rescue and, taking up a position about 600 yards from them, opened fire. This temporarily checked the Usutu main body but as their horns were still advancing there was a danger of being surrounded. Realising this,

Pennefather ordered a general retreat for by this time their ammunition was running short.

The police had barely been rescued from their dangerous situation when more Usutus swarmed out of the bush and attacked with the greatest resolution. In an attempt to drive them back a charge was made by the Dragoons but so fierce was the Usutu onslaught that police and troops turned tail and fled with the Usutus chasing them right up to the Black Umfolosi River, by which time darkness had fallen.

Mansel, reporting later on this fight, wrote, 'The Usutus were wonderfully well handled and showed the greatest courage and confidence' – this in marked contrast to the 400 of Mnyamana's men who had flatly refused to join in the conflict.

Although police and troops had suffered an ignominious defeat their losses were slight: Dragoons, two killed, two wounded; police, one wounded and several horses killed. Casualties would no doubt have been heavier but for the poor markmanship of the Usutus; their losses were unknown but it is thought they must have been considerable as many of their warriors were seen to fall.

The situation now assumed a serious aspect, for although the Governor had made every effort to pacify the people (a promise had been made that Sibebu's boundaries would be readjusted and full compensation had been offered to all who had suffered loss of corn or crops) both Ndabuko and Dinuzulu, encouraged by their success, determined to continue resistance. All who failed to give them support had their kraals raided and their cattle seized: other raids were also made on trading stations, stores were looted, and trader Louw and his son Klaas were killed for assisting Government forces.

Fortune seemed to favour the Usutus for the moment, and they were now presented with a splendid excuse for an attack upon Sibebu. A collision had occurred between Umsutshwana, a Usutu headman, and Sibebu in which the former had been killed together with ten of his followers. Though Sibebu may in this instance have acted under provocation he had been repeatedly warned against aggression and at this time was under distinct orders from Osborn not to move from the Ndunu Ridge where he and his men had been stationed. When news of this attack reached the Governor he issued instructions for a judicial investigation and told the Commissioner that Sibebu must be brought to book,[19] but as Sibebu was his special protégé the whole matter was conveniently pigeonholed and no official action taken until insisted upon at a later date by the Governor.

This certainly was not the attitude adopted by Ndabuko and Dinuzulu: one of their headmen had been killed along with ten of their countrymen; it was a golden opportunity to settle old scores and drive Sibebu and his hated Mandhlakazi from their country.

At 6 a.m. on the morning of 23 June the magistrate and police in the rough little earthwork fort at Ndwandwe (Sub-Inspector Osborn commanding) were woken by their buglers sounding the alarm: a large body of Usutus had been sighted advancing upon them from the north. The garrison, consisting of about fifty Europeans and natives, took up their positions and prepared for the attack, as did Sibebu who had now returned to his station on the Ndunu Ridge, about 1,000 yards from the police camp. Ten minutes later the Usutu *impis* swept over the Ridge and then divided into two parties, the smaller, consisting of approximately 1,000 warriors, advanced in the direction of the fort but on reaching a point about 600 yards away and being met by the rifle fire of the garrison they wheeled swiftly to the left in the direction of the Imbebe *spruit* which ran below them. This move not only placed them out of the range of fire from the fort but effectively cut off a line of retreat for Sibebu's warriors.

Meanwhile the larger *impi*, of about 3,000 men, came steadily forward towards the Mandhlakazi and when about 400 yards away charged headlong into them, yelling their battle cry '*Usutu*'. It was a fierce struggle while it lasted for both sides were fired by hatred, but soon the greater numbers of the Usutus began to tell. As headman after headman fell amongst the Mandhlakazi their resistance broke and they turned tail and fled in all directions hotly pursued by the Usutus. Once again Sibebu managed to escape and made his way with some of his men to the fort, where he knew he would be assured of a welcome.* His losses had been severe: not only had many of his headmen been slain but according to his own estimate 200 of his warriors had been killed and sixty wounded. The Usutu force, led by Dinuzulu who was in the forefront of the action and had himself been responsible for the death of five of Sibebu's warriors,† lost about forty killed.

After rallying their forces Dinuzulu and Ndabuko collected the booty which consisted of large herds of cattle and some women and children, and retired to the fastnesses of the Ceza Mountain, passing the fort but taking good care to keep well out of the range of rifle fire. A small party of mounted police followed them and managed to recapture some 200 cattle and a number of women and children but this loss was more than compensated by the Usutu seizure of a number of police horses.

When news of Sibebu's defeat reached Osborn he ordered the immediate evacuation of the Ndwandwe Fort and although Addison protested against this move (for which Osborn was later censured by the Governor[20]) it took place the following day.

Military and police reinforcements were now summoned from every available source but before they could arrive trouble broke out in another part of the country. Some fifteen miles from Nkonjeni, near the White Umfolosi River, was another mountain fastness, Hlopekulu. Here Tshingana, urged on by Ndabuko and Dinuzulu, had collected some 250 of his men and, using the dense bush and ravines of this stronghold as a base of operations, was leading forays on the cattle and property of all who were loyal to the Government. As the strength of Tshingana's force was daily increasing it was realised that it presented a serious menace to the Government lines of communication, for Hlopekulu was situated directly in the rear of Nkonjeni. Consequently it was decided that

---

* Not, as has been stated in Lugg's *Historic Natal and Zululand*, p. 149, 'seeking refuge in the Ndunu bush, defying capture and later turning up at Nkonjeni'. Osborn's official report to the Governor stated, 'The Resident Magistrate [Addison] informed me by heliograph at noon today [24 June] that *Sibebu who, it appears, took refuge in the police camp* . . .' (B.B. C5522, Encl. 1 in 52, p. 88); there is another reference to 'Sibebu himself taking refuge in the police fort' (Col. H. S. Stabb's report, B.B. C5522, Encl. 2 in 60, p. 99).

† This information was given to the author by Chief Gatsha Buthelezi.

before any concerted action could be taken against Dinuzulu and Ndabuko the rebels in this area must first be crushed.

Accordingly about 6 a.m. on the morning of 2 July the following troops under the command of Col. H. S. Stabb, accompanied by the magistrate Addison, left Nkonjeni for Hlopekulu: 134 officers and men of the 6th Dragoons under Captain Pennefather; 64 officers and men of the Mounted Infantry, 64th Regiment (North Staffs and Inniskilling Fusiliers) under Captain Purdon; approximately 100 Zululand Police under Commandant Mansel; 140 Basutos under Major McKean; 1,000 Eshowe Native Levies with 5 European officers; 400 Mnyamana's men with 4 Europeans – a total of approximately 1,850 men. Their destination was reached a little before noon and after a short rest the troops were allocated their respective tasks. The Eshowe contingent were ordered to the east of the mountain and Mnyamana's men to the west so that Tshingana's warriors could be completely surrounded. Whilst these movements were taking place a number of armed natives were spotted watching from several high points.

To reach the mountain itself it was necessary to cross a narrow neck; the police, supported by the Basutos, were ordered to advance along this route and take up a position immediately below the dense bush which covered the higher slopes: the Mounted Infantry were to follow and occupy the neck. The moment the police commenced their advance the Usutus opened fire from a ridge of high ground on the left which overlooked the neck and from this vantage point they were able to make things most uncomfortable for their attackers. Taking every advantage of the natural defences of the place, the Usutus had concealed themselves, some in the dense bush and others behind the many boulders scattered around, and from here they kept up a steady fire. It was immediately realised that this dominating position would have to be cleared before any real advance could be made and an order was given to the Dragoons to drive the Usutus out.

This was accomplished without much difficulty and when the ridge had been taken it was seen that the enemy had hidden their cattle and women and children in some deep gorges far below. Now, driven from their vantage point, the Usutus withdrew into the dense bush and as they moved swiftly from place to place it was hard to ascertain their exact whereabouts. An attempt was made by a section of the police to clear them out but the firing was so fierce they were compelled to retire. A second attempt met with a similar fate. Mansel then summoned his whole force and gave the command to fix bayonets; by a spirited charge that section of the bush was cleared at last.

Yet the struggle was by no means over. Though that area had been cleared there was ample opportunity for the Usutus to conceal themselves in other equally difficult parts of the mountain. This they did with great alacrity and from these various points kept up a heavy fire. The conflict by this time had assumed a desperate character for the Usutus fought with great determination and courage, but as only a very limited number of them had guns, and these were mostly antiquated muzzle-loaders, the odds were greatly against them and it was only a matter of time before they were driven from their hiding places down into the deep kloofs far below where they were pursued by both police and native contingents who inflicted severe losses on them. Yet time and again they turned on their foes, inflicting heavy casualties in hand-to-hand fighting. But in the end the order and discipline of trained troops prevailed. Usutu resistance weakened, then broke, and as they scattered they sought refuge in the caves and recesses with which the mountain abounded.

The objects of this expedition had been threefold: to arrest Tshingana, to disperse his armed forces and to seize his cattle, most of which had been stolen. Two of these objectives had been achieved, Tshingana's resistance had been broken, his *impis* scattered and many cattle had been seized, but Tshingana himself had eluded them and as darkness was fast closing in nothing more could be done as it was essential that all sections of the troops and police be reassembled before night fell. It had been a decisive defeat for the Usutus, as later events proved, and marked the turning-point of the whole rebellion, for their leaders realised that if they continued their resistance they would have to stand up against the trained troops of Britain, against whom they were no match. In any case their quarrel was not so much with Britain as against the maladministration of the Natal officials which had resulted in the reinstatement of Sibebu; they could now withdraw from further conflict, having forcibly demonstrated their opposition to the policy of these officials by soundly thrashing their favourite.[21]

## CHAPTER 10

# Dinuzulu's Exile

AFTER the fight at Hlopekulu heavy reinforcements poured into Zululand; these were posted at scattered strategic points, a large force being retained at Nkonjeni for use in the projected attack on Ceza, Dinuzulu's stronghold. Although there were a few sporadic outbreaks in various places they were easily quelled and as numerous chiefs and their followers were surrendering daily it was felt that the hard core of resistance had been broken. Nonetheless vigilance was necessary. Dinuzulu and Ndabuko were still at large with a considerable following and Tshingana had not yet been captured; rumour had it that he had escaped to the New Republic.

Scouts, sent out to reconnoitre around Ceza, found the whole area deserted; later it was discovered that Dinuzulu and Ndabuko, with about 1,600 followers had fled over the border. A telegram was then sent to President Kruger requesting him to disarm and send these men back to Zululand. He replied that they would be disarmed but he was not prepared to grant extradition 'for so-called political offences'.[1]

A message was also sent to the Swazi King urging: 'Should Dinuzulu and Ndabuko escape over border to Swaziland Governor relies upon you to arrest and hand them over to Zulu authorities.'[2] The King replied (on the instructions of T. Shepstone, his adviser) that: 'He would do as the Government says.'[3]

Harriette Colenso (daughter of the late Bishop Colenso) now appeared on the scene, taking up the cudgels on behalf of Dinuzulu and his chiefs, thus causing great annoyance to the Zululand officials who resented any outside interference. This courageous but over-zealous woman wrote direct to the Governor:

The Zulu Chiefs are not rebellious towards H.M. Government but are simply driven to despair and bewilderment by the conflict between Your Excellency's expressed intentions and the exasperatingly cruel miscarriage in the execution thereof. . . . Sympathy with Dinuzulu is strong even among the tribes in the Reserve. . . . Sibebu has no more right to be moving about with and using an impi than had Dinuzulu to follow his example. May it be ordained for Your Excellency to restore to the Zulus and the surrounding tribes some belief in the justice of England.[4]

At the same time she also addressed a letter to 'The Heads of the Zulu people' pointing out that at the present juncture there were two roads open to them, either to die holding their weapons, or to go of their own accord and give themselves up to the English authorities. As they were charged with the crime of rebellion they would have to suffer punishment. Yet should they surrender, a policy which she recommended, there were certain circumstances in their favour:

1. The Governor promises that if they surrender their case will be examined.
2. Their surrender would enable their sympathisers to expose the treachery by which they were hemmed in and so bring punishment on those who were destroying and slandering them.
3. The case of a man who is seized fighting is very different from that of one who gives himself up believing in his innocence.[5]

This letter on reaching Dinuzulu and his followers produced a profound effect, for Harriette Colenso was revered and deeply loved by the whole Zulu nation and a message from her invariably carried great weight.

Miss Colenso followed this up with another letter to the Governor informing him that her two messages urging surrender had been favourably received: 'As the Usutus did not wish to fight against the English but against Sibebu who has brought back his assegai red with our blood as before.'[6]

Meanwhile as Dinuzulu was now in the Republic telegrams were being exchanged between the High Commissioner in Capetown and President Kruger. On 14 August the High Commissioner wired: 'Urge Your Honour to disarm Dinuzulu and Ndabuko and intern them at a distance from frontier sufficient to prevent hostile movement from south-east of Republic. Hope request will be carried out.'[7]

On 11 September 1888 Havelock informed the Secretary of State (Lord Knutsford) that the President of the Republic had received news from Vryheid of the surrender of Dinuzulu and the disarmament of his followers. He was stated to have surrendered on the assurance that he would not be handed over to the English. Ndabuko was believed to have fled, more or less on his own, to Tongaland.[8]

In later messages, first by telegraph and then in a dispatch, the Governor told the Secretary of State that on 16 September Ndabuko had come voluntarily to the military camp at Mona, near Ivuna, and given himself up unconditionally to Lt-Col. Martin, the O.C. of the troops stationed there. He had been sent under escort to Nkonjeni where he was now closely guarded. Col. Stabb had been instructed to conduct a preliminary investigation into his case as it was felt that Addison, the Resident Magistrate, was too closely connected with the offences with which Ndabuko was charged and thus would be unsuitable for this duty. The investigation would be held at Nkonjeni.[9] It had also been ascertained through Col. Stabb that Ndabuko had sent two messengers to Dinuzulu urging him to come in and surrender to the British without loss of time.[10]

A few days later President Kruger sent news to the High Commissioner that it had been decided to intern Dinuzulu and Tshingana, who had now joined him, in the district of Lydenburg,[11] far away from the border; his followers would be dispersed 'amongst the Kaffirs in the district of Piet Retief and H.M. Government could rest assured that it would be impossible for them in future to be a threat to the authorities in Zululand.'[12]

Evidently Ndabuko's messengers reached him about this time and Dinuzulu determined to act upon his uncle's instructions. Along with Tshingana and their followers, he vanished during a night when the Republic's police were none too careful in the guarding of their charges and although the hue and cry was raised and an extensive search organised not a trace of them could be found. This happened in late October and it can readily be understood that it created no little sensation both in Zululand and in the Transvaal.

The next we hear of Dinuzulu is that on 1 November he had reached the border of Zululand accompanied by a large number of his men. From there he sent a message to Addison begging permission to give himself up. Addison telegraphed the Governor who replied: 'Dinuzulu has placed himself in the hands of the Republic. I absolutely decline to have any communication with him; if he enters British territory he will be apprehended and detained as a prisoner.'[13] Consequently Dinuzulu vanished again and the last that was heard of him was that he was seen going in the direction of the Transvaal with about twenty mounted men. His other followers had scattered; Tshingana also had disappeared.

Tshingana was the first to be found. After parting from Dinuzulu he had made his way back to his home near Hlopekulu where on 6 November he was arrested and taken as a prisoner to Eshowe. Instructions were issued to Mr Saunders, the Resident Magistrate, to institute a preliminary investigation into the charges against him with a view to his being brought to trial.[14]

On the night of 13 November the Governor received a telegram from Major Pennefather, magistrate of Nqutu, reporting that Dinuzulu had crossed the Buffalo River into Natal on the morning of the 12th and was making his way to Maritzburg. Instructions were immediately issued to all magistrates on the borders of Natal to be on the look-out for him and Col. Dartnell was requested to give orders to the police for his apprehension.

An interesting account of his journey to Maritzburg is given by Wilhelm Petrus Meyer, a farmer of the Republic who, acting on the instructions of a Vryheid attorney, accompanied Dinuzulu from his kraal at Mahashini to Bishopstowe, the residence of the Colenso family:

I met Dinuzulu at his kraal on Sunday 11 Nov. 1888; we left there about 11 a.m. and accompanied by a number of his headmen crossed the Buffalo River at Rorke's Drift about 4 a.m. on Monday morning; we slept that night near Bleu Bosch Laagte. On Tuesday we went as

far as Sundays River, about 3 miles from Elands Laagte and slept
there in the veld. On Wednesday morning we went to Elands Laagte
and I telegraphed to the magistrate at Ladysmith for passes for all
Dinuzulu's followers and got the following reply: 'Which way are you
travelling? They must apply in the usual way for passes and pay fees.
If they are coming through Ladysmith let them use this telegram as
authority for travelling.' Upon receipt of this telegram I got into
the train with Dinuzulu and 12 of his men at about 4 p.m. and
proceeded to Ladysmith, stopping there about 20 minutes and
then coming on by train to Maritzburg where we arrived about 1.30
a.m. on Thursday morning [15 November] and went straight out to
Bishopstowe.[15]

Mrs Colenso told the story of their arrival at Bishopstowe and
entry into Maritzburg:

On Thursday morning last Dinuzulu arrived with no previous notice
and with some 20 followers. Agnes came to tell me of it as soon as I
was awake and we settled that it was best that she should go in as soon
as she could to town to announce our young friend's arrival and to
say that he came to give himself up to the Governor. . . . Very soon
Agnes was gone into town but before she came back a party of mounted
police arrived with an arrest for Dinuzulu. They, or rather the presiding
officer, was most civil and willingly consented to wait till Agnes
returned. They had seen her on the road coming home and she
appeared very soon and nothing could be more civil and friendly than
every one was. It was rather comical to see 5 or 6 mounted men
called to make a cordon round the house to prevent the escape of a
boy who announced himself as having come to give himself up to the
Governor and accept his decision. . . . He is treated with really great
kindness at the police barracks where he is detained and his people
allowed free access to him and Miss Colenso especially but he does not
like to see guns on every side of him.[16]

Sergeant-Major Shekleton, Natal Mounted Police, describes the
actual arrest:

On arrival I saw a lady whom I believe to have been Miss Giles and
asked her if Dinuzulu was there. She replied 'Yes'. I told her that I
had come to arrest him and she asked me to wait until Miss Colenso
returned from town. I consented to wait and posted sentries round the

house. Upon Miss Colenso's arrival I told her that I had a warrant for Dinuzulu's arrest. She did not ask to see it but said 'You have come for Dinuzulu. I will go and tell him.' She then went into the house and after a short time came out with a native and a white man named Meyer who said to me 'That is Dinuzulu.' I then took charge of him. He said nothing and made no resistance; he appeared to come willingly. I asked Miss Colenso to tell him that if any of his followers wished to be with him that they could follow him in and accommodation would be found for them in the barracks. He then said he was ready to go and got upon the horse we had taken for him and we rode into town. He did not speak on the road.[17]

As soon as Dinuzulu had been incarcerated the Colensos took upon their shoulders the responsibility of briefing the firm of Messrs Dillon and Labistour as solicitors for his defence; Miss Harriette had already contacted Harry Escombe, who was also acting on their behalf, in London where he was at the time of the arrest.

The following day Dinuzulu learnt that he was to be moved almost immediately to Eshowe where arrangements had been made for him to undergo a preliminary examination at the hands of Col. Thompson of the Royal Scots, prior to his trial. This move was strongly opposed by Dinuzulu and his solicitors. They were most anxious that the trials should take place in Natal and not in Zululand, for it was felt that there witnesses for the defence would fear reprisals from Osborn, Addison and other officials should they attempt to expose official maladministration.

As the officials were doing their utmost to rush proceedings Dinuzulu's supporters realised that they must act quickly. Accordingly, on the Saturday morning (17 November) an urgent application was made to the Supreme Court at Maritzburg for an interdict preventing the removal of Dinuzulu for a period of fifteen days. This was granted with the proviso 'That this order may be moved to be set aside or altered on Tuesday next before this Honourable Court.'[18]

Needless to say the prosecution took immediate steps to upset this arrangement. Pressure was brought to bear upon Dinuzulu by Henrique Shepstone, Secretary for Native Affairs, to gain his consent to the move, but as this was unavailing an appeal was made direct to the Governor and on Tuesday the 20th the matter was again brought before the Supreme Court by the Attorney-General, acting on behalf of the Governor as Governor of Zululand. The result was inevitable and the previous order of the 17th was discharged.

The prosecution were now free to act and they lost no time in doing so. Without giving a clue to Dinuzulu's counsel or his friends, he was removed secretly that night and by 1.25 a.m. on the morning of the 21st was safely installed on the Durban train with an escort of Natal Police en route for Eshowe. Arriving at Verulam at 8.50 on the morning of the same day he was lodged in gaol till noon when he was conveyed with one attendant by post cart to Bond's Drift. Here the Tugela, which divides Natal from Zululand, had to be crossed. The Natal police handed their prisoner over to the Zululand police in the middle of the river and, escorted now by the latter, Dinuzulu rode the rest of the way into Eshowe on a horse. There he was lodged under guard in a tent set apart for him on instructions from the Governor.

Proceedings were again hurried forward with the object of allowing as little time as possible for the defence to prepare their case and in order to prevent too deep a probe into the administration of justice in Zululand. The preliminary investigation under Col. Thompson was begun on the morning of the 24th.

Meanwhile Dinuzulu's attorneys had not been idle. Leave to appeal against the discharge of the interdict was lodged but refused by the Supreme Court, so it was decided to submit the case to the Privy Council in London. Further, as it became obvious that the prosecution were determined to race through all the cases connected with the recent troubles, the defence, in desperation, appealed direct to the Secretary of State urging a postponement.

On 3 December Lord Knutsford telegraphed Sir Arthur Havelock: 'Strongly inclined to opinion in favour of adjournment of trial of Dinuzulu for 1 month or 6 weeks. Of great importance that they should have counsel and thorough examination in each case so that no possibility of raising question whether fair inquiry being made.'[19]

To this the Governor replied on 5 December: 'Having communicated your telegram to the President of the Court have received the following answer: "In deference to Secretary of State but contrary to our views we grant adjournment for 7 weeks. Trial of Ndabuko already begun. Dinuzulu not committed to trial. Preliminary proceedings near completion." ' It was obvious that he too only grudgingly agreed to this postponement, for he concluded his telegram by adding: 'Trial of Dinuzulu will also be postponed. Expenses of commission will be very largely increased by adjournment.'[20]

Thus as far as the Special Court was concerned the trials were adjourned till 23 January 1889, though the preliminary investigations were pushed ahead with all speed.

For the conduct of these trials a Special Court of Commissioners was constituted by the Governor in consultation with the Attorney-General, Sir Michael Gallwey, and the Secretary of State, for it was realised that neither Osborn nor any of the Zululand magistrates were fitted to act in a judicial capacity as they had been too closely connected with the events in question, and moreover they would also be required to give evidence. Consequently Mr Justice Wragg, Senior Puisne Judge of the Supreme Court of Natal, assisted by Messrs Fannin and Rudolph, resident magistrates of Natal, were appointed as Commissioners. Confirmation of these appointments was duly received from London on condition that each of the accused should be allowed to defend himself by counsel should this be desired. Further, full notes of all evidence must be transmitted to H.M. Government and if the accused were found guilty: 'The sentences must in no case be carried into effect until H.M. Government had had an opportunity of considering the evidence against them and the Queen's pleasure is known.'[21]

Miss Harriette Colenso now reappeared on the scene protesting most strongly to the Governor against the composition of this Court on the following grounds:

1. As the recent disturbances were the direct result of the maladministration of Zululand, of which the Governor was the

head, the Special Commissioners should not have been appointed by him.

2. As Dinuzulu surrendered in Natal he claimed the protection of the Courts of Natal and should not have been forcibly returned to Zululand.

3. The Court should sit in Natal to enable witnesses to give their evidence freely and without fear of persecution by the Zululand officials.

Similar objections were also submitted direct to the Colonial Office by Advocate Harry Escombe who was still in London, to whom the Colonial Secretary replied that although the Court of Special Commissioners had been appointed by the Governor as the representative of the Queen in Zululand, nevertheless the selection of its members had been made on the responsibility of H.M. Government: 'Who were satisfied of the fitness and impartiality of its members. All sentences already passed on other Chiefs are suspended pending their consideration by the Secretary of State. Trials must be resumed on dates arranged.'[22]

Meanwhile the preliminary investigation of Ndabuko at Nkonjeni had been completed and he had been committed for trial on the charges of high treason, rebellion and public violence. Tshingana's preliminary investigation was also concluded at Eshowe and had resulted in his being committed for trial on similar charges. Dinuzulu's case, after due consideration by the Attorney-General, had resulted in his being indicted on charges of murder, high treason, rebellion and public violence.

Before the Special Court trials commenced lengthy arguments were carried on between counsel for the defence and the prosecution, and undoubtedly the defence had reasonable grounds for complaint. Very briefly these may be summarised as follows:

1. By the Proclamation (IV of 1888) constituting the Special Court the accused had been deprived of their right of trial by jury.

2. The *causes* of the recent disturbances were not allowed to be brought before the Court.

3. Witnesses were compelled to answer *all* questions even though

such answers might incriminate themselves and no indemnity was granted them.

4. All Sir Arthur Havelock's dispatches, the reports of Osborn and all other Zululand Native Commissioners as published or referred to in the Blue Books were excluded as evidence.

As already indicated the objections under (1) were overruled.

Regarding the second objection it is obvious from a careful perusal of the records that the Zululand officials had on numerous occasions acted beyond the powers delegated to them and in some cases inflicted punishments far in excess of those merited by the guilty parties. Some of these officials were a law unto themselves, often acting not according to the law but guided by their own sentiments. On several occasions glaring injustices had been brought to the notice of the Governor and resulted in severe reprimands and in some cases the quashing of the sentences.

The case of Somkele and his people may be quoted.[23] The tribe had been fined by Pretorius, the magistrate of Umfolosi, 2,000 head of cattle for rebellion, with an additional fine of 100 head for each chief. On complaints being made the Attorney-General reported: 'Tribal fines should be imposed only by the Supreme Chief. The action of the magistrate was arbitrary and unconstitutional in imposing any fine without trial. There is no deposition in the case, there are no notes of evidence and no records.'[24] When brought to the notice of the Governor the conviction was quashed and the magistrate reprimanded.

A second case concerns Siziba, Sikwata, Ngunya and Mahlatini, arraigned before Tyrrell, acting magistrate of Ndwandwe, for building on forbidden ground, an offence which according to the Native Law of Zululand was usually heard by a chief who had the power to impose a fine – a case somewhat similar to our contempt of court. The judgment inflicted by Tyrrell was: Siziba fined five head of cattle; Sikwata five head of cattle and twenty-five lashes; Ngunya and Mahlatini, twenty-five lashes each. The lashes were inflicted at once – illegally, for the sentence had not been submitted for confirmation as the law directed.[25] On the case being reported to the Resident Commissioner the other part of the judgment was quashed and the magistrate suspended; when later this case reached the ears of the Secretary of State he ordered a special circular to be issued to all magistrates: 'explicitly informing them that corporal punishment should under no circumstances be ordered except in the cases in which it may be clearly prescribed as the statutory punishment.'[26]

A further case may be instanced in which counsel for the defence had summoned three witnesses to Eshowe. The men (Mafukwini, Mfunzi and Pakate) had on arrival been arrested on the instructions of Osborn who then sent them away to a remote district. When this was reported to the Governor the Commissioner was rebuked for his action:

It has been more than once intimated to you that it is not intended to punish others than the leaders in the late outbreak. . . . You were informed that the judicial commission was to be specially appointed for the purpose of trying those amongst the *leaders* of the Usutu party who might be charged with offences. Under these circumstances it seems to me questionable whether proceedings should have been instituted against Mfunzi and Pakate and the fact that their attendance at Eshowe had been procured as witnesses for the defence made it all the more necessary to use caution in arresting them.[27]

On the Governor's instructions the men were ordered a safe conduct to Eshowe and back.

The third man, who had given evidence unfavourable to the prosecution in the preliminary investigations, on his return to Eshowe was re-arrested without any warrant and lodged in gaol on a charge of incitement to murder. Here he was kept until the Special Court had concluded its sessions; the defence were not allowed to call him as a witness and the prosecution, fearing that he would again give evidence unfavourable to them, kept him safely under lock and key and though charged with inciting to murder he was never brought to trial before the Special Court.

One of the most severe of the Zululand officials was Addison, the magistrate at Ndwandwe. So many complaints had been lodged against him that on two occasions questions were asked in the British House of Commons regarding statements made by certain witnesses for the Crown in the trials at Eshowe that

Addison had endeavoured to extort evidence: 'By torture, flogging, isolating men and then firing a gun to make each separate man think the other was shot.'*[28]

Though these charges may have been exaggerated there is no doubt that Addison acted in an unconstitutional manner. After reports on his case had been submitted and all the circumstances duly considered the Secretary of State wrote to the Acting Governor: 'After making full allowance for the difficult position in which Mr Addison was placed ... I feel compelled to regard his conduct as deserving of censure.'[29]

Concerning the third objection that witnesses were compelled to answer all questions, with no indemnity granted, counsel for the defence felt with much justification that this severely limited the evidence of many witnesses, and when the position was explained to Dinuzulu the young chief instructed his counsel 'Not to imperil the life or liberty of any of his people.'[30] Even Mr Justice Wragg recognised the possible hardship to witnesses resulting from this clause and offered to do what he could to prevent future prosecution, but the Crown prosecutor was adamant in insisting that no indemnity would be granted.

With regard to the fourth complaint, of the exclusion as evidence of all dispatches and reports in the Blue Books it is obvious that this was done to cover up the maladministration of Zululand by its officials, for had these reports been brought before the Court and certain officials cross-examined many irregularities and much injustice would have been revealed.

Thus there can be little wonder that there was a general demand on the part of the public and the Press that there should be a full inquiry into the administration of Zululand. Even the *Natal Mercury*, 'always an able and relentless opponent of the Usutus',[31] wrote on 8 December 1888:

The defence must, on the face of it, rest on only one basis, namely, that the accused had been forced by circumstances to take up arms against the Queen's forces. These circumstances can be nothing less

* This type of punishment had been used some years earlier to extract information as to the whereabouts of Cetshwayo's hiding place. See my *The Last Zulu King*, p. 170.

than blundering and provocation on the part of the representatives of the Crown. An inquiry into these circumstances means nothing short of a complete and searching inquiry into the administration of Zululand.

But officialdom had too firm a grip of the situation, being fully aware that if such inquiry were instituted many heads would fall, so in spite of the general outcry the iron curtain descended and no further investigations were allowed once the Special Court had completed its sessions.

The Court reassembled on 23 January 1889 and after several minor cases had been dealt with the trial of the ringleaders commenced on 13 February and lasted to 27 April.

In the case of Tshingana (the son of Mpande, half-brother of Cetshwayo, and thus an uncle of Dinuzulu) the prosecution pointed out that on 7 July 1887 he was present at the hoisting of the flag at Nkonjeni where he heard and assented to the terms of the annexation of Zululand; from then to the end of April 1888 he had remained loyal to his oath and had regularly received his stipend as a chief, but during the following month, when Dinuzulu and Ndabuko moved to Ceza and numerous messages had come to him from them, his attitude underwent a complete change. Soon after he held meetings at his kraal and at these gatherings he strove to undermine the loyalty of his people. After the Ceza fight on 2 June he and his followers moved to Hlopekulu and, though warned by the magistrate, openly defied his orders and prepared to resist by fortifying various strong points on the mountain. From this time he became openly aggressive, plundering kraals and raiding the cattle of all loyal Zulus in that area. After Dinuzulu's victory at Ndunu he prepared his men for active resistance against the forces of the Government, had them doctored for war, confined his cattle in selected hiding places, stationed his warriors at strong points on the mountain and when the clash with Government forces occurred, offered such stubborn resistance and fought with such determination that about seventy loyal troops were killed; he himself lost close on 300 of his warriors. After this fight he escaped to the Republic and continued his hostile activities by recruiting four new companies with which he joined Dinuzulu at Ceza. When these disloyal forces dispersed he fled to Hlopekulu where his rebellious career was terminated by his arrest.

Although the defence (conducted by Messrs Dumat and Samuelson) argued that it was through fear of Sibebu that Tshingana had acted as he did the Commissioners were fully convinced of his guilt and sentenced him to imprisonment for twelve years without hard labour.

The trials of Ndabuko and Dinuzulu followed. In the case of Dinuzulu the murder charge had been dropped and both prisoners refused to give evidence on their own behalf.

There were five main charges:

1. On 26 April 1888 when the police went to the Usutu kraal to arrest certain offenders known to be sheltering there they were openly defied, insulted and followed for miles by armed men under the leadership of Ndabuko who only restrained them from bloodshed because Dinuzulu's and his plans for open rebellion were not then matured, for Dinuzulu was still away recruiting men in the Republic.

2. On 13 May 1888 Dinuzulu and Ndabuko assembled their united forces at Ceza; all were fully armed and were wearing the *tshokobezi* badge (fighting head-dress). They had selected this mountain as a convenient stronghold affording them an easy line of retreat into the Republic in case of necessity.

3. On 2 June 1888 they resisted H.M. forces sent to arrest them and in the struggle two soldiers were killed. Dinuzulu and Ndabuko were both present, personally directing their men and when the Government forces retired 2,000 of their warriors pursued them to the Black Umfolosi River, endeavouring to surround them. Dinuzulu was seen urging his men on and only checked them when they ventured too far on the southern side of the river.

4. On 23 June Dinuzulu and Ndabuko led a force of between four and five thousand men from Ceza, twenty-five miles away, to 'finish Sibebu and if Dick [Addison] was there they would fight him as well.' A section of this *impi* approached

the Ndwandwe fort, where a small number of Zululand police was stationed, but on orders from Dinuzulu they turned away and attacked Sibebu, killing 300 of his men and seizing many of his cattle, his women and children.

5. During the months of May and June, from their stronghold at Ceza they raided cattle from the kraals of Mnyamana, Siwetu and other loyal Zulus; they murdered Dirk and Klaas Louw, white storekeepers and several loyal Zulus.

There were numerous minor charges including that of inciting others to rebellion and threatening them with death if they disobeyed and though the defence put up a strong case, pointing out that the accused were goaded on to these unlawful acts by the maladministration of the Zululand officials and by the restoration of Sibebu, yet it was proved to the satisfaction of all the Commissioners that both Dinuzulu and Ndabuko were guilty and Mr Justice Wragg announced the verdict of the Court in the following words:

Dinuzulu, we find you guilty of high treason. After a patient hearing of your case we are justified in saying to you that we are convinced that at the time of your determined resistance to H.M. officers in Zululand and of the attacks upon H.M. forces which you led in person, that you were endeavouring to regain that power to which the annexation by Her Majesty had put an end and that your intention was to overthrow the existing form of government in Zululand. You are sentenced by this Court to imprisonment for ten years.[32]

The same applied to Ndabuko who was sentenced to the heavier penalty of fifteen years but in both cases the imprisonment was to be without hard labour; before being carried out these sentences would have to be confirmed by the Secretary of State.

Within a few days of the rising of the Court Harry Escombe, who had acted as Senior Counsel for the Zulu Chiefs, submitted an application for bail pending the decision of the Secretary of State or, if this was impossible, that their imprisonment be made 'as little irksome as possible'. The request was forwarded to the President of the Court who replied as follows:

To grant this request would be, in my opinion, prejudicial to the peaceful settlement of Zululand and most dangerous. If the Zulu Chiefs are released on bail the whole of Zululand would be startled and be speedily in a state of ferment. The effect upon the law-abiding section would be pernicious. As President of the Court I deem it my duty to observe that it is not within the power of Your Excellency or of the Secretary of State to enlarge these prisoners on bail while the sentences remain valid and the prerogative of pardon has not been exercised.[33]

Towards the end of May 1889 the Governor wrote to Osborn requesting his views on the expediency of removing Dinuzulu, Ndabuko and Tshingana from Zululand in the event of their sentences being confirmed; Osborn's opinion was as follows:

I certainly consider it would be expedient to remove the three Chiefs from Zululand and I do not think it would be advisable to keep them in Natal for they would undoubtedly find means to communicate with their partisans and to carry on intrigue. The very fact of their being in either of the two places would be sufficient to keep alive a smouldering current of active disloyalty and expose the loyal element to the dangerous intrigues which are sure to be carried on by partisans of the Chiefs. . . . Should the sentences be confirmed I am of the opinion that the three Chiefs should be removed to some safe place across the sea and be kept there during the term of their sentences.[34]

This opinion the Governor forwarded to the Secretary of State with the comment: 'Osborn's views are also held by the President and members of the Special Commission. I too am convinced of their soundness.'[35]

Six months elapsed before a reply was received and it was not until 5 December that the Secretary of State wrote to the new Governor, Sir C. B. Mitchell, stating:

A careful perusal of the evidence leads me to anticipate that I shall be unable to advise a remission of the sentences of imprisonment in the case of the three Chiefs: in these circumstances I quite concur in the views expressed that the prisoners should not remain in Zululand during the term of their confinement. I arrive at this opinion not only on political grounds, connected with the tranquillity of Zululand, but from a feeling of what is best in the interests of the Chiefs themselves. If they remain in Zululand there will be no alternative but to subject them to strict and irksome incarceration, whereas in a more isolated British Possession, they may, subject to good behaviour, be allowed a large degree of freedom from personal restraint. I am advised by the Law Officers of the Crown that their removal may be lawfully effected and I have selected St Helena as the British Possession which, on climatic and other grounds, is best adapted for the purpose.[36]

On 18 December the sentences of imprisonment were confirmed and in the same dispatch[37] the early removal of the three chiefs to St Helena was ordered. Each chief was to be allowed one male attendant and Ndabuko and Tshingana, who were married, could be accompanied by one of their wives; due provision was also to be made for the wives and children left behind. Interpreters were to be provided and the St Helena Government was to select one or two guardians who would be responsible for the safe custody of the prisoners.

Once a definite decision had been made arrangements were launched and the officer administering the Government at St Helena was instructed to find suitable accommodation for the three chiefs and their retinue. As it was intended that they should reside in the country three different places were suggested, Rosemary Hall, Primrose Lodge and High Knoll, the first-named being eventually selected as the most suitable. It was a sizeable, well-built house in large grounds, about 1,700 feet above sea level, with stables which could be adapted to meet the requirements of some of their staff; it was situated about four miles from Jamestown, the capital. An order was issued to get the premises ready for the arrival of the prisoners. Full instructions for their accommodation, food, clothing, medical supervision and police control were given by the Secretary of State to Sir C. B. Mitchell who was also requested to:

Explain to the Chiefs generally what will be their mode of life in St Helena, pointing out that the comparative freedom and comfort of their future lot can only be accorded to them in some place other than Zululand and outside of South Africa, so that their transfer to St Helena really constitutes a most material mitigation of the punishments which they have incurred.[38]

They were to be allowed to move about the island and receive such visitors as could be approved of from among the residents; they were forbidden to go into Jamestown without permission and only on special occasions. Reports on their condition were to be sent to London from time to time.

On 17 January 1890 the Colonial Secretary telegraphed to the Governor: 'Unless inconvenient, send whole party together, including women and children and order passages for them to their destination by Union Steamship Co. mail steamer Anglian.'*[39]

Meanwhile Osborn had been making the necessary arrangements at Eshowe for the deportation and selection of their attendants. He had met with some difficulty in the choice of a European interpreter-custodian but eventually managed to secure the services of E. R. W. Saunders, the clerk and Zulu interpreter to the resident magistrate at Umlazi and a younger brother of the Eshowe magistrate.

Strict security measures were taken in conveying the party from Eshowe to Durban as the correspondence between the Governor, the Resident Commissioner and Saunders indicates,† but everything was carried out according to instructions and in due course the *Anglian* arrived at St Helena at eleven o'clock on the morning of 25 February; the prisoners and their party, however, were not allowed to land until the following morning when they were at once taken to Rosemary Hall.

On 28 March the Administrator reported to the Secretary of State: 'The behaviour of the prisoners has been very good since their arrival. They have given no trouble and have expressed themselves as pleased with the arrangements made for them.'[40]

Once settled in St Helena Dinuzulu abandoned his appeal to the Privy Council and no further moves were taken in this direction.

Sibebu, on whose account most of the trouble had started, was in due course brought before the resident magistrate at Eshowe (C. R. Saunders) for a preliminary investigation into his conduct

---

* It had earlier been suggested that the wives and children should follow later.

† See Appendix VIII.

and the murder of Umsutywana. After a fairly lengthy trial he was, somewhat surprisingly, acquitted. This caused a storm of disapproval, and the Attorney-General himself took strong exception to the decision of the magistrate, but as no further action was taken in time the storm subsided and Sibebu, though not allowed to return to his old tribal lands, quietly resumed his chieftainship, a much subdued man as a result of his recent experiences.

## CHAPTER 11

# The Return from St Helena

AFTER the Special Court had closed its sessions full reports on all the cases had been submitted to the Secretary of State for confirmation and in numerous instances sentences had been considerably reduced. Though the Usutus appeared to have settled down after the exile of the ringleaders there still existed a strong undercurrent of resentment. One of its causes was the boundary question between the Usutu and the Mandhlakazi. As has been told, Sibebu, after his return, had illegally seized certain lands and although he had been driven out by Dinuzulu the matter had never been settled.

Some months earlier Addison had made a rough survey and indicated certain boundaries but as these were unsatisfactory it was decided to appoint a Special Commission, consisting of Osborn, Cardew and Gibson, to go carefully into the whole matter and reach a final settlement.

A thorough investigation was made. This necessitated the removal of a number of kraals, both Usutu and Mandhlakazi, but in order that no undue hardship should be inflicted their removal was not to take place until after the harvest. It was also recommended that a new magistracy, separating Sibebu's people from the Mandhlakazi, be established at Lower Umfolosi; this would remove another cause of friction by preventing the Mandhlakazi crossing over Usutu territory when a visit to the magistrate was necessary.

At last a genuine attempt was being made to settle some of the outstanding differences between these two tribes and thus bring about a more peaceful atmosphere.

Hardly had the Commission completed its task when once more

all efforts towards a settlement were destroyed by an extremely foolish move on the part of the Governor, on Osborn's recommendation, to reinstate Sibebu forthwith on his old lands. News of this scheme quickly reached the Usutus, for reports were already current of Sibebu's gathering his people together in preparation for their return. Their reaction was immediate: 'Can the English be going to send back Sibebu? Is the spear to be flung back? Is there to be no end to the stabbing one another? Fighting can never cease if Sibebu is sent back.'[1]

Fortunately, Knutsford though 6,000 miles away displayed far more wisdom than some of his officials in Zululand and nipped this move in the bud:

With regard to the question of restoring Sibebu to his country I have to observe that the mere fact that the Commission has made a satisfactory report which has been approved does not seem to me sufficient occasion for taking action in the matter at present.[2]

Sibebu's restoration is a question which I am not at present prepared to entertain.[3]

At about this time rumours were being circulated among the Usutus that the British Government were about to return Dinuzulu as *King* and Gibson, the Nongoma magistrate, had to let it be known publicly that there was no foundation whatsoever in these rumours. Possibly they may have arisen from exaggerated reports of the news which occasionally filtered through from St Helena. (Dinuzulu had been allowed to write, through his doctor, to his mother.)

Few restrictions had been imposed upon the prisoners and as they were all behaving in an exemplary manner they were allowed to do pretty much as they chose. A tutor had been appointed for them. Dinuzulu had learnt to read and write quite well (as the signature reproduced from a letter of his shows on p. 152). He had also taken up music, learning to play both the piano and American organ; visits were made from time to time to Jamestown and many hours spent in riding over the island, for Dinuzulu was an accomplished horseman.

Unfortunately Saunders, his interpreter, after a stay of about six months had to return to South Africa owing to a severe illness and his place was taken by a local official. Some time later it became necessary to send to Zululand for a midwife and an interesting letter written by Daniels, Dinuzulu's secretary, to Saunders states:

We have had an increase of 7 persons since you left; the new Guardian and his wife and daughter; the Zulu midwife and three babies:

> Mrs Tshingana, a son, born in November 1890.
> Miss Umka Silomo, a son born in November 1890.
> Miss Uhlazile, a daughter, born in December 1890.*

Dinuzulu had fathered the two last from each of his 'Female Attendants'.

Back in Zululand plentiful rains had fallen so the people were kept well occupied in cultivating their crops; pasturage was excellent, the cattle in good condition and a fine harvest was expected. Naturally, this put the people in a good frame of mind and being kept busy they had little time to spare in discussing their grievances.

Meanwhile Natal had been moving steadily, though sometimes stormily, towards Responsible Government. Protracted negotiations had taken place between the Colonial Office and the local Legislature with this in view; two of the conditions insisted upon by the former were that:

* Quoted from the original kindly loaned to the author by Mrs M. M. K. Robinson.

1. There should be a nominated Upper House as a check upon hasty legislation.
2. A sum of £10,000 must be reserved annually to promote the welfare and education of the Natives.[4]

The Colonial Office also insisted upon the condition that Responsible Government meant 'defence from all danger, external as well as internal'. This posed a big problem for the small Colony, for it was realised that in the event of trouble she had not the forces to cope with it. However, after lengthy negotiations a promise was extracted from Lord Knutsford: 'To maintain for a period not exceeding 5 years after the introduction of Responsible Government, a certain number of troops in Natal and Zululand to facilitate the organisation of colonial forces.'

Though strong opposition to the granting of Responsible Government was encountered in Natal itself (opinion was about equally divided and two strenuously contested elections had taken place), the Colonial Office finally decided in its favour and on 4 July 1893 Natal entered upon her career as a self-governing Colony. Her first Ministry was sworn in by the new Governor, Sir W. Hely-Hutchinson, on 10 October 1893 with Sir John Robinson as its first Premier.

Another change took place about this time, a change that closely affected Zululand. In July 1893 Melmoth Osborn retired, his place as Resident Commissioner being taken by Sir Marshall Clarke. Undoubtedly this had far-reaching consequences, for though Osborn had had a difficult role to fill, his continuous favouritism of Sibebu coupled with his autocratic manner, had made him many enemies, particularly among the Zulus who hardly had a good word for him.

Marshall Clarke's advent was marked by a period of quiet in the country and the people appeared to be settling down to the new order. The land was no longer torn by strife and its people had been able to reap their crops without fear of raiders who stole their cattle and swept away their corn. Content prevailed. After years of semi-starvation their grain-pits were well filled and they could brew and drink their *tshwala* (Kafir beer) to their hearts' content.

Unfortunately these days were numbered: the *Amadlozi* – the spirits of their ancestors – must have been angry. The new season's crops had been planted, the spring rains had fallen, the hills and valleys had shed their winter coats and fields of growing corn had taken their place – all indicated another good harvest.

One morning of 1895 as the women were going out into the fields a dark cloud appeared on the horizon which travelled towards them with great rapidity; it grew blacker and more dense as it approached, accompanied by a sound rather like that of the whirring propellers of an aeroplane; it blotted out the sun, casting an ominous shadow over the countryside. Suddenly the cloud disintegrated into millions of fragments and the locusts descended on the fertile fields, transforming them in a short hour or so into blackened ruin with every vestige of growth consumed; not a leaf was left, not a blade of grass, not an ear of corn, all devoured by the voracious pests which now, reassembling into another ghastly cloud, swept on to further devastation, leaving behind a people faced with starvation in the cold winter months ahead.

Spring came again and the people looked to the skies for the gathering clouds that would herald the approach of the much-needed rains after the long, dry winter. Day after day they watched and waited. As the days lengthened so the sun grew fiercer, scorching up the new grass. But there was not a drop of rain and the country became a desert. The rivers turned to trickles and the streams dried up as the sun blazed down from a pitiless sky. Cattle died in their thousands and the land became strewn with carcases; even men had great difficulty in staving off a cruel death from thirst and were in many cases only saved by their womenfolk tramping miles over the baked earth to draw water from stagnant river pools or muddy holes where once had run gushing streams.

But their tribulations were not yet over. The following year, 1897, the murderous rinderpest came down from the Zambezi to the Cape and Natal and wiped out almost every beast that lay in its path. It was as if the plagues of Egypt had descended upon Central and Southern Africa. This was a terrible time for the Zulus whose wealth lay in their herds and it was several years before they recovered from the repeated blows which had fallen so heavily on them.

During the time of these disasters events of considerable importance had been taking place in St Helena, Natal and London. Early in 1895 the British Government had indicated to the Governor of Natal that they desired to apply a policy of clemency to Dinuzulu and were seriously considering the question of his return to Zululand. Marshall Clarke was requested to find out whether this could be done without endangering the tranquillity of the country and also:

What designs were harboured by Dinuzulu and his partisans regarding British rule and by the sections of the Zulus with whom they had been at enmity. If he was allowed to return Sibebu should also be permitted to go back to his own country. How far could he be trusted to confine himself to his own proper sphere of authority or whether there was any danger of his taking measures of retaliation against those of the hostile faction who lived near him.[5]

Having given careful consideration to these queries Marshall Clarke concurred with the view of the Colonial Office that 'the time had come for the exercise of a policy of clemency towards the Zulu Chiefs at St Helena'. Zululand had quietened down and in his opinion all danger of rebellion was over. Possibly there might be certain risks but these could be averted by prudence in laying down conditions as to the position to be assigned to Dinuzulu after his return.

To instal him as a tribal Chief having authority over a strictly defined district inhabited by his most devoted followers would be open to objection for the internal politics of Zululand were such that Dinuzulu might in course of time be drawn into a false and embarrassing position with respect to the Government however desirous he might be at the outset to work loyally under it.[6]

He therefore suggested the following as offering the best prospect of a satisfactory settlement:

Dinuzulu should be taken into the service of the Government of Zululand in the position of Government Induna and Adviser; a house should be provided for him in the neighbourhood of Eshowe with a salary of £500 per annum attached to his office. He must clearly understand that he does not return as Paramount Chief but would be subject to render obedience to the Government. . . . Ndabuko and Tshingana should also be allowed to return to Zululand.[7]

These were wise suggestions, which were adopted by the Colonial Office, and steps were taken to put them into operation with as little delay as possible. Accordingly on 28 December 1895 the Governor of St Helena was informed of the proposed move and told that a vessel would call at the island on 10 February to take the three exiles back to Zululand. Needless to say Dinuzulu and his uncles were greatly cheered by the news and preparations were made for their departure.

But they were to suffer disappointment. Shortly after Natal had gained Responsible Government she had persistently urged upon the Colonial Secretary the necessity for the incorporation of Zululand and when intimation was received of the proposed return of Dinuzulu the Natal Ministers telegraphed the Colonial Secretary on 18 January that unless there was an assurance that this incorporation would take place *before* the return of the exiles there would undoubtedly be serious trouble in Natal.

On this point Natal was adamant, for the Government was still sore over the peremptory manner in which they had previously been treated by Havelock and Osborn and the way in which they had been excluded from all matters connected with a country which was so inextricably bound up with their interests. So strong was their antagonism and so firm their refusal to sanction this move that the Colonial Office had to bow before their opposition. Consequently the Governor of St Helena had to be informed that the order was countermanded and the return of the exiles was postponed for the present; to make amends for the disappointment which Dinuzulu and his uncles would understandably suffer by this decision, the Governor of St Helena was instructed: 'To accord to the Zulus as much liberty as may be possible within the island and to meet all their reasonable requirements in even a more liberal spirit than heretofore.'[8] At the same time London told Natal that Dinuzulu's return would have to take place at an early date and the question of annexation must not be discussed in connection with the return of the exiles.

Little notice was taken by Natal of these instructions and on 26 August 1896 the new Colonial Secretary, Joseph Chamberlain, wrote again to the Governor about the repatriation of Dinuzulu and suggested that arrangements should be made for this to take place 'about the end of the present year if no native disturbances occur'.[9]

This brought the reply, by telegram: 'Unsafe to bring Dinuzulu back at this time; locusts and drought last two seasons; famine in Zululand and locusts still bad; rinderpest has appeared in Natal and Zululand. Loss and suffering may dispose natives to disorder owing to despair.'[10]

This was followed later by a dispatch from the Governor enclosing a statement from his Ministers in which they expressed their views as follows: 'We consider it desirable that the incorporation of Zululand with Natal should, if the exiles return, take place first so that they may return under the wing of the Natal Government.'[11] At the same time the Ministers stated their willingness immediately to submit to Parliament their proposal for such annexation.

To these suggestions the Colonial Secretary replied that the Ministers should inform Parliament that there was good reason to hope that a satisfactory settlement could soon be reached on condition that they accepted the terms proposed by London, which would include a decision on the repatriation of the exiles. On receipt of the above the Governor telegraphed on 23 April 1897: 'Can you inform me before May 15 [close of Parliamentary Session] of nature of conditions of incorporation.'[12] On 4 May the Secretary telegraphed his reply indicating these conditions, of which the following is a brief résumé:

1. The existing system of land tenure in Zululand to be maintained for five years and no grants of land to be made during that period. In the meantime a joint Imperial and Colonial Commission to be appointed to delimit sufficient land reserves for native locations, which locations will be inalienable

without the consent of the Secretary of State. At the end of the period of five years the Natal Government to be at liberty to deal with the unreserved land; the Natal Government to be at liberty, during such period of five years, to proclaim townships with the consent of the Secretary of State, if such townships should become necessary in consequence of progressive mining enterprise.

2.  Native jurisdiction as provided for under the Zululand Proclamation No. VI of 1894 not to be abolished but provision to be made for a Court of Appeal for native cases.

3.  The restriction upon the sale of liquor to natives to be maintained.

4.  The obligations which have been incurred by the Government of Zululand for payment of grants and pensions to native Chiefs to be taken over by the Colonial Government.

5.  Buildings and land connected with mission stations to be secured.

6.  The position of Government officers who may be retained or whose offices may be abolished, to be safeguarded.

7.  The return of the Zulu exiles to Zululand must take place either before or soon after the incorporation and must not be further postponed.[13]

On 17 May the Governor wired: 'Ministers assent to proposals and give assurance that they will not press for any alterations in conditions which could not be accepted by Secretary of State.'[14]

The Natal Legislature was dissolved on 15 May and a General Election took place in September; the Government was defeated and the Country Party under the Premiership of Henry Binns was returned to power. In spite of this change the new Government, after requesting a further delay in Dinuzulu's return, reaffirmed its assent to the Secretary's proposals.

London sent a quick reply to their request (20 October 1897): 'Cannot consent to postpone return of Zulu exiles beyond end of this year.'[15] On the 23rd of the same month a reply was sent to the Secretary: 'Ministers accept position.'[16] So at long last the question of the incorporation of Zululand with Natal and the return of the exiles was settled.

The Secretary of State, determined that there should be no further procrastination in Dinuzulu's return, clinched the matter by cabling the Governor on 28 October: 'Exiles will return by steamship 'Umbilo' calling 19 Dec. at St Helena, reaching Natal Dec. 30'[17] and the following day instructions were forwarded to Governor Sterndale of St Helena to make the necessary preparations for their departure; a statement was also enclosed explaining the nature of the position which Dinuzulu would occupy on his return. The conditions, as already stated, were that he would return, not as Paramount Chief but as Government *Induna*. These were now elaborated: his salary would be held during the pleasure of the Government and would be strictly dependent on the manner in which he behaved and obeyed the laws laid down for his guidance but would not be withdrawn without the approval of the Secretary of State. He would be employed in native matters, such as questions of inheritance and others in which it might be desirable to obtain independent evidence and opinion. He would be chief over those people residing in the location marked off for the Usutu and would rule them by the same laws and form of Government as other chiefs in Zululand, whilst he himself, like other chiefs, would be under the laws of the Government of Zululand.

These conditions were read over to Dinuzulu and his uncles by Governor Sterndale and in order that there should be no misunderstanding they were also interpreted to them by Daniels and Miss Agnes Colenso who was staying at St Helena at that time.

The Governor's reply to the Secretary of State is amusing:

To arrange for their departure is no slight matter; they came here savages in karosses; they are leaving with Gladstone bags and packing cases. Dinuzulu has a more varied assortment of suits of clothes than I have and his drawing room furniture contains books, pictures, ornaments and an American organ on which he plays with considerable skill. Miss Colenso has asked to accompany them at her own expense to which I have offered no objection as she may be most useful to them on the voyage.[18]

Arrangements meanwhile were made to meet the vessel on its arrival in Natal and instructions were given to S. O. Samuelson, the Under-Secretary for Native Affairs, to be in Durban on Tuesday evening, 4 January 1898.

Having carried out these instructions Samuelson on the Wednesday morning made his way to the shipping agents to ascertain the time of arrival of the *Umbilo* and later proceeded to the Public Works Department to obtain the loan of three tents for Dinuzulu's use between the railway terminus and the Tugela. He also purchased '19 ordinary and 6 better class blankets' for the trip. He had then to arrange with the General Manager of the Railways for a special train to leave Durban early the next morning.

Accordingly, about 7 p.m. that evening (5 January), accompanied by W. P. Wheelwright a Zululand magistrate, the two made their way to the docks where they were met by Otto Siedle, the shipping agent, and later boarded the tug *Lion*. Although 'the utmost secrecy had been enjoined' Miss Harriette Colenso was there along with some of Dinuzulu's adherents, one of whom was an old Zulu general.

None of these men had ever been afloat before and when the vessel rolled during the crossing of the Bar their antics were most amusing. Instead of holding on to the rail of the tug they clutched at the deck on all fours and rolled about getting very seasick. Arrived alongside the Umbilo negotiating the rope ladder to get on board was another problem which was overcome with difficulty.

Arriving on board about 8 p.m. our party made for the saloon while the natives fraternised with the exiled natives. We found Dinuzulu awaiting us, accompanied by his two uncles Ndabuko and Tshingana. The former of the two was an imposing figure with a Napoleonic cast of features, whilst Tshingana was rather squat and rotund. Dinuzulu himself looked very fit and proved later not to be suffering from an inferiority complex in consequence of his exile, rather the contrary. Settling down eventually at the Captain's table the Indaba [round table talk] began, Samuelson taking the lead and expressing the future plans with regard to Dinuzulu's movements after landing.[19]

After Dinuzulu had been told of the incorporation of Zululand with Natal and it had been explained that the two countries would henceforward be under the same Government, the conditions of his return, in both Zulu and English, were handed to him which, having read, Dinuzulu returned with the remark that they were the same as those explained to him at St Helena. Ndabuko and Tshingana were told that each would be paid £60 per annum during good behaviour by the Government of Natal. Dinuzulu then said to Samuelson that he wished to spend some time in Durban to have a look around and to do some shopping but when informed that all arrangements had been made for their departure by special train at 6.15 the next morning:

He became very aggressive and gave many disapproving clicks when he heard the intentions with regard to himself. It transpired that he wanted to parade the town making a sort of triumphal procession through the streets. However, after a heated discussion he was emphatically told that the Government would not agree to anything of the sort and our party left for the shore, landing at the Point about 10 p.m.[20]

At this *indaba* Dinuzulu had also mentioned his luggage and its transport to Zululand and Miss A. Colenso informed Samuelson that it consisted of '40 tons of furniture, 6 donkeys, 10 dogs, some rabbits, fowl pens, a canary, a parrot and a monkey.'[21] Poor Samuelson was flabbergasted for there were only three wagons to meet them at Tongati. However, he told Dinuzulu that he must select such things as would be required on the way and arrangements would be made to send along the rest later.

Next morning the *Umbilo* steamed into port at an early hour and the whole party – about forty – were put into the special train which was at the Point to take them on to Tongati. Everything passed off smoothly and after as much of the luggage as possible had been stowed away they moved off about 6.30 a.m. A brief halt was made at Durban where Sir Marshall Clarke was waiting to greet the exiles and to bid them farewell, for his term of office as Commissioner had expired on 31 December 1897, his place being taken by Mr (later Sir) Charles Saunders. During this interview Dinuzulu expressed regret that no visit was to be made to the Governor but it was explained to him that there could be no delay on this occasion as Mr Saunders was awaiting them at Eshowe. Dinuzulu and his uncles were then warned to be careful whose counsels they followed, to regard the Government of Natal as their friend and to write to them when in difficulty and to visit the office of the Secretary at Maritzburg should the necessity arise for consultation. A friendly and respectful atmosphere had prevailed and after good wishes had been exchanged the party proceeded to Tongati which was reached about two hours later.

At this point Samuelson returned to Durban having handed his charges over to two Zululand magistrates, Wyndham and Wheelwright. The last part of the trip was made by mule wagon and it was here that the tents and blankets were put to good use, for this ride took the best part of four days. Eshowe was eventually reached about 4 p.m. on 10 January. Adequate arrangements had been made for their reception, a house having been built for Dinuzulu at some distance from the Residency and furnished at Government expense.

The following morning Dinuzulu had his first interview with the new Commissioner, Charles Saunders, and there was a frank discussion of all points covering the future welfare and work of the repatriated exiles. At the outset Dinuzulu was told that it was the Commissioner's intention to be perfectly open in all his dealings with him and he expected the 'same demeanour on Dinuzulu's part towards himself'. The question of the recent annexation of Zululand with Natal was considered, particularly in its relationship to the future administration of Zululand, the Commissioner stressing the fact that should Dinuzulu be faced with any problems or difficulties he must not hesitate to ask for guidance or advice. This was very different treatment from that which Dinuzulu had experienced at the hands of Osborn. Everything possible was now done to make his duties clear and his path as smooth as possible.

Dinuzulu's task was certainly not an easy one. His primary duties, as specified in the conditions of his return, were 'to act as Government Induna and Adviser': this meant that he would be the principal Native Executive Officer on the Commissioner's staff and as such he must reside near Eshowe; although this was not expressly stated it was an understood condition, otherwise a furnished house would not have been provided. At the same time he was appointed chief of a tribe which lived nearly a hundred miles away and although the task was not insuperable, to exercise proper control of its affairs when living at Eshowe would present many difficulties. In addition, it was only natural for him to want to live at his old home and amongst his own kith and kin.

When this problem was placed before the Commissioner and referred by him to the Minister of Native Affairs (Sir Liege Hulett) it was given sympathetic consideration, and on 22 January word came through granting the returned exiles the necessary permission on condition that Dinuzulu made frequent visits to Eshowe. At the same time Sibebu also was to be allowed to return to his old kraal; it will be remembered that whilst the exiles were at St Helena he had been compelled to reside in the Eshowe district. Strictest injunctions were given to both parties that 'the assegai must now be buried' and they must learn to live harmoniously side by side. A full reconciliation having been effected and a solemn promise extracted from both to observe this condition they were allowed to return to their respective kraals as soon as satisfactory arrangements had been made.

Thus the principal condition laid down by Sir Marshall Clarke for Dinuzulu's return to Zululand was practically ignored, with disastrous consequences as later events proved only too conclusively.

## CHAPTER 12

# Dinuzulu as Government Induna

Six weeks after Dinuzulu had arrived in Eshowe he and his uncles were on their way to Nongoma in wagons provided for them by the Government; they were accompanied by Agnes Colenso, Maxwell and Daniels and all who had been with them on St Helena.

During the eight years of Dinuzulu's absence the duties of chieftainship had been carried out by his mother, Oka Msweli, assisted by his Prime Minister Mankulumana; the latter had taken over much of the actual work of civil and minor criminal cases but Oka Msweli had kept the power. Their kraal, Ekubhazeni, was situated in the Ngome district and fell under the jurisdiction of the Nongoma magistrate. When rumours of the return of Dinuzulu reached their ears preparations were made for the erection of new huts at the royal kraal of Usutu and a number of young men were enlisted to form two regiments which were to welcome him home and act as his bodyguard. These regiments received the names of the Inqubokakundlazi and the Udakwakusutha (commonly known as the Udakwa).*

Great were the rejoicings amongst the Usutu at the return of their chief, for in spite of his long exile his position as their *Inkosi* (King) had been in no way affected and his authority was still regarded as supreme.

A European who witnessed the event gives us a description of the chief's appearance: 'I was at Nongoma when Dinuzulu returned from St Helena in 1898; a fine, well built figure [he was then thirty years of age] dressed in a shooting suit of that period. He entertained his visitors at the Usutu in good style and was able to rattle off some tunes on his piano.'[1]

* Information given to the author by Chief Sangwene, Nongoma district.

164

Unfortunately, this adulation and the return to kraal life had a bad effect on the prince. From this time onwards there was a marked deterioration in his character. Away from the restraining influences of civilisation and in spite of the steadying influence of Ndabuko and, in a lesser degree, of Tshingana he lapsed into evil ways; not content with a considerable number of wives he took to himself an even greater assortment of concubines; casting aside his European clothes but without resuming the picturesque garb of his younger days, he appeared before his subjects in a slovenly and untidy dress; living luxuriously on his patrimony, plus the ample allowance (for those days) of £500 a year, he spent much of this on liquor, drinking inordinate quantities of European spirits.[2] Naturally this told on his health and though repeatedly warned he paid little or no heed. By 1905 he had grown so corpulent that he weighed 330 lb and by then was suffering from so severe a dropsical condition that it became almost impossible for him to walk without assistance.

For the first few months after his return from St Helena he visited Eshowe fairly frequently to carry out his duties as Government *Induna* but whether these duties were not understood by the Natal Government or whether they were deliberately allowed to lapse is a pertinent question. What actually happened was that Dinuzulu's visits to Eshowe grew less and less and after a while stopped altogether. Maybe the lack of insistence on his regular visits was due in some measure to the unsettled state of affairs in South Africa, for the country was on the verge of war, but whatever the reason it was a serious omission and one which later was to produce results of great gravity.

His appointment as Government *Induna* surely meant that in addition to his duties as tribal chief to the Usutus Dinuzulu was to occupy the position of a central official under the District Commissioner and would be in some measure the confidant of the authorities. Thus he was to act as a connecting link between the Government and his tribe and through his tribe to the nation in general. This is certainly what Sir Marshall Clarke had in view when he suggested this post as one of the conditions of Dinuzulu's return, for it was of vital importance that the lines of communication be kept open between the authorities and the Zulu people. Sir Marshall foresaw the need of one who should act as the intermediary between the Zulu nation and the Government, one who should voice their sentiments, express their opinions, state their grievances and in return ascertain the Government's reaction to these and the remedies, if any, that they suggested. The Government on their part could inform their *Induna* of any new Native legislation that they proposed to introduce, any fresh taxation, in fact, any matters that concerned the Zulus and he could in turn present these to his people. It needs little imagination to realise the significance of this link. Under the old regime the Zulus had their King assisted by a privy council of some half-dozen leading chiefs and a general assembly of elderly men; their deliberations were public and anyone could listen, even take part; in this way the laws were enacted which governed their lives. Since the annexation the King was replaced by the Governor, the privy council by an executive committee, the public assembly by a legislative council, all consisting entirely of white men, most of whom were completely out of touch with the Zulu tribesmen and their needs. Hence the necessity for this link, and because of its absence laws were enacted without any native consultation or representation. Little wonder that the resultant state of affairs caused bitter resentment, a resentment that was later expressed by Dinuzulu in the following stirring words:

We are people who have no representatives in the councils of the country, no one to speak for us and the laws of the country simply come over us by surprise; they are promulgated to us and we are ordered to do this and that. We simply hear the laws without having any opportunity of discussing them. We have no representatives in the affairs of the country.[3]

Both the Government and Dinuzulu himself were to blame for the development of this situation, the Government even more so than Dinuzulu, for it was in their power to have insisted on his taking his rightful position as *Induna* and seeing to it that he kept in constant touch with the authorities. Dinuzulu's blame lay in having taken up permanent residence at Usutu instead of Eshowe and so letting slip the one and only opportunity that was given for keeping in close contact with the movements of the Government in so far as they concerned his people. Both the Government and Dinuzulu were to live to regret that Sir Marshall Clarke's condition had not been more strictly observed.

At the time Dinuzulu no doubt felt that he had scored by moving to Usutu. Here he was to a large extent free from the prying eyes of officials and could do more or less as he pleased. Always susceptible to flattery, his vanity was now fed to a dangerous degree; not only was he lionised by his own people but others came from near and far to pay their respects, and although the law proclaimed that their Supreme Chief was now the Governor of Natal, yet so deeply was their veneration for the royal family ingrained in them that they still regarded the son and heir of Cetshwayo as their *Inkosi.**

This forced Dinuzulu into a situation which the Government wished to avoid and which they could have avoided had they insisted on his assuming the position of Government *Induna*, for it soon became obvious that the Zulu people as a whole looked on him as more than the mere head of the Usutu tribe and, naturally, Dinuzulu played up to this and encouraged the various chiefs to visit him by treating them with lavish hospitality. It is probable that he had in mind the regaining of his old position, but whether this was so or not he certainly wished to increase his status from that of a mere petty chief over one tribe. He was shrewd enough to know that the path to power was beset with many difficulties; it had been amply demonstrated to him by experience that the use of force was out of the question, so other means had to be adopted. He therefore set about the task of attempting to create such a situation, by currying favour with all the various tribes of Zululand, that he should have behind him the solid backing of the whole nation and thus make himself the undoubted leader of his people; then, should the opportune moment arrive, he could

---

* The author had a striking manifestation of this veneration on a recent visit to the Princess Magogo, a daughter of Dinuzulu. An *Indaba* was being held at the chief's kraal and as the Princess appeared instantly every man jumped to his feet, raised his hand and gave the royal salute '*Bayete*': it was spontaneous and enthusiastic.

press his claim to paramountcy with a reasonable prospect of success.

As the Boer War dragged tragically along a sudden and unexpected opportunity presented itself to him for the advancement of his ambition.

During the early stages of the war there had been a tacit understanding that none of the African races should become embroiled – it was a white man's war purely and simply – and as far as the Zulus were concerned the Transvaal–Zululand border would not be violated. For many months this understanding had been observed but in the later stages, when guerrilla tactics were adopted by the Republican forces in a last desperate attempt to stave off defeat, this boundary condition was broken. The British Military Command in an attempt to check the guerrillas issued orders for the seizure or destruction of all enemy cattle in order to deprive them of their food supply. Raids were to be organised by the military along the north-western boundaries of Zululand and Col. Bottomley was sent to arrange them. To carry out these plans he went to Dinuzulu, without obtaining the consent of the Natal Government, and ordered him to arm and assemble his men. Dinuzulu reported these orders to the magistrate, who objected to them in the strongest terms; he was, however, overruled, for the country had been placed under martial law and Dinuzulu was forced to obey. Having collected twenty-four companies – about 1,500 men – he sallied forth and at a hill called Dhleke accomplished his task, losing two of his warriors in the attempt; a Boer wagon was also raided and a number of firearms seized. In the outcry that followed it was reported that this raid had prevented a Boer attack on a nearby magistracy.

This little episode enormously enhanced the reputation of Dinuzulu in the eyes of the Zulu people, for it was then widely reported amongst the tribes that Dinuzulu had been asked to undertake this duty because the military powers recognised him as the head of the Zulu nation.

The incident had serious consequences. The Boer guerrillas, now faced with the cutting off of their food supplies, commenced

to raid native cattle in the district of Vryheid and being embittered by the Dhleke incident, they also burnt down a number of
native kraals. It so happened that these kraals belonged to the
AbaQulusi tribe, one of the fiercest enemies of the Boers and,
though not under the chieftainship of Dinuzulu, among his
strongest and most loyal supporters. Little or no notice being
taken of their losses, the men of this tribe determined to take
revenge. Accordingly Sikobobo, their chief, gathered together
about three hundred of his warriors and having ascertained that
a party of some seventy Boers, known as Potgieter's commando,
were bivouacked near the foot of a mountain called Holkrantz
(modern spelling Holkrans) some twelve miles from Vryheid, he
led his men out to the attack.

The Boer field-cornet had been warned that the AbaQulusi
were on the war path and although there was a measure of
uneasiness among some of the commando, for odd Zulus had been
sighted on the heights, yet no precautions were taken and no
sentries posted. These were deemed unnecessary as an armistice
had already been declared between Boers and British.

That night they lay down to sleep as usual and at about four
o'clock on the morning of 6 May 1902 several of the burghers were
awakened by the sound of a shot; before an alarm could be raised
the AbaQulusi were upon them with rifle and assegai and, as is
well known, when the Zulus can get in at close quarters with their
assegais they are indeed a deadly foe. It was a sharp and bloody
encounter. The Boers had been taken completely by surprise and
when the count was finally taken it was discovered that of the
seventy-two burghers fifty-six had been killed, but the AbaQulusi
had also left about seventy dead on the field.

Naturally the disaster alarmed the Boers but at the same time it
created a profound and dangerous impression upon the whole
Zulu nation; once again they remembered Isandhlwana and other
actions of the war of 1879, and now Holkrantz!

One of the immediate results was the seizing of some rifles by
the AbaQulusi, a number of whom made their way to Usutu
taking the guns with them. Later, on being questioned about this
Dinuzulu replied that he had summoned the men to his kraal in

order to restrain them from further acts of violence. No doubt there was considerable truth in his statement, for open hostilities were what he most wished to avoid at this juncture. Nonetheless this was a danger signal and a warning to those who were supposed to keep a watchful eye over their Government *Induna*.

Shortly afterwards Dinuzulu strengthened his authority in another direction by re-establishing the Nobamba kraal in the Emakosini Valley. This was an extremely important site to every Zulu. It had been originally founded by Jama, the grandfather of Shaka, and was situated in what Dr Bryant has aptly called 'The cradle of the Zulu clan, the birthplace of the Zulu Nation.'[4] Lugg also refers to it as 'Hallowed ground, reserved for Royal kraals only'.[5] Once this kraal had been established its inmates regarded themselves as belonging to the royal house and no longer under the authority of their local chief. The kraal of Tshingwayo was situated nearby and it was but natural that his people too should offer their allegiance to Dinuzulu. So, quietly and unostentatiously, Dinuzulu was consolidating his position amongst the tribes scattered in various parts of the country.

The year 1902 was a most important one for Natal but a sad one for Zululand. It will be remembered that the first of the conditions of the annexation stated:

The existing system of land tenure in Zululand shall be maintained for 5 years. In the meantime a joint Imperial and Colonial Commission to be appointed to delimit sufficient land reserves for Native locations. . . . At the end of the period of 5 years the Natal Government to be at liberty to deal with the unreserved lands.

Undoubtedly, the main object of an influential number of the Natal colonists in pressing for the annexation of Zululand was not so much to bring the Zulus under their administration as to gain possession of a large tract of their country. For many years Natal farmers, amongst whom were a number of Members of Parliament, had cast envious eyes on a wide belt along the Zululand coast which was admirably suited for the cultivation of sugar and they eagerly awaited the expiry of the time stipulated in the condition of incorporation so that their Government would then 'be at liberty to deal with the unreserved lands'. Before any action could be taken in this matter the joint Imperial and Colonial Commission had to be appointed and their findings presented to both Imperial and local Parliaments. This Commission was to consist of two men and in due course Sir George Dartnell was nominated by the Secretary of State as the representative of the Imperial Government and Sir Charles Saunders, the Civil Commissioner of Zululand, was appointed by the Governor of Natal, Sir Henry McCallum, as representing the interests of the Colony.

These men at the outset were placed in an invidious position and their task was a most difficult one. Right on their doorstep were the land-hungry farmers with the backing of Parliament, eager to snap up the rich sugar-growing land on the coast the moment the opportunity offered, irrespective of the fact that these same men had only a few years earlier raised their hands in horror at the action of the Boers who had seized a large slice of Zululand for their New Republic; now they were adopting the selfsame tactics, filching more land from the Zulus without even the excuse of having helped them crush their foes.

On the other hand there was the Imperial Government which was infinitely more to blame than the Natal farmers. Theirs was the responsibility for having ever allowed such a situation to develop in view of their solemn pledges to the Zulu nation.

On 9 October 1879 Sir Garnet Wolseley, addressing Zulu chiefs and headmen, the leaders of the people, had expressly promised: 'That no sale, transfer or alienation of land in Zululand would be permitted as the British Government was anxious to prevent white people from settling in the country.'[6] This was later confirmed by the Secretary of State: 'I also concur in your prohibition of the acquisition of land by white people in Zululand.' About the same time each of the thirteen Kinglets was made to promise on solemn oath: 'I will not sell, or in any way alienate, or permit or countenance any sale or alienation of any part of the land in my territory.'[7]

Sir Theophilus Shepstone laid down in his Report of 27 February 1883: 'That these reserves of land . . . were for the Zulu people, not for the white men and that no portion was to be sold or alienated.' When the Boers at a later date pressed their claim for about half of Zululand solemn pledges were forgotten under the excuse of political expediency, regardless of the fate of a brave nation.

Now in 1902 history was repeating itself. The Commissioners were instructed 'To delimit sufficient land for Native locations' and the Natal Government was then at liberty to deal with the rest. Not one single cent was offered to the Zulu people by way of compensation.

The Commissioners did their best. Of the 6,695,000 acres 3,887,000 were reserved for the exclusive occupation of the Zulus and 2,613,000 acres were handed on a platter to Natal, the small balance being set apart for townships, etc. Although the Zulus appeared to gain a considerably greater acreage it must be remembered that much of this land was unsuitable for human occupation; either it was mountainous, arid and stony, or it was unsuitable for stock on account of the ravages of the Tsetse fly, or it was low-lying and malaria-ridden.

The Commissioners made their recommendations subject to an important condition, viz. that the Zulus *also* should have the right to purchase land in the area thrown open for European settlement, should they desire to do so and should they be able to afford it; in other words, to pay money to the Government for land which rightfully belonged to them. The recommendation of the Commissioners is worth quoting:

The Commission presumes that Natives, in common with other British subjects, will be allowed to purchase if they wish to do so, and considers that the fact of their being landowners would be a guarantee of loyalty against future disturbances; indeed, in view of the pledges given from time to time by H.M. Government that the country would not be taken from the Zulus, we do not see how they can in common fairness be prohibited from purchasing land, notwithstanding the fact that Reserves are now being delineated for their occupation.[8]

The recommendations in due course received the approval of H.M. Government and the land thus thrown open for European settlement was surveyed into farms not exceeding 500 acres apiece and sold to sugar farmers or land-grabbing companies for a mere song.

Nine years later even the right to purchase was taken away from the Zulus: 'Except by special permission of the Governor-General, which special permission, so far as is known, has never been given save for the 1,000 acres of Amatikulu lots.'[9]

Thus Natal commenced her government of the Zulu nation by sowing the seeds of lasting bitterness, for it can hardly be wondered at that these intelligent people deeply resented the handing over for European settlement of another huge tract of their country, containing some of its most fertile areas, in spite of repeated assurances that the land belonged to them.

It has remained for the Nationalist Government to attempt in some measure to rectify the position and hand back a portion of their country to them, in face of very bitter opposition from a section of the people of Natal. To attain this end hundreds of thousands of rands have been paid to farmers in compensation and money is being spent lavishly year by year to help the Zulus make the best possible use of the areas which are now reserved for them in perpetuity.

To aggravate the position still further, once the farmers were settled on their newly acquired land a number of Zulus whose kraals had been there for generations were ordered to clear out and seek new lands; others were regarded as squatters and compelled to pay a monthly rent, or in lieu of rent, to give their services for so many months (three to six) in each year. Although the majority of farmers charged a nominal rental there were numerous instances where these charges were exorbitant, some even demanding as much as £12 a month, and when it is borne in mind that the average pay for native labour on the farm was at that time about ten shillings a month, plus rations, the injustice is obvious. The result was that many Zulus got hopelessly into debt and in an attempt to extricate themselves from their difficulties put their cases into the hands of various country lawyers who were unscrupulous to a degree, charging enormous rates of interest on their loans. So bad did the position become and so great was the outcry against these men that the Government was compelled to take action and legislation was passed limiting their interest charges. This gave immense relief to many of these poor people and saved their cattle, their only wealth, from falling into the hands of these grasping rogues.

Another source of unrest among the Zulu people was a system in vogue at that time known as *isibalo,* which is a modified form of *corvée.* To understand this it is necessary to go back to the days of the Zulu kings. It was then customary for the monarch to call up various regiments from time to time to the royal kraal; these men would have to undertake certain duties, such as the building and repair of the royal apartments, erecting cattle kraals for the King, hoeing and weeding his lands. For these tasks no wages were paid and no regular food supplied, though occasional beasts were slaughtered as a special gratuity, otherwise the relatives of the soldiers would have to see to their feeding. The regiments submitted to these tasks without demur; it was the law of the land and therefore it was their duty to obey.

In later days, when the kingship was abolished and the Governor had replaced the King as Supreme Chief, this system was continued, though in a different manner. Natives were then forced to work for the various Government departments and the chiefs were compelled to supply a certain quota from their tribes each year; if they failed to do so they were fined. The Commissioner's report for 1902 states: 'During the year close upon 3,500 Natives have been ordered out in the Province for services under the Public Works, Railways and Harbours and Military Departments.'[10]

True, the hours and conditions of labour were good, regular wages were paid and plentiful rations were supplied, but the whole system was unpopular and rankled with the Zulus, largely on account of the bribery practised among the chiefs, for should a man wish to get out of this duty he could readily do so by giving a beast or some other bribe to his chief.

A further injustice suffered by the Zulu people at the hands of the Natal Government lay in the iniquitously small sums spent on their general welfare and education. It had become increasingly apparent since Annexation that the Government were doing their utmost to get everything they could out of the Zulus but give as little as possible in return. It will be remembered that one of the conditions imposed by the Imperial Government was that a sum of £10,000 a year was to be set aside 'for the promotion of the welfare and education of the Natives'. In spite of the large rise in their population and the consequent big increase in the revenue accruing to the Government, this annual expenditure had remained static; this meant that with a Zulu population standing (in 1906) at 938,472 only £10,000 was set aside to cover all education, hospitalisation and general welfare. Yet the Government was extracting an annual sum of about £250,000 in direct taxation from these unfortunate people, thus making an annual profit out of them to the tune of approximately £240,000, which money went to relieve the European taxpayer.*

Thus as time passed and as the wrongs under which the Zulus suffered seemed only to increase, so the people more and more felt the necessity for a protector, for

Someone of their own flesh and blood whom they could trust to voice their interests and one who, because of his rank, would ensure adequate attention being given thereto. The more Dinuzulu allowed these exhibitions of feeling to go on, the more Natives in an ever-widening circle looked on him as their natural champion, as the one who in every way *ought* to lay their grievances before the Government. They wanted him to stand up for them with a view to the ancient life, habits and customs – with which, for so many centuries, they had been intimately associated – being allowed to continue with less restrictions and innovations than had become customary.[11]

Quite possibly Dinuzulu was pleased with the situation in which he now found himself but had he consistently made use of his position as Government *Induna* he could have proved himself of much more service to the nation. Had he kept in close touch with the authorities, as was his duty, and raised his voice in strong protest from time to time against the many repressive measures

---

* In 1905, according to the official returns for that year, the total taxation extracted from the Zulus in Natal and Zululand amounted to £247,455.14.8. In 1906 this amount had increased to £306,484.18.7. (*Annual Reports, Department of Native Affairs, Colony of Natal*: 1905, p. 155; 1906, p. 75.)

which were adopted against his people, he might have done something towards averting the catastrophe which later befell them. But he let slip his opportunities, being too much engrossed in the flattery of the chiefs who visited him. Already murmurs were heard against the attitude which he had taken up; soon these came to a head in the person of his old antagonist, Sibebu, who came forward with a demand for the return of certain cattle which, he stated, were owed him by Cetshwayo and he held Dinuzulu, as Cetshwayo's son, responsible for the debt. It was just an excuse and a rallying point for action to be initiated against his former enemy. Dinuzulu contemptuously repudiated the claim and once again the animosity of many years flared up. Others gathered round the standard of the old warrior and Manzolwandhle, the posthumous son of Cetshwayo, joined his ranks. Quite a number felt that he had a better claim as Cetshwayo's successor than Dinuzulu. Things looked ugly and the possibility of another civil war loomed. Fortunately this was averted by the death of Sibebu which occurred on the evening of 27 August 1904 at his kraal at Banganomo, and the whole movement collapsed.

So ended the career of one of the most remarkable and most belligerent men that Zululand had ever produced.[12]

## CHAPTER 13

# The Crisis Breaks

ONCE the quarrel with Manzolwandhle had died out there appeared little real opposition to Dinuzulu and his star was in the ascendant. This could hardly be attributed to his personality for, though gifted with considerable intelligence and much shrewdness, his life of indolence and his intemperate habits unfitted him for the leadership of that nation. It was only the prestige of his position as the King's son that made so many of the chiefs turn to him in their hour of need as their one hope.

Since 1879 the nation had suffered years of agony; their country had been ravaged by the horrors of civil war; much of their land had been taken from them, their homes destroyed and many of the once proud warriors of Cetshwayo were now forced by circumstances to eke out a miserable existence as serfs to the white man whose word, from sore experience, they had learnt could not be trusted. With the passage of time their afflictions seemed just to increase; they had been scourged with drought, locusts, rinderpest and East Coast fever and what little remained to them of their rich and beautiful country had become a land of sorrow: 'The joy of their hearts was ceased; their dance was turned into mourning.' (Lamentations 5: 15.) They were denied the privileges of education except on the mission stations, for the Government looked on them as nothing but an unlimited source for the supply of cheap labour. For the few who had received the advantages of an elementary education there was no possible hope of advancement, for every step in this direction was blocked by job reservation – positions were strictly reserved for white men only.* They were

* Fortunately in recent years this appalling state of affairs has been largely remedied and though job reservation is still enforced it is to a lesser degree

obliged to carry a multiplicity of passes whenever they moved from their kraals and these could only be obtained at a magistrate's office; this often entailed a walk of many miles – twenty or even more was no uncommon occurrence – and when they reached the office, more often than not they faced hours of delay, were treated with rudeness and frequently told to come back again another day. Should they be caught without the required pass they were often brutally handled by the police and flung into gaol alongside hardened criminals. Their womenfolk too were unsafe, for often they were interfered with by white men. Naturally this caused angry resentment, particularly amongst such a race as the Zulus who in their tribal life had laid so great an emphasis on chastity.

To add to their burdens, since the Boer War the whole country had been in the grip of a dreadful depression, prices for their produce had slumped to an extremely low level, jobs were scarce but their numerous taxes had still to be paid; the hut tax had already been increased from 7s. to 14s. and now there were rumours of fresh and heavier taxation.

In the year 1904 the Government decreed that a census of the people should be taken. Up to this time no enumeration of the Zulus had ever been attempted and 'there is nothing that a Zulu will take umbrage at more quickly than when he, his family and belongings, are being counted. It appears to him tantamount to

---

than of old and there are now many openings for the educated African, large numbers of whom hold positions of responsibility with great credit to themselves. Millions of rands have been and are being spent annually upon vast housing schemes; hospitalisation and welfare services far surpass those of any other native territories in the world; their system of education advances year by year and though much remains to be done it must be remembered that, though the Africans contribute largely, a big percentage of this expenditure comes out of the pockets of a very limited European population. In the Province of Natal alone there are now 1,939 native schools employing 6,485 teachers with a total of 335,253 scholars (1964 figures). In addition there is a fine University College at Ngoye with a staff of forty-six professors and lecturers and an enrolment in 1964 of 180 students which number has steadily increased since its inception in 1960. In Natal there are also six training colleges for African teachers and two vocational colleges (a third is soon to be opened) where the respective trades are taught, and each of these institutions is filled to overflowing.

The scene of the Mpanza Fight. The rock on the right is where Bambata's
warriors hid. The old road ran just above this

Fort Yolland

Sigananda (left) and a native sergeant of police

The Bambata Rebellion. A group of captured rebels: (l. to r.) Mesini, one of Bambata's *indunas*; Nkomo, Bambata's chief *induna*; one of Sibindi's rebels; Cuyaganya, implicated in the mutilation of Sergeant Brown

placing himself entirely in the hands of another and of being surrounded',[1] as he used to surround his enemies in warfare. This resentment was aptly expressed to the magistrate at Greytown who, when explaining the regulations to an assembly of Zulus, was asked: 'What guarantee have we that, in being enumerated in the fashion proposed, it is not in the mind of the Government, making use of the information gained, to do us an injury in the future?'[2]

Yet another disaster befell the Zulus. On 31 May 1905 a terrific hailstorm, the worst in living memory, swept over the country, destroyed the crops and caused untold damage.

The cumulative effect of all these troubles, coupled with the increasingly repressive policy of the Natal Government and the farmers, was seen in several directions.

In the first place many of the chiefs, urged on by their headmen and councillors, adopted the age-old custom of interviewing the head of the state to discuss their many problems with him. As there was no longer a King they naturally turned to his heir – Dinuzulu. A large number of them had called on him previously, on the occasion of his return from St Helena; that visit was purely of a social nature, to welcome him home; now they came seeking guidance and help, for they were full of anxiety about the future.

During these interviews there were lengthy discussions of the Government's repressive laws and the generally callous treatment to which all were being subjected. Whether Dinuzulu encouraged the spirit of resistance or one of appeasement is a moot point, but from what ensued it appears that he adopted the latter policy, for many of the chiefs returned to their kraals disappointed and embittered men. Possibly this was in part due to a feeling of frustration as they realised that though Dinuzulu listened with much sympathy to their problems he could do nothing and the only advice he could give was 'Take your troubles to the Government – I am only a petty Chief.' This was indeed small consolation, for they knew from experience that the Government would turn a deaf ear to all their appeals.

In the towns too the same spirit of unrest was stirring. Here an economic and social revolution was being forced on the African people by the white man's rule. Poverty, disease and taxation had driven great numbers of men and a limited number of women out of their kraals into the busy cities where there were opportunities of employment. The gold mines of Johannesburg were yearly absorbing thousands of Africans for work underground and many of these came from the hills and valleys of Zululand. In most cases the object of these men in seeking employment on the Reef and elsewhere was to earn money to help support parents, wives and families.

But life on the mines meant being herded into compounds, cut off from all intercourse with their womenfolk and from the friendly atmosphere of the kraals which had been their home and the home of their fathers for centuries. Many broke under the strain of such a violent change and tried to forget their loneliness in the arms of prostitutes or in the shebeens run by the many 'queens' who concocted soul-searing brews with a potency like the kick of a mule. In the thrills of this new life obligations to those left behind in the kraal were completely forgotten; the discipline of life which had been a tradition with them for generations was blotted from their minds and in its place was born a spirit of defiance and hatred for their white overlords.

This spirit was encouraged by Ethiopianism, a quasi-religious movement imported from America. It was a type of fanaticism that had a particular appeal to the Zulu in the discontent of that time. Primarily it was a separatist movement based on an entire breakaway from all European control in ecclesiastical affairs and had as its clarion call 'Africa for the Africans'; under the guise of religion it became a fiery political movement, preaching sedition at most of its services. Though small numerically, it embraced within its ranks several fanatics who with blazing tirades against the oppression of the white man stirred up their congregations to semi-hysterical outbursts. One of their leaders was a man called Moses who later drifted into Natal and Zululand where he openly preached rebellion and had a considerable following, including a number of chiefs.

As mineworkers and city labourers drifted back to their kraals so they not only brought back with them stories of the sophisticated life they had led and of the many low-grade Europeans with whom they had come into contact on the mines but they carried in their hearts an increasing hatred of the white man for his oppression of their race. One of the results of this impact was the conversion of a considerable number of Zulu women to Ethiopianism and they soon came to exert an important influence in the life of the kraals.

The importance of the influence of Zulu women has often been overlooked by those who have written about this people; many of them have regarded women as of little or no account simply because they were not allowed in the councils of the nation. This has been a serious omission, for a careful survey of Zulu history indicates very clearly the great power and influence which Zulu women wielded in the affairs of their nation, as they undoubtedly did at this time.

Thus the cumulative effect of these varying forces soon became concentrated in a display of antagonism against white men in every part of the land.

The first sign of this spirit was a mysterious order that spread over the whole of Natal. (It must be noted that the first steps towards an open breach were taken in Natal, *not* Zululand.) The order read as follows:

All pigs must be destroyed, as also all white fowls. Every European utensil hitherto used for holding food or eating out of must be discarded and thrown away. Anyone failing to comply will have his kraal struck by a thunderbolt when, at some date in the near future HE sends a storm more terrible than the last, which was brought on by the Basuto King in his wrath against the white race for having carried a railway to the immediate vicinity of his ancestral stronghold.[3]

To grasp the full significance of this strange order an explanation is necessary.

Pigs, though largely kept by the Zulus, were never eaten by them; they were retained solely for the purpose of barter or sale to Europeans. That white fowls were to be killed and European manufactured utensils had to be destroyed was a sinister but clear indication that the author of this command wished the white man to be killed.

The reference to the 'thunderbolt' was a direct pointer to the Zulu King whose acts were often compared with the fury of the elements; more than this, he was supposed to control those elements and could bring or withhold rain. Sometimes this necessitated the assistance of other native kings and a tribute of ten oxen was usually sent to get them to exercise their skill. The Swazi kings were reputed to be able to bring gentle copious rains whilst the Basuto monarchs, by the use of certain secret drugs, were said to cause devastating storms and bring down deadly thunderbolts.[4]

Since the order appeared to emanate from one holding a position of supreme authority the Zulus would naturally conclude that it came from Dinuzulu and within a very short time of its proclamation numbers of chiefs flocked to the Usutu kraal to ascertain whether he was indeed the author. To all these chiefs the reply was the same, a flat denial, but if they wished to conform to the order, that was *their* business. In the end Dinuzulu became so exasperated that when Tilonko, a chief from mid-Ilovo, visited his kraal he took him around and, pointing to numerous pigs that were running about the place, said to him: 'Look, pigs exist here.' In order to convince him fully Dinuzulu then ordered one of his servants to bring some white dishes which were regularly used by himself, affirming at the same time that he knew nothing about the order. From a careful examination of all the facts it appears certain that he spoke the truth; its origin, even to this day, remains an unsolved mystery.

As the Zulus of Natal in increasing numbers obeyed these mysterious commands, so Dinuzulu became more and more perturbed, so much so that he pressed for an official inquiry into its origin but as the Government could find no substantial grounds for connecting him with it he was completely exonerated.

The persistence of the Natal natives in carrying out the order was a pretty clear indication that they were about to take action in some way or another, yet in spite of this warning the Government took no notice nor did they attempt in any way to investigate the root causes of the brooding unrest that had spread all over the country. On the contrary, there were some who welcomed the idea of an outbreak of violence, as was proved by reports from both the Chief Commissioner (C. R. Saunders) and the magistrate of Vryheid (A. J. Shepstone). The latter on 1 June 1904 wrote to the Secretary for Native Affairs:

I know that it has been remarked quite recently by ex-burghers that the best thing that could happen would be a Native rising, that it would do the Natives good as they were getting insolent, it would draw the Englishmen and the Boers together and give the Boer an opportunity of recouping losses sustained during the war.[5]

Then came the spark which caused the explosion – the imposition of the Poll Tax.

The financial depression which followed the Boer War had told very severely on Natal and the Colonial Treasurer was faced with the difficult and unenviable task of finding a means to reimburse an empty treasury. Various new taxes had been passed by the Legislative Assembly (a House Tax, a Bill to tax adult natives, another dealing with unoccupied lands) but all of them had been thrown out by the Legislative Council and as the end of the session was drawing near it became imperative that a new tax of some sort be passed without delay. So the Treasurer fell back upon the Poll Tax, a tax which had been gazetted but shelved some months earlier. This was now reintroduced, rushed through both Houses and became law in August 1905.

By this tax an amount of £1 per head was imposed on all White, Coloured, Indian and African residents in Natal and Zululand of the age of eighteen and upwards, the only concession being the exemption of Africans who paid Hut Tax.

Immediately it became law it was met by a storm of opposition from all sections of the African population. The young men on whom the burden chiefly fell resented it because they could not see why a tax of one fixed sum should be imposed alike on Africans and on Europeans in view of the fact that the European's income was on the average at least twenty times greater than that of the African. A further reason for their resentment was the fact that many of them were already paying the Hut Tax on behalf of their parents.

The parents resented it because they feared that their sons would now throw off all their obligations on the plea that they could no longer afford to send money home as they had their own tax to pay and as these sons were in distant cities it would thus mean a complete breakaway from all parental control.

Feeling was particularly strong in Natal, for the Zulus felt that the census, against which they had so resolutely objected, was now being used to their disadvantage in spite of Government assurances.

On 22 November 1905 instructions were issued to the various magistrates to summon all chiefs and tribesmen and explain to them as fully as possible the implications and provisions of this new law, laying particular emphasis on the fact that though payment of the tax would fall due on 20 January 1906 they would be allowed till 31 May before any action would be taken against them for non-compliance.

By the beginning of 1906 dissatisfaction 'had reached such a pitch that outbreaks of defiance and violence were inevitable. . . . Dinuzulu must have been aware of this and must have known that if ever he was to use the antagonism of the Natives towards the Natal Government for his own ends, that time had arrived.'[6] But instead of taking advantage of this crisis he remained quietly at his kraal and before the due date not only had he paid the tax himself but had seen to it that all his own tribesmen had done the same. (They began paying on 17 January.) So convinced was the Chief Commissioner of the prince's loyalty that in one dispatch after another he assured the Government that Dinuzulu was in no way connected with the rebellious spirit which was being shown throughout Natal, and of all men Sir Charles Saunders could surely speak with authority, for he knew Dinuzulu intimately, was himself an outstanding Zulu linguist and since 1888 had held important official positions in Zululand which had brought him into frequent personal contact with the chief.

Whatever attitude we may adopt regarding Dinuzulu's entanglement in the troubles that were about to follow, it is certain that the brooding spirit of sullen resentment amongst the Natal

African population burst into open rebellion mainly through the imposition of this Poll Tax and certainly not through the instrumentality of Dinuzulu.

The first indication that the people were about to take the law into their own hands occurred on 17 January. Henry Smith, a farmer of Umlaas Road, on that day had accompanied his natives to the magistrate's office at Camperdown to see that they paid their tax. That evening whilst standing on the veranda of his home he was handed a note by one of his servants. Turning to the lamplight to read it he was stabbed with an assegai and mortally wounded. The servant was later arrested and in the trial which ensued it was ascertained that the only motive which prompted him to commit this murder was resentment at the payment of the new tax, for it was proved beyond question that Smith was a good master.

Sporadic outbursts followed in many parts of the country. On 22 January the magistrate of Mapumulo and his staff had, by previous arrangement, proceeded to a certain store for the collection of the tax. Soon after their arrival Chief Ngobizembe turned up accompanied by three hundred fully armed warriors, a gross breach of etiquette, for by an unwritten law amongst the Zulus all arms must be laid aside before appearing in the presence of a chief, and a magistrate held such rank. The men, when sternly reprimanded, roared in reply: 'We won't pay.' An ugly situation developed as they surged forward bent on mischief and had not the chief and some of his *indunas* set about belabouring the offenders with their sticks it is more than likely that the officials would have suffered a grim fate. Similar incidents occurred at a store on the Insuze River and at another on the Umvoti, and by the end of January reports of serious unrest came in from almost every part of the Colony.

On 7 February at Henley, a small station about eleven miles from Maritzburg, another episode of a similar nature took place, this time with fatal consequences. Warrants were issued for the arrest of the ringleaders and on the evening of 8 February a posse of mounted police under Sub-Inspector Hunt proceeded to carry these into effect. A fierce struggle ensued during which the Africans used their assegais and the police their revolvers, and in the conflict Hunt and one of his troopers were stabbed to death.[7] A force of about fifty police were then sent out to recover the bodies of the two men who had been killed and to search for the rebels.

By contrast the situation in Zululand should be noted. Sixty-two chiefs had been called upon to pay and of these forty-six had responded by 26 January and other payments were being made daily, the only exception being at Nkandhla where one of the chiefs displayed some insolence to the magistrate. The Minister of Native Affairs, who was at Nongoma at this time, expressed his view that the successful collection of the tax in Zululand had been 'in a measure due to the good example set by Dinuzulu'.[8]

As a result of these outbreaks Natal became panic-stricken and the authorities went to extremes. On 9 February they called out the militia and the day following martial law was proclaimed, to include Zululand. On 13 February two tribesmen accused of complicity in the murder of the police were tried by court martial, found guilty and shot at once.[9] Some days later twenty-four tribesmen were arrested, tried in a similar manner and twelve of them sentenced to death. When England heard this news – by cable – a storm of criticism broke and the Secretary of State for the Colonies cabled an order to stay the executions pending further investigations. The Natal Prime Minister (C. J. Smythe) refused to accept this order; the Governor, Sir Henry McCallum, then fell back on his prerogative powers and ordered the suspension of the death penalty. In retaliation the Prime Minister and his colleagues resigned; cables sped to and from England but in the end the Secretary of State gave way, the Ministers withdrew their resignations and on 2 April the twelve men were shot at Richmond. 'As if in defiance of humanitarian protests, the executions took place in public, even schoolboys being allowed to look on, and, with questionable taste and morality, the firing party was made up of comrades of the two murdered men.'[10]

In spite of the uproar caused by these executions the Government in no way attempted to put a curb on the actions of their military commanders nor did they even now in the face of so serious a menace endeavour to ascertain the causes of these outbreaks. Whilst it is acknowledged that stern measures were necessary to maintain law and order it is certain that the harshness adopted by the authorities incited others to take increased action against the Government. Had there been some effort at conciliation, however small, even at this late hour, it could have produced a beneficial effect and possibly stimulated Dinuzulu to back the authorities and the enormous influence which he undoubtedly wielded might have been used to such effect that the lives of hundreds of his people could have been saved. But the Government showed themselves utterly indifferent to the many injustices and the grinding poverty under which the majority of its subjects were compelled to live.

## CHAPTER 14

# The Fight at Mpanza

WHILST these outbreaks were occurring trouble of a far more serious nature was brewing in another part of Natal.

For some months past a minor chief, Bambata by name, whose kraal was situated about sixteen miles beyond Greytown, had been causing the authorities considerable anxiety by his unruly behaviour.

Bambata had been a general nuisance since boyhood, not so much from an over-exuberance of boyish spirit as from a quarrelsome nature which led him into frequent fights in which he was invariably the victor; he grew up to be a fine athlete, an outstanding runner, a good shot and an expert in the use of the assegai. These qualities, coupled with his irascibility, made him a dangerous customer.[1]

Some years after the death of his father, which occurred when Bambata was twenty-five years old, he was appointed chief of the AmaZondi tribe and hardly had he assumed this position when he was accused of stealing three head of cattle belonging to a Boer; he was arrested and severely punished but saved from imprisonment by his tribesmen paying a fine. This had an embittering effect on his attitude towards the white man and intensified his difficult disposition, making him even more harsh, reckless and extravagant than ever; he became a heavy drinker and as a result was invariably in debt, a state of affairs which was accentuated by his landlord demanding the somewhat exorbitant rental of £3 per hut per month; to extricate himself from his financial difficulties Bambata borrowed from lawyers who, as was customary, charged the usual extremely high rate of interest, which resulted in his constantly being sued; instead of making some sort of an effort to meet his obligations he plunged even more deeply into debt and became a greater nuisance than ever both to Europeans and his own tribesmen, for the latter were constantly being called upon to get him out of his difficulties. At the time of the census he roused the ire of the magistrate by his somewhat offensive remark: 'If there be anything behind all this, we shall be angry.' In August 1905 he was mixed up with a faction fight in his own ward, brought into court, convicted and sentenced to a fine of £20 or three months' imprisonment; this, along with his general misconduct, resulted in a recommendation to the Government that he be deposed from his chieftainship.

As I have described, the African population throughout Natal had taken strong exception to the Poll Tax and amongst the AmaZondi the spearhead of resentment lay strangely enough not in Bambata but in his headman, Nhlonhlo. He, by one of those queer twists of fate, brought about a chain of circumstances which led his chief directly into open rebellion.

For some weeks past the magistrate of Greytown had been receiving reports of serious unrest in the Mpanza Valley as a result of which, rather than face an ugly demonstration, he issued an order to Bambata to appear personally, along with his tribesmen, at his office on 22 February 1906 for the payment of their tax. On the appointed day Bambata had arranged that before proceeding to the magistrate's office all taxable members of his tribe should assemble on a ridge just outside the town. A number of the older men having reached this place sat down to await the arrival of the others. Bambata himself was following and when within a few miles of Greytown a messenger informed him that his young men, under the leadership of Nhlonhlo, were hiding in a wattle plantation a little way ahead, all armed with shields and assegais and in a very defiant mood. This was disquieting news, so Bambata sent back the messenger ordering the young men to lay down their arms, proceed to Greytown and pay their taxes quietly. They refused to do so. Meanwhile Bambata continued to the appointed rendezvous to find that some of the older men had gone on to the magistrate's office; others told him it was useless for them to do so as they had no money. He remonstrated with them and ordered them to return to their homes, sell some of their goats and so pay their tax. The remaining few who had brought the necessary cash were sent on to Greytown with instructions to inform the magistrate that he himself was unable to come that day owing to sickness but would follow later.

Bambata was in a dilemma; a large number of his people were in a dangerous mood and had threatened that if he went to Greytown and any attempt were made to detain him they would resist by force of arms. Thinking it was better for him to try to pacify his young men rather than proceed to the magistrate's office, he decided on this course and so put himself in the wrong, for had he reported this insubordination the onus of preserving peace would have fallen on the shoulders of the Government. Yet it must be remembered to his credit that he acted as he did to save his tribesmen from the severe punishment which was certain to have followed had he reported their conduct to the magistrate.

Events now moved rapidly. Bambata's non-arrival at the magistrate's office, together with a series of alarming reports that he and his people intended to attack Greytown that night (reports which later were proved to be without foundation), were telegraphed to the Secretary for Native Affairs who replied with a summons ordering his immediate appearance in Maritzburg. After some difficulty Bambata was found and the order conveyed to him personally by two native policemen; he promised to comply but his headman, Nhlonhlo, refused to allow him to go because, he stated, once Bambata set foot in Maritzburg he would be arrested; to check such a move he and his *impi* carried Bambata off to another kraal. Later messages met with a similar refusal on the grounds that it was reported that the white men had taken up arms against him. Hearing of all this trouble Bambata's attorney now sent a message offering assistance, promising to accompany him to the authorities and explain matters to them. But once again Nhlonhlo stepped in saying: 'I prefer he should die in our own hands rather than be shot by Europeans out of our sight.' A heated argument ensued in which the older tribesmen supported the view that Bambata should surrender himself to the authorities, but the threats and defiance of Nhlonhlo and the younger men prevailed and Bambata peremptorily ended all further discussion by stating: 'I won't go. Some of you want me to be killed by myself; when they kill me it will not be until some of you have been laid out.'

The die was cast; Bambata and his followers took to the dense bush where they remained in hiding, awaiting developments.

They had not long to wait. On 9 March a force of 170 Natal police together with a troop of Umvoti Mounted Rifles arrived at Mpanza to arrest Bambata but as their approach had been seen the whole body retreated deeper into the almost inaccessible bush and the police, unable to find their quarry, were forced to return empty-handed.

It is important to note that concerted military action was resorted to by the Government some considerable time before Dinuzulu knew anything about the outbreak of trouble amongst the AmaZondi tribe.

Realising that a conflict was inevitable Bambata decided, as so many other chiefs had done before him, to go to Usutu and ask advice of Dinuzulu and his *indunas*. Accordingly, on 11 March he vanished from the district, but from evidence given later at the trials of the rebels it is possible to trace his movements. For two days he and most of his people hid in the bush, men and women apart, but on the morning of the 11th, Moses, the Ethiopian pastor who had been working among the tribe for some time, acting on Bambata's instructions, summoned Siyekiwe (Bambata's wife) and told her to be ready, along with her two small sons, Ndabayake and Nonkobotshe, and Kolekile, his daughter by another wife, to accompany him to Zululand, as it was his intention to set out immediately for the Usutu. Bambata himself was accompanied by Mgoma, his *inceku* (personal servant and mat-carrier) and a young man named Nkantolo. As he knew the journey would involve considerable risks, for he was now a hunted man, it was decided that all travelling should be done by night. Since none of them were sure of the way, Jolwane, one of his tribesmen, was to act as guide.

Their progress was slow, for Siyekiwe, his wife, was pregnant at the time. Thus the journey must have been somewhat of an undertaking for them, sleeping by day, sometimes at odd kraals but more often in hiding on the veld, and travelling by night. Eventually they reached the kraal of Gezindaka, a short distance from Usutu. As Gezindaka was the father of Cakijana, who became an important figure in the events which were to follow, it is essential to know something about this young man.

For some time past he had been working on the mines in Johannesburg together with four of his brothers, one of whom, Nqatshana, had been seriously ill. As there was no sign of improvement it became necessary for him to return home. Evidently he was in a bad way; not only had the journey to be undertaken hastily but one of his brothers had to accompany him. That brother was Cakijana and, as he himself later said, it was his full intention to return to his work as soon as possible for he had left all his belongings at the mine together with some of his pay. On reaching his father's kraal he was told he would not be able to go back to Johannesburg until he had paid his Poll Tax. This he did without objection but before resuming work he decided to visit his girl. On his return he found visitors at the kraal, 'three men, a woman, a girl and two young boys and their guide Jolwane' (Bambata, Nkantolo, Mgoma, Siyekiwe, Kolekile and the two boys). In evidence given later he stated explicitly that at this time he knew none of these people but was asked by their guide to show them the way to Usutu; he went with them as far as Dhlebe, left them at Nsukuzonke's kraal and returned home. Evidently he was much in love with his girl, for he set off to see her once more before going back to Johannesburg. For the time being we must leave him with her and continue with Bambata and the others.

On arriving at Nsukuzonke's kraal Bambata decided to leave his wife, daughter and one of the boys behind whilst he, his *inceku* Mgoma, Ndabayake and Nkantolo went on to Usutu which they reached on Sunday morning, 25 March. According to custom he immediately sought out one of the *indunas*, Mgwaqo, to whom he made himself known, at the same time asking that his presence might be reported to Dinuzulu with whom he desired an interview, for he wished to be allowed to remain at Usutu as he was in trouble with the white men about his rent.

Before such an interview could be granted, however, it was necessary for Mgwaqo to know more about this man who was a complete stranger to him and who, as he related, 'did not look like a Chief'. Consequently Bambata had to submit to extensive questioning.

It must be remembered that the *indunas* were very shrewd men, accustomed to making searching inquiries before presenting any petitioner to their chief, and in the disturbed state of the country they would wish to obtain full particulars of anything of moment that might be happening in other parts of the country. Mgwaqo was no exception to this rule and it is more than likely that he ascertained from Bambata much of the story of his escape from the police and troops sent out to effect his arrest.

Mgwaqo conveyed a brief message to Dinuzulu, who was ill at the time, and received the reply that it would be better for his Prime Minister to interview the newcomer, but as Mankulumana was away Bambata must await his return. In the meantime Mgwaqo was instructed to see that their guest, according to custom, was provided with food and shelter. This gave him further opportunity for another lengthy conversation during which there is every likelihood that Dinuzulu's illness was discussed and Mgwaqo was told by Bambata of his own 'great doctor' who lived near Mpanza. Consequently when Mankulumana returned the following day Mgwaqo would be in possession of all the facts of the case regarding their guest, for he had had practically a whole day to carry out his investigations and these, unquestionably, would be retailed to the Prime Minister at the very first opportunity.

That Bambata was welcomed at Usutu with customary Zulu hospitality is evidenced by the fact that on the morning after his arrival he was allowed to send for his wife and children who, on reaching the kraal that afternoon, were also given food and shelter.

Later the same day Mgwaqo reported to Dinuzulu that not only had Mankulumana returned but that Bambata's wife and family had also arrived and been provided with accommodation. Hearing this, Dinuzulu immediately sent a message to Mankulumana ordering him to interview Bambata and let him know the result as soon as possible.

It is most probable that before this interview took place Mgwaqo and Mankulumana had discussed the whole question of Bambata's visit and his desire to remain at Usutu and that both of them realised the utter impossibility of acceding to such a request, for to harbour indefinitely a man who was at that moment being hunted down by the police would be courting disaster for both Dinuzulu and themselves, particularly in view of their past experiences of rebellion against the authorities and of the frequent visits to Usutu of the Nongoma magistrate. However, a loophole of escape from the difficult predicament in which they found themselves had been presented to them; they could get rid of their unwelcome guests by sending him back to Natal with the request that he obtain the services of his 'great doctor' to try to effect a cure on Dinuzulu. No doubt when he reached his kraal he would be pounced upon by the police. That would be the end of the trouble as far as they were concerned, for they could then quite truthfully assert, if ever questioned on the matter, that he had been sent away from Usutu with the sole object of obtaining a doctor for Dinuzulu. In support of this plan it was decided to call in the services of two of the 'King's messengers' who would be told to accompany Bambata with orders to get hold of Malaza, the 'great doctor', and bring him back to Usutu.

The two King's messengers chosen were Ngqengqengqe and Cakijana. The former, who was living at Usutu, was immediately summoned to be present at the forthcoming interview and there receive his instructions, later to be confirmed by Dinuzulu himself, the latter was to be picked up by Ngqengqengqe on his way down to Natal.[2] Consequently when Bambata was called before Mankulumana, both Mgwaqo and Ngqengqengqe were also present.*

* At this stage it is important to note that this was the first time that Ngqengqengqe had met Bambata. In his evidence he stated: 'I found with the Induna Mgwaqo a stranger whom I then did not know but I afterwards found out was Bambata.' This contradicts Stuart's version that Ngqengqengqe had been sent by Dinuzulu to fetch Bambata from his home in Natal to Usutu as he (Dinuzulu) wished to see him. I base my version of the events on the verbatim evidence taken down at the trial of Dinuzulu and it appears that this is more likely to be the correct one, for the Judge President in summing up the case took a similar line, throwing out the other version as unreliable. (See *Criminal*

Dinuzulu, 1903

Mankulumana, Dinuzulu's
prime minister

W. P. Schreiner

Sir Charles Saunders

When Bambata was asked the object of his visit he stated that he had come to *konza* (pay his respects to) Dinuzulu and request permission to be allowed to live either in or near his kraal as he was suffering sorely at the hands of the white people.

Mankulumana in reply laid great stress on Dinuzulu's illness for obvious reasons, even going into details and telling him that Dinuzulu's 'feet and legs were swollen, his chest was sore, he had difficulty in breathing and was unable to pass water', but Bambata's request would be reported to him and Dinuzulu would no doubt grant an interview as soon as he was feeling better. With this Bambata was dismissed.

As Dinuzulu was awaiting the result of the interview Mankulumana and Mgwaqo presented themselves before him and gave an account of what had happened so that he should be in possession of the facts of the case before Bambata himself was summoned. That Dinuzulu concurred with the course of action suggested by his *indunas* is obvious from the interview which took place on the following morning.

When brought before Dinuzulu and asked the reason for his visit to Usutu, Bambata stated that he had come 'because he was constantly in prison because of high rents and wished to settle at Usutu; he was a Chief and had a large kraal in Natal.'[3] Without hesitation Dinuzulu answered that he had no place to put him; he must present his case to the Government. The reply was similar to that which he had given to many other chiefs who in the past months had brought their difficulties to him and made requests for assistance. He was, he continued, though the late King's son, now only the chief of the Usutus just as other chiefs were but the heads of their respective tribes, and should he interfere in the affairs of others than the Usutus he would bring down the wrath of the Government on his head and on the heads of his own people. Whilst Bambata was at Usutu he would be given hospitality as was their custom. Dinuzulu would also offer him assistance in his return to Mpanza if he on his part would search out his 'great doctor' Malaza and get him to come to Usutu to exercise his skill

---

*Records, Special Court, 1908–09,* Vol. I, *Rex vs Dinuzulu,* and compare with Stuart's *A History of the Zulu Rebellion,* pp. 166ff.)

in trying to effect a cure on Dinuzulu. To guarantee Bambata's safe return he would send with him two of his messengers. In their company, every assistance would be given on his journey and none would dare harm him. Meanwhile he could leave his wife and children behind where he could rest assured that they would be well looked after. Dinuzulu would discuss his case with his *indunas* and send for him again when final arrangements had been made for his return. With that the interview terminated.*

* I here strongly differ from the account of this interview as given by Stuart (p. 167). He states Bambata's wife was *concealed* at Usutu and 'Through Mankulumana, Bambata was given instructions to go back to Natal, commit an act of rebellion and then flee to Nkandhla Forest where Dinuzulu's men would join him. *Bambata was at the same time given a Mauser rifle and some ammunition* [author's italics]'. The Judge President in his summing up, with which his Assessors agreed, stated explicitly:

'With regard to the incitement of Bambata we have to decide whether we can place sufficient reliance on the credibility or accuracy of the three witnesses Siyekiwe, Kolekile and Ndabayaka as to the identity of the gun. If we feel that we cannot rely upon the evidence of these three then undoubtedly this charge against Dinuzulu must fall to the ground. With regard to the verbal incitement the considerations I have mentioned lead me to the conclusion that it is absolutely incredible, that it must be untrue and that it is either a deliberate invention for some motive which I cannot divine or else that she is repeating and adopting what had been told to her by someone else, believing herself that it is true.

[The Judge's reason for throwing out Siyekiwe's evidence was because it was obviously false, for native etiquette and Zulu custom would never have allowed a woman to have seen or heard much of what she reported.]

'With regard to the question as to whether Bambata did obtain a gun at Usutu, after giving a careful consideration to all the evidence both for the prosecution and the defence, I have arrived at the conclusion that it is not established that he did.

'Under the circumstances existing in this case I find it difficult to believe that on the chance arrival of this unknown man at Usutu Dinuzulu would fix upon him as a proper instrument to commence a rebellion, if he were contemplating such a step. If he did he would, I think, have taken steps to see that other chiefs of greater importance were ready and willing to join. I think it is clearly established that within the preceding two months a number of chiefs sent messengers to Dinuzulu telling him of the unrest amongst their people caused by the Poll Tax and asking him for advice, and I think it established that Dinuzulu advised them to tell their people to pay. If Dinuzulu were contemplating rebellion, here was an occasion ready to his hand; he had only to tell them to resist and I think from the evidence before us that he would have been obeyed and a serious revolt would almost certainly have ensued.' (*Criminal Records, Rex vs Dinuzulu.*)

Realising that he had no hope of remaining at Usutu and that he would have to return to Natal where there was every possibility of a conflict, for the police were after him and his young men were only too eager for a fight, being urged on daily by their Ethiopian pastors, Bambata determined to make the best possible use of his time at Usutu.

It must be remembered that he stayed four days at Dinuzulu's kraal during which time he moved about quite freely and met many of the residents, amongst whom were a considerable number of malcontents, people in whom there also burned a fierce spirit of resentment at the general oppression of their nation, a resentment which had been greatly inflamed by the recent imposition of the Poll Tax. A man of Bambata's cunning, particularly in his present revengeful mood, would naturally turn to such kindred spirits and as he discussed matters with them he laid his plans for future action. There were many guns at Usutu at that time and it would not be difficult to persuade his newly-found friends to procure one or two for his own use. That he was successful in this quest is proved by later events, for by the time he left Dinuzulu's kraal he had obtained possession of a .303 magazine rifle, a double-barrelled breech-loader and a carbine.[4] It was now an easy matter for a man of such character to go back to his people and stir up their fighting qualities by telling them that he had received these arms from Dinuzulu, when in reality they had come not from Dinuzulu but from the malcontents in his kraal. Further, as if in support of his statement, he could point to the two King's messengers who accompanied him and so convince anyone who had a doubt of the truth of his words.

All that remained now was the final interview with Dinuzulu and his *indunas* and this was of brief duration. Bambata was instructed to set out immediately for Natal to obtain the services of his 'great doctor' Malaza; two King's messengers would accompany him and the doctor must be brought to Usutu as soon as possible.

Accordingly, early on the morning of 29 March he set out for Mpanza accompanied by his two servants Mgoma and Nkantolo and the King's messenger Ngqengqengqe. Acting on instructions they made for Gezindaka's kraal where they were to pick up Cakijana, the second messenger.

On arrival they discovered that he had returned from his final visit to his girl and had just killed the customary goat preparatory to his departure for Johannesburg on the following day. After a preliminary conversation with Gezindaka, during which Ngqengqengqe explained the purpose of their visit, Cakijana was summoned by his father and told by Ngqengqengqe, whom he knew well, that they had been directed to go and fetch a doctor in Natal and he was to accompany them. Cakijana's reaction was immediate: he refused to go on the grounds that he was about to start for Johannesburg to return to his work. Ngqengqengqe insisted on his coming, telling him that he had been ordered by Dinuzulu to do so. Cakijana was so disgusted that he walked out and went to another hut but was called back by his father who said: 'You *must* go; don't you wish that Dinuzulu should recover from this sickness from which he is suffering?'[5] Realising that Ngqengqengqe was a King's messenger and refusal to obey his orders would result in heavy punishment, possibly death, Cakijana grudgingly submitted.*

---

* Refusal to obey the orders of a King's messenger was a most serious crime as was testified by Arthur J. Shepstone at the trial. *Inter alia* he stated: 'Messages from the Zulu Chief to his subjects were conveyed direct or through a messenger. These messengers would not be asked for any details nor could the orders be questioned. Implicit obedience was demanded; non-compliance would result in death. A mere hint to the hearer would be sufficient to require obedience. . . . They now recognise the Governor of Natal as Supreme Chief but if they received an order from Dinuzulu they would obey that order rather than the order of their Supreme Chief and take the risk of punishment. In spite of the changed circumstances they still look on Dinuzulu as King, for he is the son of Cetshwayo. If they disobeyed an order from him they would live in fear of their lives and no man would dare to act as an impostor as a messenger for the King – that meant certain death.'

Shepstone's evidence is supported by the evidence of Kafula, the *induna* of the Magistrate's Court at Greytown, a man who had held this position for over ten years and was a trusted servant of the Government. When questioned by the Judge President on this matter he replied: 'If I got an order today from my Chief [the Inkosi] to do something against the Supreme Chief [Governor of Natal] I would do it and then mislead the White Chief and say I did not know. I would ignore the white authority and obey the black one even though I knew it was wrong. If I disobeyed my Chief it would be my last

Accordingly, after Gezindaka had killed a goat for their journey, as was the custom when visited by a King's messenger, the five of them set out for Natal.

Their first stop was at Ntabanhlope where it was decided to split into two the obviously heavy bundle which Mgoma was carrying. As this was being done Cakijana observed that three guns had been concealed amongst the mats and quite naturally his suspicions were aroused; however, he said nothing as it was not his concern. It was here that he learnt from Ngqengqengqe that their companion was Bambata, a chief of Natal. Up to this point he had only known him as one of the party which he had guided some days earlier to Nsukuzonke's kraal *en route* for Usutu. After the bundles had been more or less evenly divided between Nkantolo and Mgoma they continued their way to Palane's kraal where another goat was killed but as they were anxious to hurry on and intended to travel through the night, only a brief halt was made.

Some hours later during a short rest Bambata ordered his *inceku* to unwrap his bundle and take out his gun for he wished to clean it and have it, as he said, in readiness 'to shoot a policeman'. He now spoke quite openly of his intention to take up arms against the white people and drive them out; 'My day has come,' he said; with the gun in his hand he turned to Cakijana, who had been a silent but somewhat astonished spectator, and remarked: '*This gun has been given me by Dinuzulu to start the fighting.*' This was Cakijana's first intimation of Bambata's intention to rebel, for although his suspicions had been aroused by the guns he understood that their journey was being undertaken solely for the purpose of obtaining a doctor for Dinuzulu.[6] Knowing nothing of what had happened at Usutu, Cakijana was completely hoodwinked and everything now assumed an entirely different complexion. If Dinuzulu had given

---

day, I would never see light again. I am so positive of this that I would submit to be hanged for it. I am talking of today, *not* of Cetshwayo's time.'

Asked by the Judge, Sir William Smith: 'Supposing you got an order from Dinuzulu to shoot me?', he replied: 'I should shoot your Lordship because I would be afraid of being shot myself. If I took the other course and did *not* shoot you I should take to my feet and run with such swiftness that I would not stop until I got in the pond of the sea.'

Bambata the guns to start a rebellion and he, Cakijana, had been ordered to accompany them as King's messenger, it would be his duty to stand by Bambata and, if necessary, fight with him. Although Ngqengqwngqe had rebuked Bambata for his statements and his conduct, Cakijana felt that as a chief Bambata would never have dared to use the name of Dinuzulu if what he had said was untrue. Thus Bambata's cunning had won him his first follower, an important victory, for Cakijana was a King's messenger and with his support it would be comparatively easy to convince others that Dinuzulu was at the back of him.

Their next stopping place was Bomana's kraal at Qudeni where they hoped to be able to snatch a few hours' sleep but in this they were disappointed, for Bambata, having previously deceived this chief over a cattle deal, was chased away and told to find accommodation elsewhere; consequently they moved on towards the Tugela, reaching it about sunset. As they were about to cross the river they saw to their dismay a number of tents clustered around the drift and their first thought was that it was a police guard. Bambata raised his gun to fire but was restrained in time, for it was discovered that the tents were only housing a road party. However, for safety's sake they split up, crossed the stream at different points and joining up after darkness had set in made their way to Matshilo's kraal.

Bambata was now amongst his own people who greeted him with the news that he had been officially deposed in favour of his brother Funizwe, his uncle Magwababa having been appointed chief in the meantime. He was so furious that, although wearied by his long trek, before thinking of rest he ordered certain of his men to set out immediately for his various kraals to summon his *impi*, bidding them assemble, fully armed, at Sambane's kraal where he would meet them on the next day.

Accordingly when he and his fellow-travellers reached this kraal on the morning of 1 April 1906 they found a number of young warriors already mustered. One of Bambata's first tasks was to send for his 'great doctor' Malaza. Already Ngqengqengqe was showing signs of uneasiness at the way events were shaping and it was obvious that he was anxious to return to Usutu as soon as possible and so dissociate himself from Bambata's rash behaviour, for the *impi* was already under orders to attack both Magwababa and Funizwe that night. However, his messengers returned later that day with the news that Malaza could not be found, so another doctor of lesser repute, Mfihlo, was ordered to take his place and accompany Ngqengqengqe who had decided to leave first thing the following morning.

Meanwhile, in spite of Ngqengqengqe's remonstrances, Bambata went ahead with his plans and ordered his local witch-doctors to sprinkle his warriors for war. By the time darkness fell all was ready and the *impi* moved off accompanied by Cakijana who, no doubt influenced by the elders of the tribe, was determined if possible to restrain Bambata from murdering his own kith and kin, Cakijana himself had also by this time made up his mind to return to Usutu the moment Malaza appeared and was allowed by Bambata to go with him.

Reaching their destination at dead of night they surrounded Magwababa's hut and smashing down the door dragged out the unfortunate man; others attempted to set the kraal on fire and had it not been for the intervention of Cakijana, who was himself wounded in the scuffle, the old man would have been killed and the whole place burnt down.[7] Wounded and badly beaten up, Magwababa was bound with reims and carried off a prisoner. At this stage some of the older men of the tribe intervened, taking up the cudgels on his behalf by pleading with Bambata: 'How will your *impi* succeed if you start by killing one of your own blood?' Their appeal succeeded and a form of trial was decided upon, but as no one could formulate any definite charge against the old man he was released; some hours later he managed to escape to Kranzkop where after having reported everything to the magistrate he was sent on by post cart to Greytown.

The *impi* now made for Funizwe's kraal, for Bambata was determined to kill his brother for having accepted the chieftainship. Fortunately, having been forewarned, Funizwe had fled and by the time the warriors arrived he was far away hiding in the bush. Determined to enlist every available man in his tribe Bambata now led his *impi* from kraal to kraal, forcing everyone to arm;

many displayed considerable reluctance but when threatened with death they had no alternative but to submit.

On his arrival at Greytown early the following morning (3 April) Magwababa related the story of his escape to the magistrate who immediately took steps to trace the whereabouts of the *impi*. Accompanied by an Inspector of Police, two troopers and a native guide, he hurried along the main road to Marshall's Hotel.* On arrival at the Mpanza they were suddenly confronted by a body of armed men led by Bambata himself, who immediately opened fire. Shots were exchanged but as the magistrate's party was so greatly outnumbered a withdrawal was ordered and they retreated to the hotel where they found three frightened women in occupation. Realising the extreme danger of their position it was decided to attempt an escape to the Police Station at Keats Drift on the Mooi River. Fortunately they were not pursued and the little party reached their destination without mishap that afternoon, the womenfolk being accommodated at a nearby store.

Once the hotel was vacated Bambata and some of his men invaded it and as a large supply of liquor was available an orgy of drinking followed; leaving some hours later loaded up with more intoxicants they returned to their hiding place in the bush. All were now in a dangerous mood of which their Ethiopian priest, Moses, took full advantage by urging them to 'Shoot the white men and finish being the servants of these people.'

Meanwhile telegrams were passing to and fro; Greytown was more or less in a state of panic when Col. Leuchars stepped into the breach caused by the absence of the magistrate and proceeded to arrange suitable defences for the inhabitants. The town hall was turned into a laager, barbed-wire entanglements were erected and trenches were dug in case of an attack; patrols were sent out, reserves called up and the Umvoti Mounted Rifles mobilised. A hundred police had arrived from Richmond and these, together with a detachment under Col. Mansel, forming a force of 146 men, set out for Keats Drift to bring in the fugitives. Leaving about

---

* Marshall's Hotel (now a farmhouse) is situated in a valley near the Mpanza River Drift. It is surrounded by high hills and deep ravines, all covered with dense bush. In this area Bambata's Mpanza kraal was situated.

3 p.m. on 4 April they reached the Drift about 4.30, having seen nothing of the enemy on the way although Bambata's spies had followed their movements and reported the passage of this considerable body of armed white men.

Foolishly Col. Mansel left again at 6.15 that evening although fully aware of the fact that an extremely wily, elusive and fleet-footed enemy was in the vicinity, one who was thoroughly familiar with every inch of the surrounding country; he knew also that the road along which they must travel was narrow and extremely dangerous, being fenced in on either side, whilst the surrounding bush was so dense – a close network of thorn and cactus – that movement was well nigh impossible unless one was acquainted with the few bridle paths; in addition several women and a child had to be escorted through the darkness when every advantage would be to the enemy.

By the time Marshall's Hotel was reached the sun had set and a halt was made; they had now to face the most dangerous and difficult part of the trip. Twenty-six men formed an advance guard, followed by the main body in the centre of which was an open carriage drawn by two horses, bearing the women and child. The extreme narrowness of the road in this locality, its fences, its hilly nature, its numerous curves and sharp bends made it impossible to throw out flankers and the whole sorry procession was compelled to move more or less in a solid mass. The inevitable happened. At about 8 p.m., when scarcely a mile from the hotel, a sudden and determined attack was made on the rear of the advance guard. Yelling their war cry '*Usutu*' Bambata's men rushed out from behind a huge rock on the slopes of the Hlenyane Hill where they had been hiding, awaiting the return of the force, their object being to cut off the advance guard and destroy them, for owing to the narrowness of the road it would prove difficult for the remainder of the force to come to their assistance. The few rebels who had rifles made good use of them, shooting down the horses and throwing their riders who were thus unable to use their guns; others nimbly cleared the fences and got to close quarters with their assegais. For some moments there was utter confusion, the remaining horses took fright and it was only with the greatest difficulty that the men managed to get back to the main body who by this time had dismounted and were keeping up a steady fire on the rebels whom eventually they succeeded in driving off. Four of the police were killed, four wounded, one dangerously, and about fifteen horses lost; in the confusion many rifles and revolvers fell into the hands of the enemy. After the dead had been picked up, with the exception of Sgt Brown who had not been missed at the time, they were placed with the wounded in the carriage and the whole column moved on, reaching Greytown about midnight without further incident.

It was later ascertained that the rebels numbered about 150 and had been led by Bambata himself, assisted by Cakijana; not one of them had been killed but ten or twelve had been wounded.

The body of Sgt Brown was recovered on 8 April and when found was lying on its back across the road near the big rock where the fight had taken place; much of the clothing had been removed whilst the body itself had been badly mutilated: the left forearm was missing, the upper lip cut off, the stomach had been opened up and the private parts were missing,[8] all evidently having been taken by Malaza, Bambata's witch-doctor (who had by this time joined the rebels), for the purpose of making *muti* (medicine) with which to doctor the warriors.

The effect of this skirmish on the rebels was considerable, for their witch-doctor had told them that as a result of his ministrations they would be impervious to the bullets of the white men. To their superstitious minds his words carried conviction. Already they had had two encounters with the white men and come through both without any loss of life. Undoubtedly this stimulated them to further efforts and enabled them to enrol a large number of recruits.

When news of the fight reached the authorities no time was lost in calling out further troops; it was realised that as matters had taken so serious a turn stern measures were necessary to prevent the rebellion from spreading to other parts of the country. Col. Leuchars was therefore placed in command and ordered to deal with the situation. His first move was to surround the Mpanza Valley and on the morning of 7 April, after he had positioned his men, a heavy fire was opened up on the various kraals but it was soon discovered that the whole place was deserted except for a few women and children. Bambata's spies had already informed him of the troop movements which they had spotted by the dust they created; consequently when firing commenced the *impi* was well on its way to the Tugela. Bambata had decided to make for the fastnesses of the Nkandhla Forest where he would seek out Chief Sigananda whom his father had befriended many years before.

Here we must leave them to follow the movements of Ngqengqengqe. It will be remembered that at the time of Bambata's attack on his uncle he had left for the Usutu accompanied by the doctor Mfihlo, the substitute for Malaza. On his way he called on Cakijana's father and told him that 'he had run away from his son and Bambata as he had found that there was going to be trouble and fighting'. Gezindaka replied: 'that he had seen when Bambata passed that things were not right but,' he added, 'why has Cakijana remained behind?'[9]

On reaching Usutu and reporting to Mankulumana he was met with the news that Mashiqele (Charles Saunders) had just preceded him and was at that moment engaged in conversation with Dinuzulu. Some hours later Ngqengqengqe, when summoned, was greeted by an obviously angry Dinuzulu with the words: 'So you have come back; it was you who went with that *uhlanya* (madman) to Natal and who I now hear from Mashiqele is fighting in Natal and has killed his uncle.' Ngqengqengqe replied: 'Yes, it must be true as I left because he was going to fight him and Bambata was saying nasty things because he told people that the rifles he had were given to him at the Usutu.' Dinuzulu reiterated angrily: 'He must be an *uhlanya*.'

Having reported that he had been unable to secure the services of Malaza but had brought along a substitute, Dinuzulu, still angry, dismissed Ngqengqengqe with the remark that he would not see Mfihlo.[10]

A few days later Ngqengqengqe was again brought before Mankulumana who in the meantime had heard from Mashiqele the full story of the Mpanza fight (telegraphed to him during his stay at Usutu). The news had thoroughly alarmed Dinuzulu, particularly as he was at that moment harbouring Bambata's wife and family at his kraal, although, fearing the consequences, he had denied all knowledge of Bambata to Saunders. As he was anxious to get rid of them at the earliest possible opportunity Ngqengqengqe was instructed to proceed to Gezindaka's kraal with a message: 'That as his son was fighting with Bambata in Natal he had better come over to the Usutu and take away Bambata's wife and children.' On receipt of this surprising order Gezindaka sent back word that: 'As Bambata was no relation of his he wished to have nothing whatever to do with him or with any of his people.'[11]

Returning some days later to Usutu Ngqengqengqe found Cakijana had just got back from Mpanza. Dinuzulu wished to see them both. Cakijana was extensively questioned as to why he had remained behind fighting in Natal and had not returned immediately with Malaza as ordered. His excuse was that he had only carried out Bambata's orders which he understood had been given at Usutu. At this: 'Dinuzulu rose up in anger against him because he had mixed himself up in Bambata's imbroglio when he had been sent on a special mission to get a doctor.'[12]

Later, when Cakijana requested permission to remain at Usutu this was curtly refused and he was ordered to leave without delay. He then returned to his home only to be told by Gezindaka: 'The white people are looking for you; you had better pass on.'[13] Consequently, thrown out by Dinuzulu and driven away by his father, Cakijana decided to rejoin the rebels and made his way back to the Nkandhla.

## CHAPTER 15

# *The Bambata Rebellion*\*

BAMBATA and his men had been making their way to the Tugela. Their route from the Mpanza had lain almost due east; passing through the wards of Gayede, Mpumela and Mangati they hurried forward, reaching the mouth of the Mome Gorge in about thirty-six hours, having travelled a distance of close on fifty miles in that time over extremely rugged country with only a short break for sleep. In the course of their progress attempts had been made, with considerable success, to augment their numbers and it was now decided to make for the fastnesses of the forest at the upper end of the Gorge, perhaps the most secure and inaccessible spot in the whole of Zululand.

A short description of the Mome and its surroundings is necessary in order to understand something of the difficulties which presented themselves to any attacking force. The Gorge derives its name from the stream which flows through it; this has its source several miles away, high up in the forest-clad mountains which cover the whole of that area; its pure, clear waters race down the steep slopes into deep ravines from which they emerge into forests so dense that the light of day rarely breaks through; flowing intermittently through these it cascades quite suddenly over the lip of a precipice to a pool far below. Forging onward, the stream twists and turns like a writhing snake before it reaches the floor of the Gorge, well over 3,500 feet below the point from which

---

\* For a detailed account of the rebellion the reader is referred to Stuart's *A History of the Zulu Rebellion, 1906* but in reading this work it must be remembered that it was written at the instigation of the Government and consequently is much biased in their favour. I am greatly indebted to Mrs M. M. K. Robinson, daughter of Sir Charles Saunders, for the loan of his Diary covering this period from which much valuable information has been drawn.

it started; it eventually pours through a ravine into the wide open valley of the Insuzi River, into which it empties its waters.

The Gorge itself is approximately one and a half miles long; its entrance is over a ridge of hills which overlook the small plain below, a passage through the ravine being impossible; the plain, the only level spot in the whole Gorge, is bounded by a loop of the Mome stream which flows on its extreme right; beyond this the walls of the Gorge rise steeply to a height of over 2,000 feet. On the left is a high ridge, the Bocoza; this bends to the right and links up with a chain of mountains which form the head of the Gorge, presenting an almost impassable barrier. As one advances the floor of the little plain rises sharply and the stream now takes an almost right-angled turn through a massive and beautiful defile whose walls on the right rise almost perpendicular. On the left, at a wide angle to the stream, is another deep canyon in which is situated a dense pear-shaped forest, known as the Dobo, which extends almost to the top of the 3,000-foot mountain. On the right of this canyon is an enormous spur, almost razor-edged, which descends precipitously to the stream, thus forming a very narrow exit to the extreme end of the Gorge. Beyond this is the area known as the Stronghold, reached by a very stiff climb along a winding path through the forest; unless one is familiar with the way it is dangerous to proceed. This track leads to a spot behind the waterfall where are numerous caves and hide-outs, forming a fortress almost impregnable on account of its inaccessibility, hence its name the Stronghold.

The Mome Gorge and its surroundings have been the habitation of the AmaCube tribe for at least 350 years, probably more, for their earlier history is lost in oblivion, no written record having been kept of those distant days. Their chief in the year 1906 was Sigananda. His descendants still live in these beautiful forests and it is through conversation with their *indunas* and headmen that I have obtained much of my information.

The kraal of old Sigananda became known as Enhlweni, 'the Poor Man's Retreat'; it acquired this name at the time when Cetshwayo, wounded and driven from his throne by Sibebu, sought and found refuge behind the cool waters of the lovely falls.

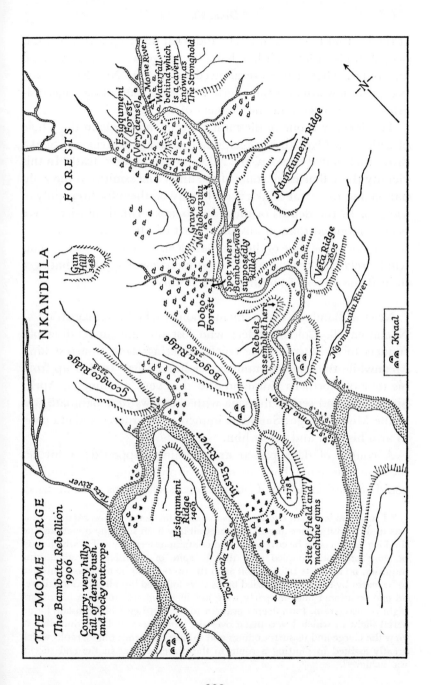

THE MOME GORGE

The Bambata Rebellion
1906

Country: very hilly;
full of dense bush
and rocky outcrops

NKAND'HLA

FORESTS

Esigqumeni
Forest
(Very dense)

To Mome River

Waterfall
behind which
is a cavern
known as
The Stronghold

Ntundhumeni Ridge

Grave of
Mehlokazulu

Gun
Hill
3489

Spot where
Bambata was
supposedly
killed

Dobo
Forest

Bogoza Ridge
2850

Rebels
assembled here

Veta Ridge
2605

Ngomankulu River

Gcongco Ridge
2238

Mome River

Insize River

Tate River

Esigqumeni
Ridge
1406

To Macala

1278

Site of field and
machine guns

Kraal

209

It retains that name even today and from the deep love which his people still bear for their late King his refuge is regarded as sacred and only a chosen few are allowed to visit it. Needless to say, very, very few attempt the pilgrimage on account of the inaccessibility of the place and the dangers of the way.*

This locality is one of the most historic and tragic in the whole of Zululand. Over these precipices the savage warriors of Shaka drove their hated enemies, the Ndwandwes, to their death. In this vicinity there flourished some of the finest blacksmiths in the Zulu nation and the great Shaka drew largely on them for his supply of assegais. In the depths of these forests more ritual murders have been committed than in any other part of Africa. In and around the Mome at the time of the Bambata Rebellion there occurred, as will be related later, one of the most merciless slaughters that ever stained the pages of South African history.

News of Bambata's movements soon reached the magistrate at Nkandhla (B. Colenbrander) who lost no time in sending out runners to the surrounding chiefs, ordering them to arrest him. Meanwhile the Chief Commissioner himself had turned up from his tour of Northern Zululand and that very morning (9 April) Sigananda had sent a message with the news that Bambata was in the Mome Gorge; Saunders immediately ordered the old chief to arm his men and arrest him.

A couple of days passed and nothing happened; a further message was sent; back came the reply stating that Bambata could not be found. The Commissioner's suspicions were aroused,

* I made no less than five attempts to reach the Gorge but on each occasion was unsuccessful on account of its inaccessibility from so many directions and the long distances to be covered over mountainous territory, all of which must be done on foot. Coupled with this, in spite of extensive and exhausting inquiries, no accurate information as to the route could be obtained; this had to be learnt by experience; varied paths were followed but all ended in failure; on one occasion I and my party were lost in the mountains on a pitch-dark night of heavy rain. I am deeply grateful to Mr Ian Lewis of Kranskop for an aerial flight in which I was taken over the whole area and was thus able to view the Gorge and its surroundings and to take numerous photographs which greatly assisted in plotting a route to the place, so that in the end success was achieved.

suspicions which were soon confirmed by reports that Sigananda's men were arming and instead of arresting the rebel leader were joining forces with him. It was also reported that messengers were being sent far and wide ordering every available man to arm and make for the Gorge; news was received of trading stations being looted and loyalists' cattle being raided; obviously the rebellion was spreading with alarming rapidity and swift action was necessary. Police and troops were summoned from all parts of the Colony, for a large force would be required to cope with the situation in such dangerous and difficult country.

Whilst the military were assembling the Commissioner kept in constant touch with Dinuzulu of whose complete detachment from these rebellious proceedings he was convinced, and though the Government attached great weight to his opinion they thought it necessary that Dinuzulu himself should take some action to convince people of his loyalty and wired Saunders to this effect, asking him whether it might not be advisable to summon Dinuzulu to Maritzburg to assist the authorities in quelling the outbreak. The Commissioner replied: 'Situation most delicate and critical at present and requires the presence of any loyal Chiefs we can depend upon amongst their own people.'[1]

Meanwhile the Commissioner had forwarded the Government's request to Dinuzulu who replied immediately:

I am not surprised that the Natal Government should have doubt as to my loyalty in face of repeated and constant accusations to the contrary effect which have been levelled against me throughout South Africa. I can only say I am perfectly loyal and am most anxious to give proof of this in any way the Government may wish. I have assured you of my loyalty by words and actions repeatedly, but apparently this is doubted, and I now ask that Government suggest means by which my loyalty can be proved absolutely and finally dispel the slurs which have been cast upon me, and which I keenly resent. I am perfectly ready to turn out the whole of my people and send them to Nkandhla at once to operate in any manner you may think fit, either in entering the Forest and capturing this dog Bambata, who has been allowed to enter Zululand and disturb the peace which we enjoyed long after Natal Natives had openly showed disloyalty. As you know, I am physically incapable of leading my people in person, being unable to move with freedom from my bed but the impi would go down in charge of my chief Induna, Mankulumana, and I myself am prepared to be conveyed to Nongoma and remain there alone with the magistrate whilst my people are operating in any way they may be required as a proof of my good faith in this matter. If Government say they wish me to go to Nkandhla I will find means to reach there notwithstanding my state of health. If this assurance is not sufficient I am sure that Government will indicate what is necessary for further proof of loyalty to our King.[*2]

This letter had a reassuring effect on all concerned and although, on the Commissioner's recommendation, the Government declined Dinuzulu's offer of military assistance it was decided that Mankulumana should go at once to the Nkandhla Forest and seek an interview with Sigananda to try to persuade him to break with the rebels and assist in the capture of Bambata.

Accordingly a message to this effect was sent to Dinuzulu and on the morning of 23 April Mankulumana with two attendants reached Nkandhla where he received his instructions from the Commissioner, later making his way down to the Forest where he spent several days. His mission was unsuccessful. Not only had he to face a hostile reception but he failed to see Sigananda who was purposely prevented by the rebels from interviewing him.

On the 27th he returned and reported to the Commissioner that obviously the whole of Sigananda's tribe was in open rebellion and he was certain that Bambata was somewhere in the vicinity. It was discovered later than the latter had moved to a spot near Cetshwayo's grave where *amadhlangala* (temporary shelters of wattle and branches) had been erected to accommodate the 700–1,000 rebels who had already assembled and whose numbers were daily increasing. Here the witch-doctors were busy with their *muti* and incantations preparing the men for war and the warriors had now donned the *tshokobezi*, the distinctive head-dress which the rebels had adopted.[†]

* Dinuzulu was at this time suffering from a dropsical complaint which completely incapacitated him from any physical exertion.

† *Tshokobezi*: the bushy part of the cow's tail which was bound round the head so as to stand erect.

By this time Cakijana also had returned from Usutu and henceforward threw himself heart and soul into the rebellion, moving around the various kraals urging all and sundry to join up with Bambata. Another important addition to the rebel ranks was Mehlokazulu, whose father Sirayo had been the commander of the famous Ngobamakosi regiment at the battle of Isandhlwana. The enrolment of such an outstanding Zulu went to show beyond all doubt how widespread was the feeling of resentment against the authorities.

Thus, for the time being it appeared that the rebels were having it all their own way; not only were their numbers greatly increasing but raiding parties were being sent out in all directions to loot cattle and grain for their maintenance.

The tardiness of the authorities in taking action was largely due to the fact that the Government forces had to be assembled from many quarters and their Commanding Officer, Col. MacKenzie, had not yet arrived at Nkandhla. An attempt was made to capture Bambata on 23 April when a force of about 250 men under Col. Mansel set off for the Manyana River, near the Macala mountain, where he was reported to be, but it ended in failure. Rebel scouts gave the alarm and by the time Mansel reached the stream the enemy had vanished in the darkness. Some days later, however (on 5 May), this same force met with a measure of success. Proceeding from Fort Yolland on a reconnaissance in the direction of Bope Ridge they encountered and defeated a rebel force, commanded by Bambata himself. The success of this fight dispelled the illusion that the *muti* of the witch-doctors was able to turn aside the bullets of the white men, for in this action more than sixty were killed and as a result Bambata had to face the wrath of many angry women who had lost their menfolk in the fray.

A couple of nights before this skirmish there occurred a tragedy which startled the whole of Zululand. About 8 p.m. on 3 May the Native Commissioner of Mahlabatini (H. M. Stainbank) while telephoning his chief at Nkandhla from his camp on the banks of the White Umfolosi was shot dead in cold blood.

During the day Stainbank and his attendants had been collecting taxes from the natives of that area, in which there were no signs of rebellion; in fact, the murder was such a shock to the surrounding chiefs that on the following day of their own accord all of them arrived at the magistrate's office to express their regret and horror at the deed and one of their number, Ngodi, volunteered to turn out his men and guard the magistracy till such time as a new Commissioner arrived to take over.

An extensive search was made of the surrounding area and four empty .303 cartridge cases were found about fifteen paces from the spot where Stainbank fell mortally wounded, but no trace of his assailant was discovered.

When news of the murder was sent to Dinuzulu by the Chief Commissioner he was extremely angry and asked permission to send Mankulumana with twenty or thirty picked men to assist in bringing the guilty party to justice. His offer was accepted and as a result several arrests were made but as the evidence against them was inconclusive all had to be acquitted; it was not until six years later that the case was finally disposed of by the Government on the arrest of a man named Matayana who was brought to trial and convicted.*

On 8 May Col. MacKenzie with a large body of men arrived at Nkandhla to take over the command of the whole expedition and sterner measures were immediately adopted. As rumours were afloat of a contemplated attack on the magistracy at Nkandhla, troops were sent out in various directions with orders to burn down all native kraals in the area, seize any cattle that could be found

---

* Matayana was the son of one of Cetshwayo's principal messengers, well known to Dinuzulu and had in collaboration with Cakijana, shot and killed a man called Gence for having committed adultery with one of Dinuzulu's wives.

The Zulus have an entirely different version from that generally accepted by the Europeans. According to them Stainbank was shot dead by a European farmer living near the White Umfolosi. This man was well known to many of them as one who had been warned repeatedly by the Commissioner for illegally grazing his cattle in the Zulu Reserve and eventually had been heavily fined for stealing Zulu cattle. This infuriated him to such a degree that as he walked away from the Court he was overheard by some Zulus to say that he would have his revenge on the magistrate 'for fining him for stealing cattle belonging to a bloody Kaffir'. This story was rigidly adhered to by Cakijana who died only recently (1963) and has been emphatically confirmed to me from various sources.

and empty all grain pits in an effort to stop food supplies reaching the rebels.

Col. MacKenzie spent a day or two reconnoitring the whole district as a preliminary to the launching of his offensive and after consultation with his staff on the latest reports of enemy movements decided to make an attack on the rebel camp at Cetshwayo's grave where Sigananda had collected a body of approximately 1,000 men; Bambata, after the Bope Ridge skirmish, had withdrawn with his followers to the Macala mountain.

This attack was to take the form of a three-pronged movement along the Insuzi Valley, all three columns to converge simultaneously on Cetshwayo's grave. In this way it was hoped to encircle Sigananda's forces and either smash them up completely or compel them to surrender. Col. Mansel was to start from Fort Yolland via Maqonga Hill and Mkalazi and work *up* the Insuzi Valley; Col. Barker, with his Transvaal contingent, was to advance from Ntingwe to Dhlolwana and proceeding through the Msukane Neck was to make his way *down* the Valley, whilst Col. MacKenzie's column, assisted by Royston's Horse, would march down the razor-edged Gcongco Spur, which drops abruptly from the top of the Nomangci Ridge into the valley 2,000 feet below, and would reach the Mome River near its junction with the Insuzi. All were timed to arrive at their destination by 11 a.m. on the morning of the 17th. Meanwhile a message was flashed to Col. Leuchars, who was then at Middle Drift, ordering him to bring up his men and co-operate in the general action by attacking Bambata's force on the Macala mountain.

The plan was admirable and had it been carried out satisfactorily might have crushed the whole rebel movement in that area but unfortunately, owing to transport difficulties, Mansel was late in arriving at the rendezvous, thus leaving a wide gap in the projected encirclement through which the rebels poured and eventually made their way back to the Mome Gorge; hence the whole movement ended in failure.

One incident of note occurred; soon after Col. Barker's force entered the Msukane Gap his rearguard was attacked by Bambata's followers who swooped down from the Macala mountain; they were repulsed without difficulty and in the mêlée Cakijana was wounded in the leg by which he was put out of action for the rest of the campaign. Col. Leuchars' column had in the meantime come up behind the Macala and thereby prevented the rebels from reoccupying their former positions but being so well acquainted with the country they were able to elude their pursuers without much difficulty and made their way into the depths of the Qudeni Forest some miles away. Although the attack had ended in disappointment Col. MacKenzie and his men were able to derive some satisfaction from the fact that a large number of cattle and goats fell into their hands, thus depriving the enemy of his main food supply.

The Colonel now decided to bivouack his troops in the vicinity of Cetshwayo's grave,\* for his men were tired after an exhausting day and that evening a heavy thunderstorm drenched them all to the skin. Rain fell incessantly throughout the night and continued for the whole of the next day, rendering any movement impossible. Fortunately the following day dawned fine and clear, so the Colonel decided on an immediate assault of the Mome Gorge. With this end in view a detachment of the Natal Field Artillery was sent in advance with orders to take up a position on the hills overlooking the Mome Valley. As the other troops followed they were surprised to see a native scout galloping directly towards Col. MacKenzie. On arrival he stated that he bore a message from Sigananda whose emissaries wished to meet him right away with a view to surrender. The troops were immediately halted and the scout sent back with orders summoning the rebel leaders who on presenting themselves were told that Sigananda and his whole force must lay down their arms in unconditional surrender by 11 a.m. on Sunday 20 May – two days hence.

---

\* Conditions at this camp were shocking and had it not been for the cattle and grain from the storage pits seized as booty the men would have suffered severe hunger. Sanitary conditions were appalling, for having had to travel as lightly as possible due to the precipitous nature of the country, no spades had been brought. To add to the discomfort of the troops the body of a rebel who had been dead for several days was discovered in the stream from which they drew their drinking water. Little wonder that this camp was nicknamed 'Stinkfontein'.

During this time the troops rested and when the appointed hour arrived and passed without any signs of a capitulation, the Colonel decided to take action, but just as the sun was sinking several men were seen bearing a white flag; they reported that they had not been able to surrender because they could not locate Sigananda owing to the density of the forest and pleaded for an extension of time. Two more days were granted on the understanding that though certain troop movements would be made in the interval these would not be of a hostile nature. These days were spent by the Colonel in making a careful sketch of the Mome Gorge and its surroundings, particular attention being given to the positioning of guns for effective shelling of the area should this become necessary.

On the day appointed for the surrender (22 May) a message was received from Sigananda himself requesting that he be allowed to give himself up at Nkandhla on account of his great age (ninety-eight) as this would save him a long and trying journey. The request was granted, the Colonel intimating that he himself would proceed to this place with some of his troops and would meet him at 11 a.m. on 24 May.

Leaving Col. Barker in charge of the remainder of the troops near Cetshwayo's grave Col. MacKenzie and his men set off early on the morning of the 23rd for the formidable Gcongco Spur up which they had to travel. Some idea of the difficulties of the climb can be gauged from the fact that in spite of its being a cold day, not less than fourteen horses had to be abandoned, three dropped dead from exhaustion and one of the native levies died from heart failure before reaching the summit. It was five o'clock that afternoon before the men reached Nkandhla, tired out but delighted to get back once again to camp and decent rations.*

Their delight, however, was soon turned to anger, for they were met with the disquieting news that a few nights before a road party

* This was clever strategy on the part of the rebel leaders: there was no intention to surrender, as was proved later, their object being to draw some of the troops to Nkandhla and so avert an attack on the Mome Gorge till Bambata's contingent, then at Qudeni, had linked up with Sigananda in the vicinity of the Stronghold from which position they felt they would be able to withstand Col. MacKenzie's onslaught.

foreman named Walters had been murdered in his tent not ten miles from their camp. Although there were no signs of mutilation the incident indicated the insincerity of the rebel intention to surrender and when the following day passed without any signs of Sigananda it became obvious that they had only been playing for time. Col. MacKenzie, justly annoyed by the deception, now decided to attack with renewed vigour and give no respite whatsoever until every rebel *impi* had been soundly thrashed.

His spies reported that Bambata was in the Ensingabantu Forest on the Qudeni mountains to which spot he was summoning all his followers, intending later to link up with Sigananda in the Mome. The Colonel determined that, if possible, he would prevent it and that very afternoon issued orders to his men to prepare for a night march so that the Ensingabantu could be encircled early the following morning and the rebels smashed before they had a chance to carry out their plans.

At sundown the whole column was on the move and though the route taken was difficult and dangerous they arrived at their destination by 4 a.m.* It was bitterly cold and a heavy mist shrouded the whole countryside but no time was lost in surrounding the bush and the movement was completed by 7 a.m. just as the mist lifted. It was then discovered that once again their wily foes had eluded them, no doubt warned by their spies. It was a bitter disappointment, for the men had been in the saddle for fourteen hours and carried out a hazardous night ride of twenty-eight miles, most of it in pitch darkness.

For the next ten days MacKenzie harried the rebels remorselessly, determined to forced them to decisive action at the earliest possible opportunity. Every day different sections of the forests were surrounded, kraals were burnt, cattle seized, but neither Sigananda's or Bambata's *impis* could be encountered, for with so intimate a knowledge of the country and so excellent a system of intelligence they always managed to evade an attack. Brushes

---

* On their precipitous descent into the Insuzi Valley a mule carrying ammunition slipped down the Devil's Staircase in the pitch darkness and crashed nearly 1,000 feet. The following morning it was found alive but dreadfully injured and was immediately put out of its misery.

occurred at the Itate Gorge and Manzipambana in the heart of the forest where a section of Royston's Horse was badly mauled and suffered several casualties, but the arrival of timely reinforcements saved the situation. The enemy disappeared once again but not before they had lost 140 killed – the biggest defeat as yet inflicted upon them.

The pace was terrific and every man was feeling the strain, for both sides realised that events were rapidly working up to a crisis. Then on the night of 9 June a spy loyal to the Government brought in the vital information that Mehlokazulu with twelve companies and Bambata with eight (a company varied from fifty to a hundred men) were leaving the Qudeni that very night for the Mome where Sigananda would meet them with all his men and early the next morning they would slip through the gap at the top of the gorge and entrench themselves in the Stronghold.*

The moment Col. MacKenzie heard this news he realised that his first task was to get in touch immediately with Col. Barker who, it will be remembered, was camped in the vicinity of Cetshwayo's grave. Accordingly he wrote the following dispatch, ordering him to:

Move at once with all available men to the mouth of the Mome Valley. Information has been received that an impi is coming down from Qudeni to enter the Gorge between this and tomorrow morning. Please try and waylay this impi and prevent them from entering and at daylight block the mouth of the Mome at once. It is anticipated that they will not enter till daylight. I have reliable information as to where Sigananda is and am moving from here to surround him. I will cut off this portion at daylight and drive down towards you, so please do all you can to prevent his escape and to co-operate with me generally. Take your 15 pounders and Maxims in case you meet the impi which is reported to be of strength.[3]

MacKenzie called for volunteers to convey this dispatch and three troopers were selected as being most suited for the task – all were

---

* The Zulu in question was in the employ of Sgt W. Calverley and the full story of his gaining the above information and his speedy escape from the Gorge in order to bring the news to the Colonel in time was related to me by Sgt Calverley's son, Mr Fred Calverley of Itala, Zululand.

Zulu linguists and thoroughly acquainted with the forest – C. W. Johnson, G. O. Oliver and W. Deeley, all of the Zululand Mounted Rifles. By 10.30 p.m. the trio were on their way and it is to their lasting credit that they succeeded in their mission. Riding through enemy territory in the dead of night for a distance of fourteen miles, in danger of ambush at any moment and through most difficult country, they reached Col. Barker's camp by 1.15 a.m.

Meanwhile Col. MacKenzie having summoned his staff indicated by means of a map his plan of attack and the positions which were to be taken up by the various regiments. The upper end of the Gorge was to be surrounded and any attempt to reach the Stronghold must be cut off at all costs; the searchlight would work all night to beguile the rebels into the belief that the troops were resting quietly in camp; a start was to be made at 3.30 a.m.: there must be no smoking or talking *en route*; where troops had to dismount on account of precipitous descents men were to be detailed not only to hold the horses but to attach nosebags with feed to prevent the animals scenting each other and giving away the presence of the troops by neighing; the signal for attack would be given at dawn by the O.C. personally, three quick shots in succession from his revolver.

These orders were carefully obeyed and as the troops moved through mist and rain to take up their appointed positions heavy firing was heard just before dawn in the direction of the Insuzi Valley. First impressions were that the enemy was fleeing up this valley but suddenly the flash of a gun was seen shelling up the Mome. At once Col. MacKenzie realised that Col. Barker having reached his objective had blocked the entrance and opened the attack. Not a moment was to be lost, otherwise their agile and elusive foes would reach the gap leading to the Stronghold and once again escape.

On MacKenzie's right, below him and between the top of the Gorge and the Stronghold was the pear-shaped area of bush known as the Dobo, which would afford shelter and retreat to the rebels. Instantly grasping the situation, the Colonel ordered a squadron of Royston's Horse to encircle the top portion of the forest and so prevent any breakthrough in that direction. The moment these orders were given he himself dashed headlong down the precipitous Gcongco Spur followed by men of the Zululand Mounted Rifles, Royston's Horse and Northern District Mounted Rifles; though some slipped and fell there were no serious casualties. Half way down all had to dismount, for it was too dangerous to proceed on horse. At the double all scrambled down as best they could and eventually reached the gap not a moment too soon; already refugees from the Gorge were beginning to stream through. In a few moments, however, the way was effectively barred and any rebel daring to show himself was shot on sight. It was near this gap that the famous chief Mehlokazulu fell mortally wounded and close to him Bambata himself was slain, though this was not known till some days later.

Finding the pathway to the Stronghold no longer available the rebels now sought refuge in the Dobo Forest only to be met by a devastating fire from the guns on the surrounding hills and from the rifles of the men guarding its upper borders. Then commenced a merciless slaughter which lasted for sixteen hours. Shells and shot rained down into the Gorge from every side and as this fire ceased the troops came in mowing down everyone on sight. No opportunity was given for surrender, for no prisoners were taken. Those who fled into the forests and tried to take shelter by climbing the trees were ruthlessly shot down; dum-dum bullets were extensively used.*

Officially about six hundred rebels were killed, though in reality the number was considerably greater, as against three of the Government forces and a small number wounded. As the historian of the Natal Mounted Police wrote: 'The back of the Rebellion was broken by the massacre – it was not a battle – in the Mome Gorge on the 10th June.'4 It was the end of the rebellion in Zululand; hostilities were yet to continue in Natal.

---

* I have live specimens of these in my possession, picked up after the massacre.

## CHAPTER 16

# The Surrender of Dinuzulu

ALTHOUGH little more fighting took place in Zululand itself, 'It was of the utmost importance to prove that the principal ring-leader, a man still believed by many of his followers to possess supernatural powers, was really dead',[1] otherwise his name might be used in another attempt to rally the shattered rebel forces. Many still firmly believed that he had escaped from the Mome, was in hiding and only awaited a favourable opportunity to strike again. Consequently every available source was tapped for information and the many who were daily surrendering were closely questioned, but without result. It was not until the third day after the fight that a young Zulu appeared before Sergeant Calverley who claimed to be the *inceku* (mat carrier) of Bambata. It seemed that at last the quest was ended, for when asked why he had surrendered he stated explicitly: 'Bambata is dead.'*

When the youth was brought before Col. MacKenzie for further examination he not only related the details of his chief's death but stated that he knew the exact spot where the body lay. Anxious to obtain concrete proof of this the Colonel ordered Calverley to proceed at once to the Gorge, taking the *inceku* as his guide, and if possible bring back the body to Nkandhla for identification so that certain of the chiefs and *indunas* who knew Bambata would thus be able to vouch to others for his actual death.

It was anything but a pleasant task. When the body was found it was already somewhat decomposed, though fortunately, owing to the cold weather, not in an advanced stage. Realising the impossibility of carrying the corpse up the extremely steep and difficult mountain slopes, Calverley decided to cut off the head as this would serve the purpose and enable those who knew Bambata

* See Appendix IX.

to verify his actual death. This was done and the head brought back in Calverley's saddle-bag.

On Calverley's return to Nkandhla care was taken to show no disrespect to the deceased. The head was not exposed to public view but kept by one of the medical officers solely for the purposes of identification and it was impossible for anyone to view it without permission. When this had been completed it was taken back to the Gorge and buried with the body.

After his return from this somewhat gruesome trip Calverley, anxious to secure the surrender of his old friend Sigananda, sent him a message that he wished to see him. The reply came in the form of a guide who was to lead him to a secluded spot in the Forest where the old chief would await his arrival. Accordingly, accompanied by Lieut. Hedges,* Calverley made his way to the rendezvous. There Sigananda greeted Calverley and said he wished to hear what he had to say. Calverley replied that he might as well make up his mind to come out and surrender because the whole of the forest was going to be set alight. After a pause the old man agreed but said he was not prepared to go at once because they would be overtaken and murdered; as soon as his absence was noticed the search would start; but he would send a messenger to Calverley when all was ready, and he could come and take him. Convinced of the chief's sincerity Calverley agreed to this arrangement and a couple of days later the messenger duly arrived stating that Sigananda was ready to surrender. Hedges and Calverley set off immediately and followed the messenger to a spot on the edge of the forest where they were asked to wait. After some considerable delay they were accosted by one of the chief's men who told them: 'Nkosi, we have brought Sigananda.' A moment later he appeared carried on a litter by some of his servants. Calverley walked over to him and picking him up like a child put him on the spare pony they had brought and took him into camp. Later, when brought before Col. Mackenzie, Sigananda stated that 'Willie' had told him to give himself up and he was glad to do so, for he was

---

* Calverley and Hedges, together with Sergeant Titlestad, were on the Intelligence Staff on account of their thorough knowledge of the Zulus, their linguistic capabilities and their familiarity with the surrounding country.

too old to continue being carried about on a raw bullock's hide.*

During the next few days the majority of the rebels in the Nkandhla district followed Sigananda's example in surrendering. The decisive blow which had been struck at Mome had led to the almost immediate collapse of hostile activities in Zululand. The old chief, though cheerful to the end and in full possession of his faculties, did not long survive his trial by court martial which took place on 25 June 1906. Although he was granted whatever he required in the way of comforts during his short imprisonment he was too old to adapt himself to his changed circumstances and passed away quietly at midnight on 22 July. He lies buried on the Nkandhla commonage where his grave can be seen today, surrounded by a ring of gum trees.

During the final phases of the rebellion in Zululand negotiations had been proceeding between the Prime Minister of Natal and the Chief Commissioner on a proposed visit by Dinuzulu to Maritzburg for the purpose of an interview with the Governor. The suggestion had been well received by all concerned but unfortunately, though Dinuzulu and his headmen realised the necessity for such a visit they were compelled to reply that 'in Dinuzulu's present state of health they feared he would never reach Maritzburg but would die on the road.' However, permission was asked, and granted, for a deputation of *indunas* to interview the Governor and at a later date, when Dinuzulu had recovered from his illness, he would be only too ready to come along himself.

Accordingly about twenty *indunas*, headed by Mankulumana and accompanied by the Chief Commissioner, proceeded to Maritzburg where they met Sir Henry McCallum on 20, 21 and 22 June. These interviews were regarded by him as satisfactory; as he stated, the men had replied in a straightforward manner to all questions put to them, so much so that both he and the Minister for Native Affairs were persuaded that Dinuzulu's name had been used as a stalking horse by different malcontents to incite their

* The above information was given to me by Mr F. Calverley of Itala, Zululand, son of Sergeant W. Calverley.

neighbours to rebellion. It was in this way that many of the false rumours of which the chief complained had arisen.[2] Yet Dinuzulu, on his part, had in some measure disobeyed orders in that he had received certain Natal chiefs at his kraal without reporting it to the Governor as he should have done. In view of this the *indunas* were to carry back a warning to their chief that he must be more careful in the future.

As the rebellion had started in Natal, so it was destined to finish in that Colony. Barely had hostilities ceased in Zululand when news was received of a serious outbreak in the Mapumulo area, another district of hills, valleys and dense bush though not so precipitous as the Mome and its surroundings.

The first indication of trouble came in the early hours of 19 June when the store at Thrings Post was attacked. A Norwegian by the name of Sangreid was killed and a guest, W. C. Robbins, who was spending the night there, shockingly wounded.

William Clark Robbins, a fluent Zulu linguist, had been sent on a special mission by the Natal Government to visit the chiefs Meseni and Ndhlovu, who lived in the Tugela Valley, with the object of persuading them not to join in the rebellion. On his way into the valley he was stopped by an armed *impi* of about 1,000 men but being known to some of their leaders and explaining to them that he wished to see Meseni about some cattle, was allowed to proceed. A little further on he was again stopped by a second and much larger *impi* of about 3,000 warriors brandishing their assegais and shields. Here again he was allowed to proceed after stating his mission. On arrival at Meseni's kraal, where he also found Ndhlovu, he told them the purpose of his visit. Both chiefs replied that they were not in favour of joining the rebellion and had endeavoured in every possible way to stop their followers from doing so, but the young hotheads, having decided to fight, would not listen to reason and had already been doctored for war. Seeing that further argument was useless Robbins decided to return at once, the chiefs duly providing him with an escort for part of the way.

Once again he encountered the *impis* and on each occasion was

225

questioned carefully as to where he intended sleeping that night. In both cases he gave the same answer, 'At Bull's Farm', where he had previously arranged to stay. Robbins, impressed by the persistency of the question, felt that there was a distinct warning in it and realised that Bull's would be the only safe place for him to spend the night. However, when passing Thrings Post the manager of the store (Sangreid) ran out and asked him to stop there as he was all alone and had a fine dinner ready, more than sufficient for the two of them. Robbins was dog-tired after an exhausting day, Bull's was still some miles distant and it was getting dark; so, forgetful of the warning, he consented to stay.

About 5 a.m. there was a heavy knocking and thinking it was the boy with the early morning tea he got up and opened the door to be faced by a crowd of armed Zulus, one of whom instantly stabbed him clean through the right side. Robbins was an extremely powerful man and grabbing his assailant by the throat pulled him towards himself and by using him as a shield prevented others from stabbing him again in a vital spot. In spite of the spear in his side he hung on to the Zulu like grim death and gradually edged his way to a corner of the room. Others swarmed around but, unable to attack him in front, one of them drove his spear from above downward right into his stomach, inflicting another dreadful wound; another thrust an assegai into his lungs whilst others started hitting him on the head with their sticks. Shouting in Zulu above the din, 'Why are you killing me like a dog? Don't you know who I am?', he was at last recognised by some of the headmen who immediately drove his assailants out of the room. Expressing their regret at his grievous wounds they asked why ever he had changed his mind about sleeping at Bull's, as had he done this no harm would have befallen him.

Now, as if to make up for their vicious attack, they did everything possible to ease his pain and laying him gently on a bed of leaves they tended his wounds as best they could. Some hours later, after a message had been rushed through to Stanger, a doctor arrived with an escort and Robbins was placed in a springless ox-cart filled with straw. An agonising ride eventually brought him to hospital where, after a stay of many months, he miraculously recovered and though never the same man again, lived for another nine years.

The store manager was murdered and when his body was found it had been pierced by fifty-eight assegais. Every living thing on the place, including Robbins's horse, had been killed.[3]

That same morning of 19 June a convoy of nine wagons in charge of Sergeant L. E. Knox and Trooper Albert Powell was also attacked. They had left Stanger the day before, outspanned at the Otimati stream, about six miles from Mapumulo and having made an early start were descending a cutting when about fifty rebels sprang out on either side. Sergeant Knox, who was on the leading wagon, received a spear thrust in his right thigh but being a splendid athlete made a run for it and soon outdistanced his pursuers. Arriving in Mapumulo without further hurt he immediately gave the alarm. Trooper Powell, who was on the last wagon, also bolted, making for Oglesby's store, near where they had outspanned, but on racing to a cave indicated to him as a place in which to hide, was overtaken and stabbed to death. Later in the day his body was discovered horribly mutilated. The Oglesbys, not being in uniform, were left unharmed, nor were the wagons looted.

Early on the same morning Corporal J. Koster, taking a short cut from Mapumulo to Stanger, was also attacked by eight of Ndhlovu's rebels who were lying in ambush and narrowly missed being killed as he rode past; galloping on for some distance he dismounted and fired several shots at his foes who promptly ran away. He then pushed on to Thrings Post where he heard of the murder of Sangreid and the assault on Robbins, whom he found in desperate straits; later, on reaching Stanger he arranged for a doctor to go to his aid as speedily as possible.

The whole of this district was now in open rebellion and a general alarm was sounded. A body of Natal Mounted Rifles under Lt-Col. Ritchie set off immediately from Mapumulo for the spot where the convoy had been attacked and as they were scouring the area an *impi* about 200 strong suddenly charged down on them. Fortunately reinforcements arrived in time and the rebels were soundly thrashed. As news was received of the approach of a much larger *impi* it was decided to break off the engagement as the number of troops was then insufficient for any large-scale conflict.

On 27 June Col. Leuchars decided to make a reconnaissance in force some three miles south-west of Thrings Post towards a hill known as Peyana where it was understood a considerable number of rebels had assembled. As the troops advanced to the crest of the hill about 400 warriors sprang out from a slight depression where they had been lying concealed and made a sudden and determined charge, advancing to within a hundred yards of the troops before they were stopped by heavy gunfire which killed many of them.

It was now known that some of the tribe of Ngobizembe, along with other malcontents, had joined up with Meseni and Ndhlovu and the rebels were thus able to muster a force of over 5,000. Consequently as soon as Col. MacKenzie arrived he split his 3,500 troops into small columns and by forced marches surrounded Meseni's territory where he had ascertained the bulk of the rebels were concentrated. The disposition of the troops was carried out very skilfully and before the enemy knew what had happened they were practically hemmed in. Unfortunately on 2 July the complete encircling movement was frustrated by a most determined attack on Col. Barker's column on the Noodsberg; however, the rebels failed to gain the mastery, and eventually the tables were turned and they suffered a crushing defeat. By daylight the following morning the encircling troops were engaged with the remaining *impis* and swept everything before them; Meseni's kraal was burnt, hundreds of rebels were killed and a large number of cattle seized. On 8 July the last assault was made and a successful drive through the bush in which the remaining rebels were concealed practically ended the rebellion; in this action it was estimated that the enemy lost about 550 killed. On 11 July Meseni and Ndhlovu, on their way to surrender, were captured and taken to Eshowe. A final scour of the country was then made by the troops and the rebellion in Natal was over.

Some 4,700 prisoners had been taken and later stood trial; the majority of sentences ranged from six months to two years with floggings added; twenty-five of the ringleaders, sentenced to long terms of imprisonment, were deported to St Helena.

It was estimated that at least 10,000 Zulus went into open

rebellion and approximately 2,000 of them had been killed; the number of wounded was never known. Of the Europeans twenty-four were killed in action or died of wounds plus six Native levies; thirty-seven Europeans and thirty Native levies were wounded.

One of the results of the rebellion, due largely to pressure on the part of the Governor supported by the British Government, was the appointment of a Commission of Inquiry into the whole question of Native administration and legislation. This Commission commenced its investigations on 16 October 1906 and continued until 18 June 1907.

Meanwhile the courts martial were kept busy and evidence submitted by certain of the rebels pointed to Dinuzulu having been implicated in the recent troubles. Suspicions were deepened by statements made by Daniels, Dinuzulu's private secretary, to the Nongoma magistrate. Daniels had had a violent quarrel with his chief and as a result he 'told a lot of sensational yarns about affairs at Osutu [*sic*]'.[4] This was manna from heaven to certain members of the Natal Government who were only too anxious to secure a charge of treason against Dinuzulu and so get rid of him, and they immediately pressed for a full inquiry into his conduct. This, however, was taken out of their hands for the time being on account of illness, which on this occasion (18 September 1906) was so severe that rumours flew around Zululand that Dinuzulu was dead. These rumours had considerable effect on the Zulus and many of them flocked to Usutu to ascertain for themselves how much truth there was in them. Amongst them were a number of rebels including the clever but elusive Cakijana, who on reaching the royal kraal were relieved to find that though Dinuzulu had been very seriously ill he was by then out of danger and on the way to recovery.

Now according to Zulu belief all serious illness could be attributed to someone having cast an evil spell over the person concerned, with the object of securing his death. It thus became necessary to find and punish the culprit before he could accomplish his purpose. Dinuzulu himself was firmly convinced that this applied to his own case and when sufficiently recovered he set about finding the person who had brought him so near to death.

Straight away his suspicions fell upon one of the doctors who had been attending him, a man by the name of Gence. These fears were further increased when it was reported to him that Gence had been committing adultery with one of his wives (Oka Maha). In days gone by Gence would have been put to death without hesitation, but realising the danger of such an act at that time Dinuzulu resorted to legal action and had both him and Oka Maha brought before the magistrate at Nongoma. Unfortunately nothing of a definite nature could be proved when the trial took place and both the accused were acquitted, much to the disgust of Dinuzulu and many of his followers. So strong was the feeling against these two that as soon as the case was concluded both fled into hiding.

The influx of numerous rebels into Usutu as a result of Dinuzulu's illness caused another quarrel, this time between the *indunas* Mankulumana and Mgwaqo (14 November). Mankulumana strongly resented the harbouring of these rebels at Usutu, fully realising the danger of such action as it was expressly against the Governor's orders. Mgwaqo, on the other hand, just as strongly supported the rebels and did all in his power to assist them.* The quarrel became so acute, especially when Mankulumana favoured the immediate handing over of the men to the authorities, that Dinuzulu himself had to intervene and he patched up the quarrel for the time being by saying that he could not turn away to certain punishment 'his father's people'.

Towards the end of November 1906, the Smythe Government which had held office for some years resigned and a new Government, with the Hon. Sir Frederick R. Moor as Prime Minister, took over. At a meeting of the Ministers on 28 December to which Sir Charles Saunders (created K.C.M.G. 9 November 1906) was summoned there was a lengthy discussion on the general behaviour of Dinuzulu, for the Governor and several of his Ministers were 'full of Daniels' disclosures'[5] and imagined that in him they had

* Bomana, a rebel, stated in his evidence: 'We were afraid to go to Dinuzulu's kraal because it was said that Mankulumana was guarding the gate of the kraal with assegais to prevent the rebels from entering. Later we arrived at night and entered without being questioned. I found many other rebels there but we did not stay long at a time.'

found a most important witness for any prosecution that might take place. Sir Charles, however, who had spoken to Dinuzulu on the telephone just before leaving Eshowe and had discussed the whole of Daniels' 'sensational yarns' with him, threw cold water on their schemes by informing them that Daniels was a most unreliable witness; many of his charges were only the result of his quarrel with Dinuzulu and had little or no foundation in fact. Two days later, on the Commissioner's return home he again telephoned Dinuzulu and had another long talk with him during which Dinuzulu 'demanded' a full inquiry into all these allegations and requested that an interview be arranged with the Governor at which he 'could unburden his heart'. The following day Sir Charles sent a code message to the Government stating that 'an inquiry into the whole of the allegations against Dinuzulu was imperative' and urged that it be held at once; he followed this up with 'a long report on the same subject'.[6]

The new year 1907 opened in a very inauspicious way for Dinuzulu. On 5 January a man by the name of Ngunguluzo arrived at Usutu, ostensibly to see his brother-in-law about some cattle. During the rebellion this man was known to have been a scout under the magistrate R. H. Addison and word quickly got around that a spy was in their midst. Without hesitation the man was set upon, bound hand and foot and flung into a hut. Dinuzulu's mother, however, hearing of this, quickly ordered his release. Needless to say Ngunguluzo took to his heels as quickly as possible and made his way to the magistrate at Nongoma to whom he gave an exaggerated account of the incident, stressing the fact that many rebels were being harboured at Usutu. Thus Dinuzulu's enemies were presented with another witness.

For the next three months little of moment occurred but early in April (the 5th) a sensational murder broke the calm. At the back of Dinuzulu's mind there was still the lurking fear that Gence, though acquitted by the Court, was plotting against him, so he determined to take action. He had ascertained from his spies where Gence was then living and, summoning Cakijana to his house, he unfolded his plans to him: 'Gence is killing me,' he said, 'I get better then he makes me ill again; he is also killing my

231

daughter, Pikisile, by making her love him with his charms; she is ill and keeps saying that she wants to go to Gence. Therefore,' continued Dinuzulu, 'you and Matayana must go and kill him. Mjiji will go with you to show you the way.'[7] Cakijana at first demurred on the grounds that his leg had not yet recovered from his wound but Dinuzulu was insistent and added, 'You are not to cheat me but to perform the deed outright.' To enforce his command he made both Cakijana and Matayana swear an oath to kill Gence. A rifle was handed to the former and a shot gun to the latter together with the necessary ammunition. Accordingly, guided by Mjiji and travelling by night, they eventually arrived at Gence's hut where, after waiting and watching for the opportune moment, both fired simultaneously, wounding their victim so seriously that he died a few days later. Returning to Usutu they duly reported the result of their mission to Dinuzulu who displayed evident relief at their accomplishment of this cold-blooded murder, thus showing his inherent belief in an age-old superstition.

In the following month news came through that the long-delayed interview between the Governor and Dinuzulu had at last been arranged for 20 May. As Sir Henry McCallum had been appointed to the Governorship of Ceylon, the meeting was to serve a dual purpose for Dinuzulu of 'unburdening his heart' and bidding His Excellency goodbye.

Dinuzulu set out from the railhead at Somkele accompanied by Mankulumana, Mgwaqo and several other *indunas*. His journey to Maritzburg was more or less in the nature of a triumphal progress. At every station and siding crowds were there to give him the royal salute and heap gifts at his feet. It was the same on his arrival at the capital where he stayed at Bishopstowe with the two Misses Colenso and on the morning of 20 May he drove up to Government House in a carriage drawn by four mules, accompanied by a bodyguard of twelve of his leading men on horseback.*

The interview itself, in addition to the Governor, was attended by the Minister of Native Affairs, the Chief Commissioner and a

---

* Information given to me by William Vere who was a spectator. He was aged eighty-one when the interview took place at Mahlabatini and still hale and hearty.

number of Government officials, Dinuzulu being supported by his leading *indunas*.

After welcoming his guests the Governor went straight to the point by urging Dinuzulu to hand over to the authorities those rebels against whom there had been issued warrants of arrest, since the Government knew that he was harbouring a number of them at Usutu.

The Governor's object was not to punish him for such misdeeds as had come to light or to probe too deeply into others that merely rested on suspicion but to show him that the Government was in possession of information which clearly proved misbehaviour on his part and to afford friendly counsel as to his conduct in the future.[8]

When the discussion came to Dinuzulu's part in the recent rebellion and his support of Bambata, Mankulumana stated on his behalf:

Is it credible that our Chief would have been disposed to give assistance to Bambata in any way in the rebellion that he created? Bambata was a Chief himself; if he felt he had strength enough to cope with the Government it was a matter for himself to deal with. Had not the British beaten Cetshwayo, the father of Dinuzulu, and was it likely that Dinuzulu would assist a Chief like Bambata, seeing that his own father had been conquered by the British and was it likely that Dinuzulu would listen to what it was reported Bambata had said, that he would restore Dinuzulu to his authority over the whole of Zululand if he would assist him?[9]

Touching his own position as merely the chief of the Usutu tribe Dinuzulu said:

I do not wish to conceal from Your Excellency that I feel it very hard on me as the son of my father who was the King of the Zulus that I have been placed on a level with all other headmen and Chiefs in the country; we are just like a flock of goats, we are all the same. My father went to war with the British Government, was beaten, but allowed to return but he was not treated as he should have been, nor I, nor the people of Zululand as other nations who have gone to war with England have been treated. The nations of India are governed and treated in a correct manner.

233

The Boers, who have recently been at war with the British Government, have also been settled down but we who were subdued before the Boers are not treated in the same manner. The laws are not the same. We cannot help feeling that we Zulu people have been discriminated against. We are people who have no representatives in the affairs of the country, no one to speak for us and the laws of the country simply come over us by surprise. We are all of us in the country like my fingers, each one has his own authority and does what he thinks right in his own district. We feel that, whilst we should own obedience and allegiance to the Government there should yet be somebody amongst us who represents the people. There is no one over us all who might be held responsible and as a superior to keep them together and to give them advice and direction.[10]

That Dinuzulu was voicing the feelings of his people is only too obvious from the reports of the Commission of Inquiry. There the chiefs expressed the same views:

Where is he who is the eyes and ears of the Zulu nation, the Guardian of the people? When a state is conquered there always remains, according to our ideas, some representative or other who carries on the Government of the conquered people. The whole Zulu people are unanimous as to the need of some person to voice their feelings. Now they were in a state of dispersion; sheep without a shepherd.*[11]

It was a lengthy but nonetheless remained a 'friendly interview'[12] and at its close the Governor told Dinuzulu that:

He had done good work; he has spoken frankly to me and I have spoken frankly to him and I hope therefore that a lot of misunderstanding has been cleared up and we part as friends and to show my friendship for him I am going to send him my photograph signed and I hope that he will let me have one of his so that I can take it away with me.[13]

A second interview took place with the Acting Prime Minister and several members of the Cabinet. That they were well satisfied

* Stuart states that though for many years many chiefs were opposed to being governed by a paramount chief, yet the desire became widespread after the imposition of the Poll Tax and at that time was held by no less than ninety-five per cent of the nation who were emphatically in favour of maintaining the tribal system on condition that its numerous abuses were removed. (*A History of the Zulu Rebellion*, p. 534.)

with Dinuzulu's conduct is shown by the simple fact that at its close he was presented with a double-barrelled breech-loading shotgun.

After a short stay in Maritzburg Dinuzulu and his *indunas* left for Zululand. Shortly after his return to Usutu, realising the extreme risk of continuing to harbour Bambata's wife and children at his kraal, he decided to take steps for their removal. During his visit to Maritzburg he had taken the precaution of sending them away temporarily to a neighbouring kraal but now he made arrangements to dispatch them to a distant spot across the Pongola River. News of this projected move reached the ears of Siyekiwe and she made up her mind to flee without delay, taking her two children, Kolekile aged sixteen and Ndabayakhe aged fourteen, with her. In her evidence she gave a description of the flight.

When we ran away we took a vessel for drawing water and we said we were going to fetch water. When we left the kraal we put the vessel alongside the path, then we remained hidden away in the grass. After dusk we crossed the stream and started on our journey along a road; we took the wagon road to Mahlabatini; we proceeded along the road till far into the night when we left it and slept in the veld. We reached Mahlabatini as morning was breaking; we saw the Induna of the Court and gave ourselves to him and he reported us to the Authorities.

Naturally this gave Dinuzulu a fright as he had already been warned about harbouring rebels at his kraal; only a few days before he had received from the Nongoma magistrate a list of eight rebels who had been seen at Usutu. Without further ado he handed six of them over as requested, hoping thereby to counteract in some measure the flight of Bambata's wife and family. Needless to say the authorities took good care of their prisoners and extracted every shred of evidence from each one.

Within a few weeks other shocking murders took place. It was most noticeable that in each case the victim was a supporter of the Government and an opponent of Dinuzulu and his regime. Though the murderers were found, even after the closest cross-examination it was not possible to fasten the crimes onto Dinuzulu;

he may have been indirectly implicated but it seems more than likely that it was a last despairing attempt on the part of some of his followers to strike such fear in their opponents that all opposition to Dinuzulu assuming the position of Paramount Chief would be subdued.

For several weeks many lived in a constant state of fear; first Sitshitshili, an outstandingly fine chief, was shot dead; this was followed up by an unsuccessful attempt on the man who was investigating the crime, Sergeant Wilkinson. In September two more were singled out for death; fortunately both attempts failed. On 20 November Mpumela was murdered and a few days later Sibiya narrowly missed being shot.

In the midst of these murders the Native Commission of Inquiry submitted its report (25 July 1907); it certainly 'did not make pretty reading'.[14]

Other murders occurred. The Government instead of relying on their police force which could easily have dealt with the situation, asked for the assistance of Imperial troops. H.M. Government replied that these would be furnished provided that:

1. There was an immediate open inquiry into Dinuzulu's doings, 'not a mere police inquiry' but such an inquiry as the chief had so often requested.
2. That this inquiry should aim at redressing grievances and ensuring future peace.
3. That the Natal authorities would co-operate with H.M. Government in carrying out the recommendations of the Native Affairs Commission.[15]

The Natal Government to extricate themselves from any 'open inquiry into Dinuzulu's doings', which they wished to avoid at all costs, decided to arrest Dinuzulu and to declare martial law, but to do this they had to have the consent of H.M. Government. In order to obtain this they affirmed that they had definite proof that Dinuzulu was at the back of both the Bambata rebellion and the recent murders. On these grounds consent was granted, with the proviso that the barrister Eugene Renaud should be allowed to proceed to Usutu to urge Dinuzulu to surrender, thus avoiding the necessity of sending troops into Zululand with the possibility of further bloodshed.[16]

Before martial law could be imposed, however, the signature of the Governor was necessary. By this time Sir Henry McCallum had left Natal and his place had been taken by Sir Matthew Nathan who when presented with the document displayed considerable unwillingness to append his signature, but as great pressure was brought to bear upon him by his Ministers he eventually did so under protest (3 December).

Almost before the ink was dry troop movements were set in motion under the command of Col. MacKenzie and preparations made for a fresh invasion of Zululand. On the same day the magistrate at Nongoma was telegraphed to instruct Dinuzulu to come in to him at once and surrender; unless this order was complied with without delay force would be used and troops were at that moment on their way to compel his submission. By 4 December Col. MacKenzie and his staff together with a considerable body of men were already at Gingindhlovu, well into Zululand, and another force was dispatched to Melmoth.

At this juncture Miss Harriette Colenso reappeared on the scene. Immediately she heard that steps were being taken to arrest Dinuzulu she left in great haste for Zululand, arriving at Gingindhlovu on 4 December just after Col. MacKenzie. She got no further, for the Colonel summarily ordered her immediate return to Natal.

Whilst the above events had been taking place the British Prime Minister (Asquith) had telegraphed to Renaud requesting him to go at once to Pietermaritzburg to see Sir Frederick Moor. In turn Moor had been asked by the Imperial Government to grant Renaud every facility to get to Usutu at the earliest possible opportunity in order to advise Dinuzulu to surrender. Renaud left right away and in the interview which ensued the Premier told him that the Government had very reliable information that Dinuzulu would *not* surrender and that he had a considerable body of men at Usutu ready to fight should an attempt be made to arrest him. Renaud, on the other hand, insisted that this information was much exaggerated. Sir Frederick, relieved to hear this, agreed to provide him with a special train to Somkele and a cape cart with six mules to take him from the rail-head to Usutu, adding that if he succeeded in inducing Dinuzulu to surrender the Government would undoubtedly confer an honour on him or pay him substantially for his services as he would have saved Natal great expense and possibly much bloodshed. (Incidentally Renaud received neither – not even a letter of thanks from the Government.)

On proceeding to the railway station at Durban Renaud was met by Col. Clarke who told him he had been commissioned by the Government to place himself at his disposal and travel with him to Zululand. On reaching Tugela Renaud was greatly surprised to meet Miss Colenso who, having heard of his trip, was anxiously awaiting him. She then related her summary order from Col. MacKenzie to clear out of Zululand, making it impossible for her to help Dinuzulu in any way. Feeling that he too might meet with considerable opposition from the Colonel, as many of the Zulus were unacquainted with him, Renaud realised the necessity of obtaining from Miss Colenso some letter or token by which the Zulus would recognise him as their friend. Miss Colenso, eager to assist in every possible way, immediately thought of a letter that she had recently received from Dinuzulu in which he had requested her to send some Chamberlain's Cough Mixture for his children who were suffering from influenza, a remedy which he stated had in the past proved most effective. Fortunately she had both letter and cough mixture with her and these she handed over to Renaud.

Although the train had been specially chartered by the Prime Minister to convey Renaud to Somkele, on its arrival at Gingindhlovu MacKenzie, again taking advantage of his powers under martial law, peremptorily ordered both Renaud and Clarke to get out under the pretext that it was required for the transport of troops. It soon appeared obvious, however, that his prime objective was to steal a march on Renaud and get to Nongoma well ahead of him, for he quickly boarded the train himself and left Renaud and Clarke standing on the platform to make their way to Somkele as best they could.

On 6 December MacKenzie arrived at Nongoma and on the 7th (Saturday) two messengers arrived from Dinuzulu stating that he wished to know the nature of the offence which necessitated his surrender; they had further been instructed to request permission for Dinuzulu himself to visit the Governor. The Colonel replied that no messenger could be sent to Maritzburg, that Dinuzulu was charged with high treason and the best thing he could do, seeing that martial law had been proclaimed, was to surrender before the troops reached Nongoma.

In the meantime Renaud had managed to reach Nongoma and the moment he set foot in the village he was issued with an order to present himself at once before the Colonel. He found him engaged in conversation with Dinuzulu's messengers; breaking off his talk with them and turning to Renaud, he asked him bluntly what was the purpose of his journey to Zululand. Renaud having explained his mission, though its significance was already well known, the Colonel turned to the men and asked them: 'Do you know this man?'

As this was their first meeting with him they could only reply in the negative. Renaud, however, was equal to the occasion and surprised MacKenzie by asking to be allowed to speak for a few moments privately with them on the understanding that he would later repeat the conversation to him; the request was grudgingly granted. It was then that the letter of Dinuzulu to Miss Colenso and the bottle of Chamberlain's Cough Mixture more than served their purpose, for they immediately worked a complete transformation in the attitude of the messengers; they were now more than willing to do anything requested of them and would follow Renaud's advice to the letter.

Returning to the conference room and giving an outline of his conversation he told MacKenzie to his obvious consternation that the men were fully prepared to listen to his advice and act upon it. Driven into a corner the Colonel had no other alternative but to ask Renaud what he proposed doing. When informed that it was his wish to go to Usutu and see Dinuzulu personally, he told him emphatically that this could not be allowed; however, under the circumstances he would permit him to write a letter, subject to its being vetted by himself before it went forward; the messengers could then take it on to Dinuzulu when they returned to Usutu later that day. Renaud, determined to get his message through at all costs, accepted this proposal. Accordingly, after expressing his regret at the illness of his children and stating that he was forwarding the cough mixture at Miss Colenso's request, he urged Dinuzulu to come to Nongoma at once and surrender himself for trial, as by so doing further bloodshed could be avoided.

The completed letter was handed over to MacKenzie for censorship if necessary. For a moment there was dead silence but when the Colonel read the passage relating to the cough mixture he flung the note down on the table, suspecting some secret code, and in a burst of anger exclaimed: 'What is this nonsense about Chamberlain's Cough Mixture?' When Renaud produced the bottle from his pocket and explained that it was in this way that Dinuzulu would realise that he had come in friendship, the Colonel became mollified and eventually allowed the letter to go forward without alteration.

After informing the messengers where he was staying and telling them that he would await their return, Renaud booked in at the hotel. At about two o'clock the following morning there was a knock on his window and to his surprise there stood the two messengers, who had hurried back on instructions from Dinuzulu to ask advice on certain points, the most important of which was: 'Would he be indicted before a civil tribunal or tried by a court martial?' Fortunately Renaud had received an assurance from Sir Frederick Moor before leaving Natal that a special court would be appointed for the trial and he was able to impart this information to the envoys. After a few other questions of minor importance the interview terminated and the messengers departed on their sixteen-mile trip back to Usutu.

Next morning about 8 a.m. when Renaud had just sat down to breakfast he was somewhat startled by the arrival of Captain Stuart accompanied by a picket of six armed men, who without further ado marched straight into the dining-room and informed him that he was a prisoner and must proceed immediately with them to see Col. MacKenzie. To protest was useless and he was marched as a prisoner through the dust and heat of a December morning for a distance of about one and a half miles to Head-quarters. Here he was ushered 'into the presence of a sort of court-martial' and was informed that he was charged with communicating with the enemy without permission of the officer commanding.

One can imagine Renaud's surprise as he had been granted a free hand to communicate with his client by no less a person than the Prime Minister of Natal who in turn was acting on the instructions of H.M. Government. This he told MacKenzie and having given a résumé of his early morning interview he stated quite frankly that it was his opinion that Dinuzulu would surrender that very day. It was obvious that he was not believed and after further questioning he was marched outside whilst the officers considered their verdict. Half an hour later he was brought in again to hear the sentence of the court; his explanation had been accepted and he would be released on the strict understanding that no further communication was to take place between himself and Dinuzulu's envoys; he must give a solemn undertaking that, if approached, he would report immediately to Headquarters. Having given his word he was released about noon, when he made his way back to the hotel.

Meanwhile MacKenzie made all preparations to move the troops to Usutu the moment they arrived from Somkele. For the rest of the day and the whole of that evening Renaud was anxiously scanning the horizon for any sight of Dinuzulu. In the interim Captain Stuart, on instructions from Sir Charles Saunders, had been sent with a wagon to meet the chief at the Ivuna Drift, about half way to Usutu.

Darkness fell and it found Renaud seated on a huge boulder on a hill facing the hotel. His vigil was suddenly interrupted by a dark form pulling at his coat; it was an envoy from Dinuzulu who had been afraid to show himself earlier for fear of arrest. In a whisper he informed Renaud that the *Inkosi* had left Usutu and would meet Stuart at the river. About ten o'clock a light was seen coming along the road; soon the wagon appeared and in it were Dinuzulu, his *indunas* and Stuart; it was escorted by about a hundred men all armed with guns and bayonets. Renaud rushed forward, jumped on the wagon and shaking hands with Dinuzulu expressed his satisfaction that without compulsion or bloodshed he had decided to surrender. Miss Colenso's letter and the bottle of Chamberlain's Cough Mixture had proved effective in more ways than one.

## CHAPTER 17

# Arrest and Trial

THE last stage of the journey to the Court House at Nongoma was
accomplished without incident and by the time the wagon reached
its destination it was 11.15 p.m. (9 December 1907). Everybody
had gone to bed except a solitary sentry who was on duty at the
door which gave access to Col. MacKenzie's room. On this door
Renaud knocked whilst Stuart was busy assisting Dinuzulu to
alight, no easy task in view of his corpulence. A few minutes later
the Colonel appeared and seeing Dinuzulu stepped forward and
shook hands with him, asking him at the same time to order his
men to stack their arms in front of the Court House after which
they could go to their quarters in the adjoining yard.

Whilst this was being done MacKenzie, turning to Renaud,
thanked him warmly for what he had accomplished and promised
to see him again in the morning. Asked what was to become of
Dinuzulu the Colonel replied that quarters were ready to receive
him, pointing at the same time to a closed door which communicated with the yard of the gaol. Bidding Dinuzulu good-night and
promising to see him in the morning Renaud made his way back
to his hotel, a tired but much relieved man.

First thing next morning he was summoned before Col.
MacKenzie and informed that as his presence was no longer
required at Nongoma Col. Clarke had received instructions to
escort him to the railhead without delay; he would, however, be
allowed a short interview with Dinuzulu before leaving and this
could take place right away. At the gaol Renaud found Dinuzulu
not only dejected at the thought of the advocate's enforced early
departure but very mortified at having been placed under lock and
key and not allowed out on parole. Renaud mentioned this to the
Colonel but was brushed off and told 'Not to mix himself up with

S

questions that did not concern him; Dinuzulu would be sent to Maritzburg where he would be allowed to see him as a client.'[1] With that he was dismissed and ordered to make his way to Somkele as quickly as possible as his escort was waiting.

On his arrival in Maritzburg Renaud duly reported the result of his mission to Sir Frederick Moor who, after congratulating him on its successful outcome again mentioned the handsome reward that was sure to follow from the Natal Government.

At 3 p.m. on the afternoon of the 10th (the day of Renaud's departure) Dinuzulu was formally arraigned before Col. MacKenzie; the only other Zulus allowed to witness these proceedings were Mankulumana, Mgwaqo and Dinuzulu's secretary, Ncapayi. After expressing satisfaction at Dinuzulu's surrender the Colonel stated that in view of the various murders which had been taking place in the country the Government had decided to take action in order to put a stop to such crimes. It was felt that Dinuzulu was exerting an evil influence and was a menace to law and order in the land. Consequently martial law had been declared, troops had entered Zululand to round up the remaining rebels and they would not leave till the prevailing disorders had ceased. Dinuzulu's offences were known to the Government and would be communicated to him in due course; it was for these that a warrant had been issued for his arrest; he would later be tried by an impartial civil tribunal and ample time would be granted to him to prepare his defence.

In his reply Dinuzulu denied all connection with the recent murders, emphasised the utter impossibility of his having taken up arms against the Government and raised his objections to the statement that he, with only limited jurisdiction over a small area, could possibly exert an influence for evil over the whole country. No further argument was allowed and within forty minutes the proceedings were concluded.

Meanwhile a large crowd had gathered outside the Court House, for news of Dinuzulu's arrest had quickly spread and many leading Zulus from the district had come in to find out what was happening to their chief. Taking advantage of the occasion Col. MacKenzie, after ordering them to sit in a semicircle around him, addressed them from the veranda. Much of what he said was just a repetition of what he had told Dinuzulu and all present were warned that should there be any opposition to the work of the troops it would be dealt with far more drastically than had happened in the recent rebellion; full powers had been given him to act as he saw fit and he was determined to use them to the limit should necessity arise. Those who were loyal to the Government would be supported and his advice to all was 'Go back to your homes and live there quietly and peaceably.'

Later in the day a large body of troops arrived at Nongoma; the men were allowed a short rest but were informed that in the early hours of the next morning they were to raid Usutu for the twofold purpose of capturing any rebels who might be in hiding and of searching for and seizing all concealed firearms; they were to split up into three columns and thus converge on the kraal from different directions. These instructions were carried out and the troops reached their destination just as day was breaking.

They were surprised to find the whole kraal in a sadly neglected state; its buildings, with the exception of the Secretary's brick office, were dilapidated, the huts needed re-thatching and what was to have been an imposing house for Dinuzulu had progressed little beyond the foundations. Over everything there was a general air of slovenliness, possibly due to the unsettled state of the country.

After the inmates had been ordered to vacate their huts the kraal was thoroughly searched, particular attention being given to Dinuzulu's apartments. Letters, documents, shields, all were seized for evidence, in fact very little was left, for though looting was nominally forbidden much took place.* Very few firearms were found and those ferreted out were discovered to be lawfully held. As they suspected that many were being concealed, instructions were issued that all guns and assegais would have to be handed in at Nongoma within a week, failing which the troops would come again.

---

* The Princess Magogo, Dinuzulu's daughter, who was a girl at the time and witnessed the proceedings, told me: 'When the soldiers came ostensibly looking for guns, they ransacked our home and looted nearly everything we had.'

An extensive search was also made for any refugee rebels in hiding; the kraal and its surroundings were thoroughly combed but none were found. Possibly this was due to the fact that Dinuzulu was said to have told those who were living at Usutu to disperse before he gave himself up to the authorities.

On 14 December, accompanied by a large escort of troops and a battery of Natal Field Artillery, Dinuzulu and his men were moved from Nongoma, conveyed by mule cart and wagons. They were destined for Maritzburg, reached two days later, where all were lodged in the local gaol; their preliminary examination began on 23 December 1907 and lasted till 30 July 1908.

After the troops had completed their raid on Usutu they were split up into small companies to scour the country for rebels and hidden arms. Much bitterness was generated among the Zulus by the persistent looting of native cattle and by the ruthless tactics of many of the troops; these facts were withheld from the public by the continued operation of martial law and MacKenzie took great care that none but those he wished should enter Zululand.

Many wanted men were rounded up in these operations and several caches of arms were discovered but the ringleader, Cakijana, still managed to elude their united efforts. An interesting and amusing story is told of one of his escapades, illustrating his quick-wittedness.* A sergeant of the police received information through one of his spies that Cakijana was at a certain kraal near Ulundi. Hurriedly collecting a hundred of his men he surrounded the place and ordered the inmates out one by one from each hut in turn, but no trace of Cakijana could be found although at the time of their arrival he was in one of the huts with an old woman and a young mother and her baby. Being secretly alerted, with great presence of mind he ordered the old woman to take off her dress and drawing this over himself he asked the young mother to hand over her baby and tie it on his back, native fashion, assuring her at the same time that no harm would befall the child if she followed his instructions; he must be given time to get right through the ring of

---

* The details of this story were given to me by Mr F. Calverley and it has been verified by several others, both Europeans and Zulus, whom I have questioned in different parts of Zululand.

police; when clear he would lay the child down under a bush and she would be able to trace it by listening for its cries. Boldly venturing forth and assuming the role of the old grandmother he made straight for the sergeant, taking the precaution to pinch the baby hard as he approached. Naturally the child, unaccustomed to such treatment, bellowed and howled, and when Cakijana reached the sergeant he was met with the order: 'Get away you old fool, I'm not looking for an old woman, I'm looking for Cakijana.' To this the so-called grandmother replied in a squeaky voice: 'I don't know anything about Cakijana; this child is sick and it is worrying me.' Angrily turning on her the sergeant booted her away. Thus Cakijana once again eluded his pursuers and got clean away.

Some weeks later Willie Calverley, knowing that there was a reward of £100 for the capture of this man and anxious to obtain it for himself, thought of a plan which he felt certain would prove effective. His spies had told him that Cakijana was hiding in the bush which surrounded his kraal and at night used to sneak down for a good meal which his mother always had ready for him. Repeated attempts had been made to seize him by scouring the bush but all had ended in failure. Calverley now decided to write a letter in Zulu, allegedly from Harriette Colenso, whom he knew to be on friendly terms with Cakijana. In this letter he was urged to 'Come to Maritzburg at once and I will hand you over to the authorities and plead for a pardon for you; even if you do get convicted you will only get a short sentence if you give yourself up.' This was sent by two messengers who stated that they had come from Miss Colenso and was in due course handed to Cakijana's mother with instructions to give it to him at the first opportunity as the matter was very important. Cakijana got the letter and made immediate preparations to follow what he thought were Miss Colenso's instructions. A beast was killed for food for the road and with two of his followers he set out for Maritzburg riding his fast white horse. Meanwhile Calverley's scouts were watching and reporting Cakijana's progress for Calverley to effect the capture as he crossed Jameson's Drift over the Tugela. Unfortunately for himself Calverley at the crucial moment received an urgent message from his wife stating that he must return home at once as his child was seriously ill. Determined not to lose his quarry he telephoned the Maritzburg police telling them that his spies had seen Cakijana cross the Tugela, that he would sleep at Kranzkop that night and would reach Bishopstowe the next day; they must therefore lie in wait for him at a place mentioned some miles outside Maritzburg. At first Calverley was disbelieved but on his promising to share the reward with the police officer the latter agreed to do as requested.

Cakijana, however, managed to elude them all and reached Miss Colenso's home in safety for the police arrived at the appointed rendezvous half an hour too late. Nonetheless, acting on Miss Colenso's advice, he was taken into Maritzburg by her and surrendered himself to the authorities on 10 March. Later he stood his trial.

By mid-March practically all the rebels had been captured and the missing guns seized, but martial law was not revoked until 11 August. The main reason for this lengthy delay undoubtedly was to impede the work of Dinuzulu's defence team, for the Natal Government was determined to secure a conviction at all costs and as long as this law remained in operation Dinuzulu's legal advisers were effectively barred from all contact with vitally important witnesses in Zululand. The Government, of course flatly refuted this, claiming that the continuance of martial law was necessary to prevent the entry of undesirable persons into Zululand, whose actions might keep alive the spirit of unrest and thus endanger the peace. Nonetheless it is noteworthy that a period of only about two months was allowed to the defence for them to proceed to Zululand for the necessary interviews, as against the many months during which the Government had been collecting their evidence and preparing their witnesses.

A further step taken by the Government at this time in an attempt to thwart the work of the defence was the cutting off of Dinuzulu's annual salary of £500 from the moment of his arrest. By this means they hoped to deprive him of the ability to finance his legal advisers. Exasperated by this niggardly act, which was immediately brought to their notice by Miss Colenso, the Imperial

Government stepped in and insisted that his salary be paid till such time as the judgment of the court had been given. A somewhat bitter wrangle ensued which was later settled by the Natal Government paying a sum of £500 to Dinuzulu's agents and the Imperial Government making a substantial grant towards the costs of the defence.

During the whole of this period Harriette and Agnes Colenso had been working assiduously on Dinuzulu's behalf. In the first instance they had briefed an English barrister, E. G. Jellicoe, K.C., to assist Eugene Renaud and Robert Samuelson in his defence. Jellicoe arrived in Maritzburg on 19 January 1908, attended two or three of the preliminary examinations and then abandoned the whole case in disgust, leaving again for England on 7 February. He made the following startling allegations:

1. That evidence in Dinuzulu's favour had been suppressed.
2. That witnesses in Dinuzulu's favour had been imprisoned.
3. That the trial was a 'judicial outrage'.
4. That witnesses signed statements supposed to have been made by them, beginning with the words: 'It is true, according to the authorities . . .'
5. That Dinuzulu was deprived of any opportunity of obtaining evidence in his favour.[2]

Naturally these allegations created an uproar but they alerted the general public to the somewhat questionable conduct of the Government in the preliminary investigations then being carried out.

As they needed to find another advocate for the defence Harriette Colenso asked Renaud to proceed to the Cape and approach the Hon. W. P. Schreiner, a former Premier of the Cape Colony, with the request that he accept the brief. Schreiner at the time was busily engaged in the affairs of the National Convention and tried to head off Renaud by saying that his fees would be too high; but Renaud persisted. Then came a further request from no less a person than the Colonial Secretary: in the end Schreiner gave his promise on the understanding that Renaud would do the necessary spade work. His main reason for undertaking this heavy task was: 'His growing realisation of the political and social issues that were focussed upon the person of Dinuzulu; the man had a history; it was not a happy one, nor did it reflect credit on the Natal authorities who were now about to prosecute him.'[3]

Meanwhile the Natal Government were taking steps to set up a special Civil Tribunal for the trial of Dinuzulu and certain other native prisoners. This they regarded as necessary, for had the case come before the ordinary Supreme Court it would have necessitated the empanelling of a jury, which they wished to avoid. Possibly there was some justification for this step, in view of the heightened feelings of a section of the population at that time. Be that as it may, a Bill was brought before Parliament shortly before the conclusion of the preliminary examinations, legalising this Special Court which was to be constituted by a bench of three judges appointed for the occasion and against whose verdicts there could be no appeal.

On 15 September the names of the three judges were gazetted: Sir William Smith of the Transvaal was to act as Judge President; he was to be supported by Judge H. G. Boshoff of the Natal Bench and Henrique C. Shepstone, ex-Secretary for Native Affairs in Natal.

Dinuzulu and his friends protested at once. No objections whatsoever were raised against the first two but there was a loud outcry against the inclusion of Henrique Shepstone who was not even a lawyer and who had been closely connected with the policy which some years earlier had led to Dinuzulu's deportation to St Helena; in addition, there had been a standing feud between the Shepstone family and the house of Cetshwayo ever since the days of the Zulu War.[4] The defence therefore lodged a protest with the Governor but the Government were adamant; the Special Court must stand as gazetted.

The trials, due to begin on 3 November 1908, were arranged to take place in the Greytown Town Hall which had been fitted out for the occasion. The building had been selected on accounts of its being in the district where the rebellion had started.

First on the list of those to stand trial was Cakijana; his case lasted from the 3rd to the 10th and resulted in his being found guilty of high treason; he was sentenced to seven years' hard labour. Jombolwana, charged with the murder of Sitshitshili, came next; he also was found guilty, sentenced to death and executed in December. The all-important trial of Dinuzulu began on 19 November. Counsel for the prosecution was led by the Attorney-General, the Hon. T. F. Carter, K.C., supported by Messrs D. Calder, W. S. Bigby and G. E. Robinson. The proceedings were conducted in English and Zulu, the chief interpreter being J. W. Cross who had been the magistrate at Greytown when the rebellion broke out.

Dinuzulu was charged on twenty-three counts and the indictment ran into no less than six and a half closely printed Blue Book pages. Commenting on this, Schreiner wrote in a letter to his wife: 'The Government are so deeply involved in getting a verdict that they are leaving no stone unturned; but the more I see of it the more I come to the conclusion that it is a persecuting political trial.'[5]

The chief charges were: high treason; public violence; sedition and rebellion; the murder of, or being accessory to the murder of Gence; incitement to murder Mapoyisa and the contravention of the Firearms Act of 1905. On all these Dinuzulu emphatically declared his innocence.

In the course of the trial, during which Dinuzulu was in the witness box for ten and a half days, ninety-five witnesses (forty-seven European and forty-eight African) were called for the Crown and fifty-two for the defence (four European and forty-eight African). During the proceedings witnesses for the Crown were compelled to turn their backs on Dinuzulu, not even being allowed to look at him lest they should be intimidated by his presence! Dinuzulu said of them:

All these witnesses appear to me mere offscourings. . . . Those appointed to care for me have gashed me in the face. . . . They have brayed against me in their newspapers, slandering me . . . moreover there are procured against me all who have ever misbehaved at the Usutu, even those who have a spite against me through having been found guilty in the courts.[6]

Schreiner commented:

There went the Crown witnesses, file after file, with their plausible well-learnt stories, piling up as the days went by. . . . A terrible mass of exaggeration and falsehood to be attacked and levelled. . . . I have never run or known run a criminal prosecution in such fashion. There is a dense atmosphere of intrigue everywhere.[7]

The prosecution closed its case on 18 January and the defence opened the following day and lasted till 23 February. Schreiner faced a most difficult task and 'had to fight the Attorney-General every inch of the way'.[8] All the forces of the Natal Government were ranged against him and the way in which the prosecution had been conducted may be illustrated by a remark of the Attorney-General to a Zulu witness: 'What! Would you dare to contradict a white man?'[9]

Schreiner with consummate skill not merely stood his ground but carried the attack deep into the camp of the enemy. On the eve preceding his final speech for the defence Dinuzulu addressed himself to 'The Inkosi Mr Schreiner':

I ask you to keep me in your armpit; leave me not in the hand of Mr Carter because he hates me exceedingly. My sole crime is that I am the son of Cetshwayo. I am being killed through ill will, there is nothing that I have done. My trouble is like that of no one else. It beset me when I was a child and my father was taken by the white people and it is still besetting me. . . . ' Nkosi, what is grievous to me is to be killed and yet alive. To die outright is nothing, then one rests and does not feel trouble. . . . I am he who trusts you, who am on your shoulder.[10]

Heartened by Dinuzulu's confidence in him and stimulated rather than daunted by the opposition of his adversaries, Schreiner in his final plea reached the climax of his outstanding career as a barrister. When judgment was given he had the satisfaction of knowing that not merely had he humbled his opponents but had succeeded in winning a great moral victory over them.

The following day, 3 March, judgment was given: of the twenty-three original counts, two had been withdrawn; on the remaining twenty-one Dinuzulu was acquitted of eighteen and a half. The Bench found him guilty of high treason in that:

(*a*) He had harboured and concealed Bambata's wife and children for fifteen months.

(*b*) He had harboured and assisted Bambata and Mangati during the actual progress of the rebellion.

(*c*) He had also harboured numerous rebels at various times between May 1906 and the date of his arrest.

In his summing up the Judge President stated:

It can be said for you with regard to the one offence that you gave no direct encouragement to these men in continuing their rebellion, and, in my opinion, at no time did you attempt to take an active part in the rebellion; but people must understand that they cannot touch pitch without being defiled, and that they cannot offer assistance to the King's enemies and claim to be loyal. At the same time, with regard to the other offence, I can understand that you were in conflict between your duty to the Government and the position which you felt you held over the Zulu people.[11]

On charge (*a*), he told Dinuzulu:

It is admitted that Siyekiwe, Kolekile and Ndabayake remained at the Usutu kraal from the time when they first arrived until the beginning of July 1907 when they left secretly and travelling through the night, arrived at the Mahlabatini Magistracy in the morning.

On charge (*b*):

On considering the whole of the evidence I have come to the conclusion, though not without hesitation, that it is established that Mangati and Bambata together visited the Usutu, that they were allowed to remain there by the prisoner and were supplied by him with food. . . . Both Mangati and Bambata were known to the prisoner to be prominent leaders of the rebel impi and when he allowed them to stay in his kraal and supplied them with food, thus assisting them to get back to the rebel forces, he was, in my opinion, guilty of an act of high treason.

Regarding charge (*c*), the Judge President continued:

Whilst I think it has been proved that the prisoner did knowingly harbour rebels at his kraal I do not think that he did so with any hostile intent against the State. . . . I think the prisoner's action in allowing these men to stay in his kraal was due not to hostile intention to the Government but to a consciousness of the position he occupied in the eyes of the Zulus, to his unwillingness to give up to justice his father's people.[12]

On count (*a*) Dinuzulu was fined £100 and on counts (*b*) and (*c*) he was sentenced to four years' imprisonment as from the date of his surrender (9 December 1907).

As a result of his conviction Dinuzulu automatically forfeited his position as Government Induna and chief of the Usutu tribe. This appeared to trouble him but little, for before parting with Schreiner he begged him: 'Let me leave the land of the Rulumeni [Government] of Natal.'

Mankulumana and Mgwaqo faced trial on 9 and 10 March, also on the charge of high treason; though neither of them was seriously implicated they were nevertheless found guilty and sentenced to short terms of imprisonment, the former to nine months and a fine of £50, the latter to fifteen months and a fine of the same amount.

Thus in spite of all the questionable methods adopted by the prosecution, the judges had remained fair throughout the long trial and it is to their credit that they displayed an impartiality worthy of the high traditions of the Justiciary. The Natal Government, smarting under their defeat, ordered the immediate destruction of the Usutu kraal and shortly afterwards split up the Usutu tribe into three, incorporating each section in adjoining tribes.

One fact remains to be noted: Schreiner's fees for his two and a half months' strenuous exertion amounted to £1,650; of this he accepted only £100 8s. 9d.; the balance of the Imperial Government's grant went to finance his colleagues and to meet the necessary living expenses.[13]

## CHAPTER 18

# *Epilogue*

LITTLE remains to be told.

Dinuzulu was removed first to Maritzburg and later to Newcastle to serve the remainder of his sentence. His term of imprisonment was, however, cut short by the advent of the Union of South Africa. Its first Premier, the kindly, unassuming General Louis Botha, remembered Dinuzulu as an old friend – he had ridden into Zululand with the New Republicans to help him against Sibebu. One of his first acts in office was to write to Schreiner informing him that he proposed to release Dinuzulu forthwith and establish him on a farm somewhere in the Transvaal. Schreiner wired back cordially agreeing with the suggestion and adding: 'Trust your known and valued friendship for him to ameliorate his condition and so win abiding goodwill of all best Zulus.'[1]

The farm, 'Uitkyk', situated about half way between Middelburg and Witbank, was soon purchased, Dinuzulu was released and there, with his wives, the faithful Mankulumana and other of his friends he settled down quietly to live out the remainder of his days. They were not many, for he was a broken man; his health steadily declined. A trip to Europe was arranged to seek medical aid but it was not to be. A serious haemorrhage set in and on the early morning of 18 October 1913 he died, expressing as his last wish:

'Bury me with my fathers at Nobamba.'

His wish was carried out and he rests near the banks of the peaceful Mpembeni River in the Zululand that he loved so dearly. His grave there is still (1966) guarded by OkaHlabane, the last remaining of his widows.

## Interview with Princess Kusabhede Soneni

As RECENTLY as 28 November 1965, thanks largely to the kindness of Dr and Mrs Hollings of Eshowe, who informed me of the presence of Cetshwayo's daughter, Princess Kusabhede Soneni (aged about 100) in the Eshowe Hospital, an interview was arranged. I obtained much valuable information from this remarkable old lady who certainly carried her years very well. Her face was barely wrinkled and it was only when one saw her shrunken hands that one realised that age had left its mark. Her voice was strong, her mind alert, her memory unclouded and as she told me of the days long gone by and related her many experiences, sometimes with a fierceness that thrilled and always with the vividness so characteristic of the Zulus, she brought that whole era to life, and through her narration shone the royal dignity inherent in so many members of that family.

When I questioned her on the history of Cetshwayo and Dinuzulu her eyes filled with tears which spilled down her cheeks as she replied, 'You have come to awaken old wounds.' She well remembered Cetshwayo's visit to Queen Victoria and related many of the incidents connected with it; she recalled vividly the procession around the wagon which conveyed the mortal remains of her father to its last resting-place in the heart of Zululand.

When asked her opinion of Sibebu her eyes flashed in anger and her whole expression changed as she almost hissed out, 'Don't mention his name to me, he was the man who destroyed the Zulu nation.' She remembered Sibebu's father, Maphitha, warning Cetshwayo, 'Beware of my son, he is very cunning', for Maphitha was loyal to Cetshwayo who always treated him as a prince because of his direct descent from Jama, one of the early Zulu kings.

Ndabuko she spoke of as a great patriot, a good and kind-hearted man for whom she had a high regard, whilst Mankulumana ranked in her estimation and in that of the whole nation as one of the most able men in Zululand. He was a splendid character, courteous and gentlemanly to a degree, extremely loyal to Dinuzulu. As the Princess said, 'the only thing which parted them was death' and it was Mankulumana who selected the site of Dinuzulu's grave close to the Mpenbeni River in the Valley of the Kings (Emakosini) and superintended all arrangements for the funeral.

# The Death of Cetshwayo

SINCE I wrote *The Last Zulu King* several new facts concerning the death of Cetshwayo have come to my notice.

That death was due to heart disease may have been the *official* view but this was almost immediately questioned in many quarters and those Zulus who had been in contact with the King and knew the full story were unanimous in their rejection of this diagnosis.

Soon after the report reached London the *Medical Times* was prompted to publish the following which was quoted in the *Natal Witness* of 2 April 1884:

After printing a sphygmographic tracing of Cetshwayo's pulse which was taken by J.K.B. when the late Zulu King was living in the Melbury Road, London, he writes:

'As ex-King Cetshwayo is stated to have died suddenly of fatty degeneration of the heart it may interest your readers to know what was the state of his heart when he was in England in August 1882. In auscultation the heart sounds were absolutely normal and the appended sphygmographic tracing will show the healthy state of the arterial system. Cetshwayo's main ailment when in England was constipation from excessive meat diet, combined with want of exercise.'

On 3 September 1962 I had the privilege of interviewing the Princess Magogo, the daughter of Dinuzulu and grand-daughter of Cetshwayo, on this matter. Her grandmother (wife of Cetshwayo) *was actually in the hut with him when he died* and she states categorically that Cetshwayo was poisoned. The account of his death was passed on orally to Princess Magogo's mother who in turn taught it to the Princess herself, as is the custom with outstanding events in Zulu history.

This story was duly related to me by the Princess in the graphic fashion common to the Zulus: 'The King's dinner was brought in to him by his servants, consisting chiefly of meat which had been prepared by those hostile to him, for his own people had been forbidden by Osborn to supply him with food. Cetshwayo took a mouthful of this meat and within seconds turned to one of his wives saying, "I feel ill"; this was followed by a terrible convulsion, the King's head dropped over to one side and he sank back in a state of collapse; water was dashed over him and everything done to revive him but he was dead.'

Sir Henry Bulwer indirectly refers to the belief in this poisoning: 'Although the Usutu Chiefs have sent for Dinuzulu several times he refuses to go to them and says that he is afraid of being poisoned as his father was.'[1]

A fact of some significance is that only two weeks before his death Cetshwayo had sought refuge at the military camp from an attempt which he said was about to be made upon his life. Sanctuary was refused him, so he fled to another retreat but was pursued by the Native Police and brought back to his former abode and a report was circulated that he had attempted to escape.[2]

About this time an attempt was also made upon the life of Mnyamana: 'It was lately reported and for some time believed that Mnyamana was dead and it appears that he was very ill and at the point of death but recovered. It is believed that, either accidentally or intentionally, poison was administered to him.'[3] It is evident that serious attempts were being made to poison the leaders of the nation who supported the royal house.

Over the years I have interviewed many Zulus in different parts of the country on the matter of Cetshwayo's death and the answer is almost invariably the same: 'He was killed by Sibebu.'

# Grant's Support of Boer Claims

GRANT, in a letter to Sir Henry Bulwer dated 4 August 1885, gave the following reasons for his support of the Boer claims:

1. His being unable to assume the grave responsibility of refusing the Boer terms because of their determination to enforce them by arms if necessary.
2. England's determination not to interfere in the affairs of Central Zululand.
3. The terrible condition of the country due to Sibebu's repeated attacks, and the necessity for an immediate settlement, particularly in view of the fact that the planting season was at hand.[1]

## Proclamation No. 1, New Republic[1]

*TO ALL WHO SHALL SEE OR HEAR THIS READ, GREETING.*

1. During the last three years war, disturbances, murders of defenceless women and children, thefts, conflagrations (or arson), and continual bloodshed have taken place in Zululand, which threw the whole country into a state of unrest, causing great divisions among the native races and in consequence of which large portions of the country became unfit to reside in, so much so that the majority of the inhabitants were obliged to hide in caves for safety and so were not in a position to provide themselves with food, and a famine in consequence resulted.

2. Whereas experience has shown that the continual wars taking place in South Africa have been damaging to trade and to the general prosperity not only in the countries where they occurred but also to the whole of South Africa, and certain portions of South Africa have been thereby completely exhausted.

3. And whereas during the past three years repeated and urgent requests for interference and protection were made by the late Zulu King Cetshwayo and his Chiefs, and again after his death by the Regents of his successor and the other Zulu Chiefs.

4. And whereas it appears that no civilised government has felt itself called upon to interfere in the affairs of Zululand to put a stop to the bloodshed of defenceless women and children and to restore peace and order there. A number of farmers from the various states and colonies of South Africa deem it a holy duty to accede to the appeals of the Zulu Chiefs, in the interests of humanity and civilisation, and with an eye to the safety of life and property of the adjoining people.

5. And whereas these farmers prepared themselves to make an effort to put a stop to the disturbances etc. in Zululand, to restore peace and order and to put Dinuzulu, the successor to Cetshwayo on the throne.

6. And whereas these farmers entered Zululand, crowned Dinuzulu, partially restored peace and an agreement was entered into on the 23 May 1884 between them and the King, and with his councillors and headmen, whereby the farmers took upon themselves the task not alone of restoring but of preserving peace and order, and whereby the King and his Chiefs agreed to give to the farmers a portion of Zululand (lines and beacons to be fixed after the ground has been inspected), in extent 1,355,000 morgen, adjoining the South African Republic and the Reserve, for the purpose of establishing an independent government and to better enable the farmers to carry out to a successful issue their engagements.

7. And whereas these farmers have decided to accept the said portion of Zululand according to their agreement and to erect an independent republican government under the name of the New Republic, and the necessary officials have been chosen and taken the oaths.

8. So it is that I, Lucas Johannes Meyer, Acting President of the New Republic, with the counsel and by the advice of the Executive Council, proclaim by these presents, and make known that the above-mentioned portion of Zululand shall form the territory of the New Republic and shall be governed by the laws of the New Republic.

All and each are hereby requested and commanded to take notice of this my Proclamation and to act accordingly.

God preserve Land and People.

(Signed) L. J. MEYER (Acting State President).
D. J. ESSELEN (Acting State Secretary).

## The Treaty between the German Land Colonization Company and Dinuzulu

(*Note:* The original document was on parchment and written in Zulu. It was found by R. G. Pearson in Dinuzulu's strong box in his kraal at Usutu, Zululand, on the day on which he was arrested for his complicity in the Bambata Rebellion of 1906. It was handed over, together with Pearson's translation, to Col. Murray Smith, N.M.R. It is interesting to note that as a kit inspection was ordered on account of one of the women having reported the loss of some belongings and as Pearson did not want to be found in possession of loot he hid the document in the ambulance wagon until the search was over. This was done with the aid of an Indian volunteer stretcher-bearer who was a young lawyer in Durban named Gandhi, later to become the famous Mahatma.)

### LAND CONCESSION.

Closed between the German Land Colonization Co. of Berlin, represented by Emil Nagel of Karlsruhe, Baden, on the one side and the King of the Zulu People, Dinuzulu, on the other side.

I.

Under today's date the ———
We, Dinuzulu, crowned King of the Zulu People, with the sanction of our under Chiefs and our People, concede the following territory:

On the North, from the Bevan, Pongola River, over the Mkuzi River to the Ocean.
On the South, from the English-Zulu frontier.
On the East, from the Indian Ocean.
On the West, from the Blood River.
With all power and right whatsoever to the German Land

Colonization Co. of Berlin or to their rightful successors for the purchase sum of £2,500.

## 2.

The payment to be made in 25 yearly instalments each of £100 or the equivalent value of weapons which shall cover the yearly sum to be paid.

Several instalments may be made at one time by the contracting company to the King of the Zulus. The payment of instalments shall begin on the day when the German Land Colonization Co. shall be installed in their rights through the agency of the High Imperial German Government.

## 3.

The German Land Colonization Co. permits the Zulu People to live free of hut taxes. The exception to this is a grant of 100,000 German *morgen*, position of which is to be more definitely fixed later, and also smaller pieces of land to be used for townships, streets, railways, etc. The whole of the remaining grant stands at the disposal of the Zulu People, to use according to their usual custom for cultivation, pasturage, etc.

## 4.

Those farms given by Dinuzulu to the Boers who have supported him in his war against Sibebu will be given over to the possessors by the undersigned Company as promised; all further grants, however, will be subject to the decision of the High German Government.

## 5.

The undersigned Company takes over the government and is the highest legal authority in the land. Any dwellers in this concession which bears the name of German Zululand shall be under the control of this government no matter to what nationality they belong.

## 6.

The undersigned Company reserves itself the unquestionable right to proclaim, dictate, instal the Zulu King. Their own proclaimed

King will not be recognised as such otherwise. The first King of German Zululand is Dinuzulu I.

### 7.

Dinuzulu I, and later his successor, shall do all in their power to maintain order and peace in German Zululand. They shall do all in their power to facilitate the discovery of such persons, whether of the native Zulu race or other race therewith connected, who may have broken the standing laws of the country and against whom evidence is substantiated. Equally, shall he or they be obliged to deliver such persons who may seek to disturb the peace of the land so that said persons may stand their trial according to the permanent laws. They shall also not facilitate, or even allow it to be possible for such persons to find refuge.

### 8.

Dinuzulu promises to encourage in every way all Mission places which are intended for the furtherance of the Christian faith in lands inhabited by the Zulus. That is to say, all such now standing and all such which may subsequently be erected. Dinuzulu also gives his word to allow any natives who may wish to live near a Mission for the purpose of exercising his religious duties etc. perfect freedom of action in this respect. Dinuzulu also promises to encourage the children of his people in that they shall attend as regularly as possible schools wherein the Word of God is read and taught. At the present time six Hermansburg Mission Stations exist within the concession, each holding six thousand English acres.

### 9.

Dinuzulu promises to make known immediately to the undersigned Co. all disputes which can lead to war. They on their side will do all they can in a conciliatory way to prevent all quarrels with neighbouring peoples. On the other hand, however, the Chief with all his *indunas* and warriors is prepared with his goods and his blood to support the undersigned Company should war be unavoidable.

### 10.

The undersigned will do all possible to guard the Zulu Nation's rights from outside and to support the Chiefs in the carrying out of any obligations which they have incurred with this Contract.

### 11.

The German Land Colonization Co. binds itself to uphold the laws with perfect equality and will exercise the law against any European or similar race who offends against the goods or otherwise of any native living in German Zululand, and if such person shall be found guilty, he shall be punished.

### 12.

The German Land Colonization Co. holds this Concession from the Zulu People under the German Government and both parties, the Company as well as the Zulus, subject themselves to the voice of the High German Imperial Government in regard to German Zululand.

### 13.

The German Land Colonization Co. binds itself to pray the German Empire to make a treaty with the neighbouring peoples which may preserve peace and help the development of German Zululand.

### 14.

Depredations from neighbouring peoples in the German Zululand Concession will be handed over to the German Government to settle.

### 15.

This Contract comes into force on the day on which the German Land Colonization Co. shall be established in their rights by the agency of the German Government.

Made in duplicate, each party holding one copy thereof in . . . on the first day of June in the year of our Lord eighteen hundred and eighty-five.

SIGNED. The German Land Colonization Co. of Berlin

EMIL NAGEL

Countersigned and sworn that this copy is correctly translated into Zulu and the contents thoroughly understood by the Chiefs.

Signed EMIL NAGEL

| | | | |
|---|---|---|---|
| DINUZULU | X | His Mark. | King of the Zulus. |
| ANDERBEKO | X | His Mark. | Brother to Cetshwayo and Successor to Dinuzulu. |
| ASTUNGAM | X | His Mark. | Brother to Cetshwayo. |

# Memorandum of Terms of Settlement between Sir A. E. Havelock, L. J. Meyer, P. R. Spies and D. J. Esselen[1]

## ARTICLE I

It is agreed that a line of demarcation be drawn between the territory to remain in occupation and possession of the settlers of the New Republic in Zululand and the territory to be left in the undisturbed occupation and possession of the Zulu Nation. This line to be as follows:

Beginning from the wagon drift where the road from the Inkandhla Mountain crosses the Umhlatuzi River:

Thence along the wagon road to the Ulundi Drift over the White Umfolozi River:

Thence following the south bank of the White Umfolozi River upwards to beacon No. 1 of the line of the 2nd inspection:

Thence to beacon No. 2 on the Idhlebe Hill:

Thence to beacon No. 3 called the Ceza, on the Impembeni Mountains:

Thence to beacon No. 4 of the line of the 2nd inspection:

Thence to the nearest source of the Impalaza Spruit:

Thence down the north bank of the Impalaza Spruit to its junction with the Umkuzana Spruit:

Thence down the north bank of the Umkuzana Spruit to its junction with the Umkuzi River:

Thence down the north bank of the Umkuzi River to the Poort where it passes through the Libombo Mountains:

Thence along the watershed of the Libombo Mountains to the Pongola River Poort.

### PROVISO A.

Provided that the right of passage with vehicles or otherwise along the road now existing or any road which may be made from

Central Zululand across the Mkuzana and Mkuzi Rivers to and across the Pongola River shall be reserved to all persons of all nationalities without let or hindrance and without payment of licence or toll.

PROVISO B.

Provided that all settlers having received allotments within the area below described may continue to occupy and possess such allotments. This area to be included within the following boundaries: From the Ulundi Drift on the White Umfolozi River, down the south bank of the White Umfolozi to a spot on the south bank opposite the Hlopekulu Hill:

Thence in a straight line southward across the Imfule River and over the Makassana Mountains down to the Umhlatuzi River to a spot on the north bank opposite the Hlokohloko Mountain:

Thence up the north bank of the Umhlatuzi River to the Drift where the wagon road leading to the Inkandhla crosses it:

Thence along the wagon road to the Drift across the White Umfolozi River called the Ulundi Drift.

*ARTICLE II.*

Lucas Meyer and his colleagues of the deputation agree, on behalf of the settlers of the New Republic, to take all such measures and to make all such arrangements with all persons claiming rights or privileges in the territory which is to be left, as provided in Article I, in the undisturbed occupation and possession of the Zulu Nation as may be required for the due carrying out of the stipulations of the said Article I, subject to conditions of Proviso B.

*ARTICLE III.*

It is agreed that a Commission be appointed, composed of four or more persons, two or more of such persons to be nominated by Sir A. Havelock on behalf of H.M. Government, and the Chiefs of the Zulu people on their own behalf and on that of the Zulu Nation, and of an equal number of persons to be nominated by Lucas Meyer on behalf of the settlers of the New Republic, to determine and mark the line of demarcation described in Article I above and also the boundaries described in Proviso B to that Article.

### ARTICLE IV.

Lucas Meyer and his colleagues of the deputation agree, on behalf of the settlers of the New Republic to abandon all claims that may have been made by the New Republic to a Protectorate over the Zulu Nation, provided that the Zulu Nation makes no objection to such abandonment of claim of a Protectorate.

### ARTICLE V.

Lucas Meyer and his colleagues of the deputation agree, on behalf of the settlers of the New Republic to guarantee to all missionary bodies of all nationalities all rights to land and other privileges, duly proved, which may have been granted to them by the late King Cetshwayo and his predecessors.

### ARTICLE VI.

H.M. Government, on being satisfied that the conditions and stipulations above set forth have been duly fulfilled, will take steps to enter into a Convention with the Boer settlers of the New Republic recognising the New Republic as an independent state, the provisions of such Convention being generally based on the provisions of the Convention made in London in 1884 between H.M. Government and the South African Republic.

In witness of the above terms the following sign this Memorandum in duplicate.

Government House,
P.Maritzburg, Natal.                                 22nd October 1886

(Signed)   A. E. HAVELOCK
L. J. MEYER
P. R. SPIES
D. J. ESSELEN

As Witness to Signatures:

(Signed)   H. C. SHEPSTONE
P. HUGO

## The Usutus and Emakosini Valley
## (situated in Proviso B)

How deeply the whole Zulu nation felt on this matter can be judged from the following:

1. After the death of Dinuzulu, some time during the year 1918, an imposing deputation of Zulu chiefs headed by David ka Zulu, on behalf of the Regent Solomon (the half-brother of Dinuzulu), called upon Mr Buntting Sr, the then owner of part of the area in question (a farm of 2,000 acres by the name of Koningsdaal) with the request that he sell it to them on behalf of the nation. To convince Mr Buntting of the sincerity of their petition several of them unstrapped two saddlebags from a pony that they had been leading and, taking these onto the veranda of the house, emptied their contents before him. To his amazement the saddlebags were filled with golden sovereigns and after these men had poured them out before his astonished gaze David ka Zulu said, 'All these are yours, Mr Buntting, if you will sell us your farm. If there are not enough here, tell us and we will bring you the balance but please let us buy from you this land that contains the graves of our Kings.' Reluctantly Mr Buntting had to refuse as the Government would not allow him to sell his farm to natives.

(This information was kindly given to the author by Mr George Buntting, a son of the former owner. He was present at the time of the above incident and witnessed the whole proceedings. His father had previously purchased this farm from a Mr van Bredaar and took over the property on the very day that Dinuzulu was being buried on the adjoining farm.)

2. Year after year when the various Governors-General of the

Union paid their official visits to Eshowe they were regularly met by a deputation of the leading Zulu chiefs with the request that the Emakosini Valley be handed back to them. When King Edward VIII, then Prince of Wales, visited this country in 1925 a particularly impressive deputation of Zulu dignitaries presented him with a petition renewing this request but it was some years later before the Government decided that the area in question should be handed back to them and in 1936, under the Coalition Government of Smuts and Hertzog, it was expropriated under the Native Land Act. Unfortunately war intervened and the whole issue was held over till 1955 when it finally passed into the hands of the Native Trust on behalf of the Zulu nation and nothing has given them greater satisfaction than to know that the burial places of their early Kings are now in their possession.

## Instructions to E. R. W. Saunders, Custodian of Dinuzulu on St. Helena*

Government House,
P.M.Burg.
25 January 1890

Sir,

Your letter of appointment and warrants are herein enclosed.

A letter of instructions will be given you by the Resident Commissioner. I have, however, thought it better to myself issue instructions to you which may be supplemented by any that the Resident Commissioner may give you.

You will report yourself to the Resident Commissioner at Eshowe not later than midday on the 2nd February and you will take his instructions as to the day and hour of leaving with your prisoners and their companions. You will, in taking over the prisoners from the gaoler at Eshowe receive from him *the original warrants on which they were committed to his charge on conviction by the Special Court.* For these warrants you will hand him a receipt.

An escort of Zululand Mounted Police or a military escort will accompany you to the Tugela and the officer in charge will, with his escort guard the prisoners across the river and, on the Natal side, you will find an escort of Natal Mounted Police which will accompany your party to Stanger where the prisoners will be lodged in the gaol during the night of the 3rd February.

The attendants and wives of the prisoners may either remain in the gaol or outside it, but they must make their election on arriving at Stanger, and if they elect to be in the gaol, they must be warned that they will not be allowed to leave it until the prisoners do so.

On the morning of the 4th Feby you will, again escorted

* These letters were kindly loaned to the author by Mrs M. M. K. Robinson a daughter of Sir Charles Saunders.

by Natal Mounted Police, proceed to Verulam where you will, as at Stanger, lodge the prisoners and, if they wish it, their companions in the gaol and await a communication from the resident magistrate, Durban, who will be charged with the duty of superintending the embarkation. At the hour named by him you will convey the whole party by special train to the Point, the escort of Natal Mounted Police again accompanying you; you will be met there by Mr Anthony Daniels, the Sub-Interpreter and Sub-Custodian and by three Natal Mounted Policemen who will accompany you and be under your orders until you are leaving Capetown, when you will dismiss them, directing them to return to Natal by the next steamer.

On arriving on board you will at once inspect the place set apart for your party and you will make all arrangements for the safety of your prisoners. These arrangements I must necessarily leave to your discretion: one of the Natal Mounted Police should always be on guard: the prisoners should be locked up at night but during the day allowed all reasonable freedom to take fresh air and exercise. Neither you nor the Sub-Interpreter should ever quit the ship until you arrive at St Helena and you should divide with the Sub-Interpreter the duties of frequent visits to the prisoners.

I need scarcely tell you that your chief difficulty will be with Dinuzulu who is young, active and enterprising and would, I think, take advantage of any opportunity afforded him of escape: the guards should therefore pay especial care to his safe-keeping and should never lose sight of him when in harbour or in dock.

Ndabuko and Tshingana are obese and indolent and there is little danger of either of them making a successful attempt at escape.

The first duty of the guards will be to make themselves thoroughly familiar with the appearance of their prisoners so as not to confuse them with their attendants who are not, of course, to be treated as prisoners.

You will, during the voyage treat the prisoners with all possible kindness and forbearance. I do not anticipate any refractory behaviour on their part but, if such should occur, you will not hesitate to use all necessary means to ensure safe-keeping and due obedience to your lawful orders.

On arrival at St Helena you will report yourself to the Governor of the Island under whose orders you will place yourself from that moment.

C. H. MITCHELL.   Governor of Zululand.


Resident Commissioner's Office,
Eshowe, Zululand.
2nd February 1890

E. R. W. Saunders, Esq.

Sir,

With reference to the instructions received by you from His Excellency the Governor for your guidance while conducting the Chiefs from the gaol at Eshowe to St Helena I have to state for your further guidance that I have appointed 5 a.m. tomorrow as the hour at which the prisoners are to start promptly from the gaol.

Two mule wagons will be in attendance at the gaol at 4.45 a.m. to receive the Chiefs and their party of wives and attendants and such luggage as they are authorised to take with them. The taking up of these into the wagons should be completed in time to admit of the start being made at five o'clock.

No person other than the prisoners and the authorised members of their party, beside yourself, and any members of the Zululand Police required as part of the guard, is to be allowed on either wagon. The three Chiefs should ride together on the covered wagon in which you should personally have your seat.

You will be this day introduced to the Chiefs by the resident magistrate, who will also cause the persons forming the rest of the party to appear in order that you may be able to identify them at any time during your journey.

A supply of cooked provisions and some uncooked will be placed on the wagons for use of the prisoners and those accompanying them during their first day's journey. I will arrange with the resident magistrate, Stanger, for the providing by him of a further supply of food on your reaching, with the party, Stanger gaol in the afternoon of the 3rd inst.

I have to caution you particularly to keep the warrants you received from the Governor, and the original warrants of Committal to prison which you will forthwith receive from the gaoler at Eshowe on your person during the whole of your journey ready to be produced to anyone who may with legal authority question your right to the custody of the prisoners.

The prisoners will be guarded from here by an escort of Mounted Zululand Police as far as the Matikulu from which point to Tugela the escort will consist of mounted Infantry. Commandant Mansel, Zululand Police, has been entrusted with the general direction of the journey through Zululand and until the prisoners are handed over to the Natal Mounted Police on the Natal side of the Tugela River. Detachments of foot police will be stationed at the following points between Eshowe and Tugela:

> Inyezane Hill (Majiya's)
> Lambs, and
> Inyoni

to remain there on duty until you have crossed Tugela with the Chiefs.

I annex hereto for your guidance a list of the three prisoners (Chiefs) and of their wives and attendants, the latter you will perceive consist of two wives, two female attendants and four male attendants including the native doctor Paul.

I request you will be good enough to send a telegram to the Governor and another to me from Capetown immediately before the steamer conveying the party leaves the Cape for St Helena, intimating the departure.

M. OSBORN.  Resident Commissioner.

## LIST OF PRISONERS AND
*ATTENDANTS ACCOMPANYING THEM TO ST HELENA*

Prisoner   DINUZULU
        Male Attendant, Nyosana ka Madwala
        Male Medical Attendant, Paul
        *Female Attendants*
        Uzihlazile ka Qetuka
        Umkasilomo ka Untuzwa

Prisoner   NDABUKO
        Male Attendant, Xamadolo ka Magidigidi
        Wife, Nozingwe

Prisoner   TSHINGANA
        Male Attendant, Usuluko ka Radasi
        Wife, Nozinyoni.

# Was Bambata killed in the Mome Gorge?

DURING my field research over Zululand in the course of the last few years, in interviews with various chiefs and headmen I have repeatedly met with the report that Bambata was not killed in the Mome Gorge encounter but managed to escape, later reaching Lourenço Marques in safety and living there for some years under an assumed name. Later, when all the trouble had blown over and the nation was calm, Bambata and his family returned to Zululand and hid in the depths of the Ngome Forest, their whereabouts being kept a strict secret and their hiding place closely guarded. Here Bambata died and was buried though the location of his grave is still maintained secret. Invariably I have heard the same story, although told by men whose kraals are widely separated.

As recently as 2 July 1966, through the kindly co-operation of Dr R. E. Stevenson, I was enabled to interview in Pietermaritzburg a Zulu by the name of Joseph Nzama. This is his story:

I am now seventy-eight years of age; when a young man I knew Bambata and his family well; I joined the rebels at about the age of eighteen and was told by Bambata, along with others, that his witchdoctor would give us *muti* which would stop the white men's bullets from killing us; for this purpose we were assembled and Malaza, the 'great Doctor', sprinkled each one of us with a carefully prepared concoction. I fought at Bope Ridge and in the Mome Gorge and was one of the lucky ones who managed to escape.

I knew Mehlokazulu, he was a big *induna*, a fine and much respected man; unfortunately he was killed in the Mome and is buried there. After escaping from the Mome I heard that Sigananda had surrendered and word went round that we were to do the same. I therefore gave myself up at the Nkandhla and later received two years' imprisonment and thirty lashes; I was sent to Durban but was released within a year. Before facing trial, when it was found out that I knew Bambata well, I was shown the head which Calverley had brought out from the Gorge and asked if I knew who it was. I said it was Bambata's because I had been told secretly by certain of my friends that I must do this in order to give Bambata the chance to escape. Although the head was something like Bambata's it most certainly was not his; I am absolutely certain of this because I knew Bambata well.

The story as related by other Zulus is that Bambata's *inceku* received instructions to surrender himself to the authorities and report the death of his chief to them; thus the search for Bambata would be abandoned and the road open for him to get clean away. When ordered by the authorities to return to the Gorge and point out the body to Calverley the *inceku* indicated that of a Zulu somewhat resembling the Chief but certainly not Bambata's.

It is significant that none of the Europeans at the Nkandhla knew Bambata by sight and so were unable to state whether the head in question was really his.

In further confirmation of his story Joseph Nzama stated that when released from prison and returning to his kraal he met Siyekiwe, Bambata's wife, and Kolekile, his daughter, but soon after his return the two women quietly and mysteriously disappeared. Some months later, however, news reached him secretly that both of them had joined Bambata at Lourenço Marques. Strict instructions were given him that under no circumstances was he to disclose their whereabouts and the secret was kept by the Zulus for many years. Only recently has it been divulged.

In an interview with some of the sons of Sigananda, all elderly men, whose kraals are situated in the Mome Gorge, further light was shed on the problem. When they were asked to show the grave of Bambata their immediate reply was 'There is no grave; Bambata escaped to Portuguese [Lourenço Marques].' The answer came quite spontaneously, for no indication whatsoever had been given them as to what was already known to us. They were most emphatic on this point and nothing would shake their belief, and as two or three of them took part in the Rebellion and fought in the Mome, their statement gives food for thought.

On being questioned further about the Mome massacre these old men were able to give a full and accurate description of the whole encounter – all the details of the fight, the position of the guns, troop movements, the shooting of those who sought refuge in the Dobo Forest etc. Finally, as mementoes of the occasion, they presented a live dum-dum bullet and a fifteen-pounder shell case picked up after the fight; both of these are now in my possession, along with more dum-dums obtained from other sources.

The need for further research on this question is indicated.

# NOTES

*Full details of the works referred to will be found in the Bibliography, p. 293. Blue Book is here abbreviated as B.B.*

CHAPTER 1

1. *Natal Advertiser*, 26 Jan. 1883.
2. F. Colenso, *Ruin of Zululand*, vol. II, p. 339.
3. Binns, *The Last Zulu King*, p. 210.
4. Samuelson, *Long, Long Ago*, p. 122.
5. B.B. C4587, Encl. 2 in 106, p. 103.
6. *Ibid.*
7. *Ibid.*
8. B.B. C4037, No. 44.
9. B.B. C4913, Encl. 1 in 50, p. 78.
10. B.B. C4037, Encl. 1 in 44, p. 50.
11. *Ibid.*, No. 44, p. 49.
12. B.B. C4913, Encl. 1 in 50, pp. 78ff.
13. B.B. C4645, Encl. 1 in 56, p. 85.
14. *Ibid.*, Encl. 4 in 61, p. 91.
15. B.B. C4913, Encl. 1 in 50, p. 78.
16. *Ibid.*, Encl. 1 in 50.
17. B.B. C4645, Encl. 1 in 56, pp. 80–4.
18. *Ibid.* and B.B. C4913, Encl. 1 in 50, p. 78.
19. B.B. C4587, Encl. 2 in 106, p. 103.
20. B.B. C4645, Encl. 1 in 56, pp. 80–6, and Encl. 4 in 61.
21. B.B. C4913, Encl. 1 in 50, p. 78. Gibson, *Story of the Zulus*, p.270, and Samuelson, *Long, Long Ago*, p. 124, also relate this incident of the oath.
22. B.B. C4037, No. 63, p. 65.
23. *Ibid.*, No. 103, p. 100.

CHAPTER 2

1. *Natal Witness*, 31 May 1884.
2. *Ibid.*, 14 May 1884, leader.
3. *Ibid.*, 24 May 1884, leader.
4. *Ibid.*, 28 May 1884, leader.
5. B.B. C4191, Encl. 3 in 11, p. 15.
6. *Ibid.*, p. 110.
7. Extract from Volkstem, quoted in *Natal Witness*, 14 June 1884.

8. B.B. C4191, p. 18.
9. *Staats Courant*, 15 May 1884.
10. B.B. C4191, p. 72.
11. See account of this interview by John Eckersley in B.B. C4191, Encl. 70, 13 June 1884.
12. B.B. C4037, No. 110, p. 117.

CHAPTER 3
1. B.B. C4191, No. 54, p. 79.
2. B.B. C4214, Encl. in 4, p. 7.
3. B.B. C4191, p. 4.
4. *Ibid.*, p. 6.
5. Quoted from Grosvenor Darke's Diary reported in the *Natal Mercury* and quoted in the *Natal Witness*, 19 June 1884.
6. *Natal Witness*, 26 June 1884.
7. B.B. C4645, No. 21, Encl. 1, p. 33.
8. *Natal Witness*, 26 June 1884.
9. Darke's Diary, *Natal Witness*, 19 June 1884.

CHAPTER 4
1. B.B. C4645, Encl. 1 in 56, pp. 80–4.
2. Extract from Volkstem, *Natal Witness*, 14 June 1884.
3. B.B. C4214, No. 17, p. 26.
4. Darke's Diary, *Natal Witness*, 19 June 1884.
5. *Natal Witness*, 26 June 1884.
6. B.B. C4191, Encl. in 70.
7. *Ibid.*, Encl. 2 in 66, p. 99.
8. *Ibid.*, Encl. 3 in 66.
9. *Ibid.*, Encl. in 76.
10. *Ibid.*, No. 66, p. 98.
11. *Ibid.*, No. 73, p. 112.
12. B.B. C4191, No. 82, p. 138.
13. B.B. C4274, No. 7, p. 11.
14. B.B. C4214, No. 73, p. 103.
15. *Natal Witness*, 20 May 1884, leader.
16. *Ibid.*, 21 May and 1 July 1884, leaders.
17. B.B. C4645, No. 21, pp. 30–3.
18. *Ibid.*, Encl. 1 in 21, pp. 30–3.
19. B.B. C4191, Encl. in 34, p. 58; also extracts from Grant's Diary.
20. B.B. C4214, No. 15, p. 22.
21. *Natal Witness*, 23 July 1884, leader.
22. B.B. C4274, p. 31; B.B. C4645, Encl. 1 in 21, p. 33.
23. B.B. C4214, No. 42, p. 63; B.B. C4645, No. 21, p. 31.

24. See extract from the *Newcastle Echo*, 21 Aug. 1884, quoted in B.B. C4214, p. 63.
25. B.B. C4274, p. 31.
26. *Ibid.*
27. B.B. C4645, Encl. 1 in 21, pp. 30–3.
28. B.B. C4274, p. 31.
29. B.B. C4214, No. 21, p. 36.
30. Statement made to Lt-Col. Cardew at Rorke's Drift on 11 December 1885, by A. Schiel, Secretary to Dinuzulu, recorded in B.B. C4645, Encl. 1 in 56, pp. 80–4.
31. *Ibid.*
32. *Ibid.*
33. *Ibid.*
34. B.B. C4913, Encl. 1 in 50.
35. *Natal Witness*, 25 Aug. 1884.
36. B.B. C4214, Encl. in 44, p. 68.
37. B.B. C4645, p. 88.
38. B.B. C4913, Encl. 1 in 50.
39. B.B. C4214, p. 9.

CHAPTER 5

1. B.B. C4587, Encl. in 114; also B.B. C4913, Encl. 1 in 50.
2. Cardew to Sir C. Mitchell, 12 Dec. 1885, B.B. C4645, Encl. 1 in 56. See also Grant's letter to Bulwer, 4 Aug. 1885, B.B. C4645, Encl. 1 in 21.
3. B.B. C4645, Encl. 1 in 21.
4. B.B. C4587, No. 40, 23 Feb. 1885, pp. 41–2.
5. B.B. C4913, Encl. 1 in 50.
6. Ndabuko's statement to Governor Havelock, 27 April 1886, B.B. C4913, Encl. 1 in 50.
7. *Natal Witness*, Sat. 4 Oct. 1884.
8. B.B. C4587, No. 40, p. 41.
9. *Ibid.*, No. 21, p. 15.
10. B.B. C4214, Encl. 2 in 52, p. 65.
11. B.B. C4587, No. 21, p. 15.
12. *Ibid.*, p. 24.
13. *Ibid.*, No. 110, p. 109.
14. *Ibid.*, Encl. in 111, p. 111.
15. *Ibid.*, Encl. 2 in 92, p. 88.
16. *Ibid.*, No. 86, p. 80.
17. *Ibid.*, No. 97, p. 90.
18. *Ibid.*
19. B.B. C4645, No. 24, p. 38, and *Natal Witness*, 1 Sept. 1885.

20. B.B. C4645, Encl. 1 in 51, p. 74.
21. B.B. C4913, No. 5, Encl. 1, p. 22.
22. B.B. C4645, Encl. 1 in 13, p. 31.
23. B.B. C4587, No. 12, p. 11.
24. B.B. C4913, Encl. 1 in 13, p. 31.

## CHAPTER 6

1. B.B. C4214, No. 21, p. 36 etc.
2. B.B. C4587, p. 46.
3. *Ibid.*, p. 41.
4. B.B. C4645, No. 35, p. 57.
5. *Ibid.*, No. 47, p. 71.
6. B.B. C4913, Encl. 1 in 5, p. 22.
7. *Ibid.*, Encl. 1 in 13, p. 31.
8. See B.B. C4645, Encl. 2 in 56, p. 24.
9. *Ibid.*, Encl. in 30, pp. 45–8.
10. *Ibid.*, No. 35, p. 57.
11. B.B. C4913, Encl. 7 in 13, p. 34.
12. *Ibid.*
13. B.B. C4645, Encl. in 60, p. 89.
14. *Ibid.*, Encl. in 8, p. 10.
15. B.B. C4913, No. 28, p. 49.
16. B.B. C4645, No. 49, p. 71.
17. B.B. C4913, Encl. 1 in 3, p. 19.
18. *Ibid.*, No. 16, p. 36.
19. See *Natal Witness*, 24 Feb. and 20 April 1886.
20. *Ibid.*, 2 March 1886.
21. *Ibid.*, 24 Feb. 1886.
22. B.B. C4913, No. 25, p. 44.
23. *Ibid.*, Encl. 1 in 25, p. 44.
24. *Ibid.*, Encl. 2 in 25, p. 44.
25. *Ibid.*, Encl. in 29, p. 51.
26. *Ibid.*, No. 29, p. 49.
27. *Ibid.*, Encl. 1 in 40, p. 59.
28. *Ibid.*, Encl. 2 in 50.

## CHAPTER 7

1. B.B. C4980, No. 3, p. 2.
2. *Ibid.*, No. 8, p. 16.
3. *Ibid.*, Encl. in 17, p. 29.
4. *Ibid.*, Encl. 1 in 25, p. 32.
5. *Ibid.*, Encl. 2 in 25, p. 32.
6. *Ibid.*, Encl. 2 in 16, p. 24.

7. *Ibid.*, Encl. in 26, p. 35.
8. *Ibid.*
9. *Ibid.*, Encl. in 37, p. 52.
10. For a verbatim account of the proceedings see B.B. C4980, No. 58 and Encls., pp. 81–116.
11. B.B. C4980, Encl. 1 in 43, p. 63.
12. *Ibid.*, No. 21, p. 30.
13. *Ibid.*, No. 23, p. 31.
14. *Ibid.*, No. 27, p. 36.
15. *Ibid.*, No. 28, p. 36.
16. *Ibid.*, No. 29, p. 36.
17. *Ibid.*, Encl. 3 in 53, p. 78.
18. *Ibid.*, No. 61, p. 118.
19. *Ibid.*, Encl. in 78, p. 158.
20. *Ibid.*, No. 93, p. 172.
21. *Ibid.*, Encls. 6, 7 and 8 in 62, pp. 127ff.
22. *Ibid.*, No. 97 and Encl. 1 in 97, p. 177.
23. *Ibid.*, No. 72, p. 150.
24. *Ibid.*, No. 73, p. 150.
25. *Ibid.*, No. 79, p. 190.
26. *Ibid.*, No. 100, p. 190.
27. B.B. C5143, Encl. 1 in 10, p. 28.
28. B.B. C4980, Nos. 101, 103, 104, pp. 190–1.
29. B.B. C5143, Encl. 1 in 10, p. 28.
30. B.B. C4980, No. 108, p. 193.

CHAPTER 8

1. B.B. C4980, Encl. 1 in 95, p. 173.
2. *Ibid.*, No. 95, p. 173.
3. B.B. C5143, No. 21, p. 40.
4. *Ibid.*, Encl. 28, p. 50.
5. B.B. C5331, Encl. 1 in 1, p. 1.
6. *Ibid.*, pp. 3–7.
7. *Ibid.*, Encl. 1 in 7, p. 22.
8. *Ibid.*, No. 11, p. 29.
9. *Ibid.*, No. 11, p. 30.
10. *Ibid.*, No. 15, p. 32.
11. *Ibid.*, Encl. 3 in 9, p. 26.
12. *Ibid.*, No. 26, p. 41.
13. *Ibid.*, p. 25.
14. *Ibid.*, Encl. 2 in 30, pp. 46–7.
15. *Ibid.*, No. 31, p. 48.
16. *Ibid.*, Encl. in 23, pp. 37–9.

CHAPTER 9

1. B.B. C5331, No. 25, p. 40.
2. *Ibid.*, Encl. 1 in 35, p. 53.
3. *Ibid.*, Encl. 2 in 37, p. 64.
4. *Ibid.*, Encl. 4 in 37, p. 67.
5. *Ibid.*, No. 37, pp. 57–69.
6. *Ibid.*, Encl. 6 in 37, p. 69.
7. *Ibid.*, Encl. 2 in 38, pp. 70–1.
8. Dispatch dated 18 December 1887, *ibid.*, Encl. 1 in 46, p. 77.
9. *Ibid.*, No. 46, p. 75.
10. *Ibid.*, Encl. 1 in 46, p. 77.
11. *Ibid.*, No. 46, p. 76.
12. *Ibid.*, Encl. 1 in 46, p. 78.
13. *Ibid.*, No. 46, p. 76.
14. *Ibid.*, Encl. 1 in 48, p. 81.
15. B.B. C5522, No. 1, p. 1.
16. B.B. C5331, No. 53, pp. 84–5.
17. B.B. C5522, Encl. 7 in 16, p. 32.
18. *Ibid.*
19. *Ibid.*, No. 72, p. 116.
20. *Ibid.*, Encl. 2 in 52, p. 90.
21. For official accounts of the Hlopekulu fight see B.B. C5522 : No. 53, p. 91 ; Encl. 1 in 66, p. 103 ; Encls. 3 and 4 in 66, pp. 106–8 ; Encl. in 67, pp. 109–11 ; Encl. in 75, pp. 120–6.

CHAPTER 10

1. B.B. C5522, Encl. 5 in 74, p. 119.
2. B.B. C5892, Encl. 1 in 2, p. 3.
3. *Ibid.*, Encl. 2 in 2, p. 3.
4. *Ibid.*, Encl. 1 in 3, p. 4.
5. *Ibid.*, Encl. 2 in 3, p. 5.
6. *Ibid.*, Encl. in 25, p. 35.
7. *Ibid.*, Encl. 3 in 5, p. 11.
8. *Ibid.*, No. 7, p. 11.
9. *Ibid.*, No. 44, p. 76.
10. *Ibid.*, Encl. 48, p. 79.
11. *Ibid.*, No. 45, p. 77.
12. *Ibid.*, Encl. in 53, p. 81.
13. *Ibid.*, No. 70, p. 107.
14. *Ibid.*
15. *Ibid.*, Declaration of W. P. Meyer, Encl. in 90, p. 131.
16. Rees, *Colenso Letters from Natal*, p. 422.
17. B.B. C5892, p. 132.

18. *Ibid.*, p. 128.
19. *Ibid.*, No. 65, p. 93.
20. *Ibid.*, No. 68, p. 104.
21. *Ibid.*, No. 31, p. 44.
22. *Ibid.*, No. 74, p. 111.
23. *Ibid.*, pp. 36–7.
24. *Ibid.*, p. 37.
25. *Ibid.*, Encl. 3 in 117, p. 170.
26. *Ibid.*, No. 164, p. 251.
27. *Ibid.*, p. 163.
28. *Ibid.*, No. 167, p. 254.
29. B.B. C5893, No. 8, p. 11.
30. See Escombe, *A Remonstrance on behalf of the Zulu Chiefs,* Part I, in the Library of the late Dr Killie Campbell, Durban.
31. B.B. C5892, No. 97, p. 152.
32. *Ibid.*, Encl. 1 in 170, p. 258.
33. *Ibid.*, Encl. 2 in 154, p. 230.
34. *Ibid.*, Encl. in 162, p. 250.
35. *Ibid.*, No. 162, p. 248.
36. B.B. C5893, No. 2, p. 6.
37. *Ibid.*, No. 7, p. 10.
38. *Ibid.*, No. 14, p. 16.
39. *Ibid.*, No. 21, p. 19.
40. B.B. C6070, No. 21, p. 38.


CHAPTER 11

1. B.B. C6684, Encl. 2 in 2.
2. *Ibid.*, No. 5, p. 51.
3. *Ibid.*, No. 10, p. 54.
4. Hattersley, *Later Annals of Natal,* p. 177.
5. B.B. C8782, No. 1.
6. *Ibid.*
7. *Ibid.*
8. *Ibid.*
9. *Ibid.*, No. 10.
10. *Ibid.*, No. 11.
11. *Ibid.*, Encl. in 15.
12. *Ibid.*, No. 18.
13. *Ibid.*, Encl. in 24.
14. *Ibid.*, No. 23.
15. *Ibid.*, No. 29.
16. *Ibid.*, No. 30.
17. *Ibid.*, No. 31.

18. *Ibid.*, No. 46.
19. Extracts from Otto Siedle's MS. *Story of Dinuzulu's Return from St Helena* in the Library of the late Dr Killie Campbell, Durban.
20. *Ibid.*
21. Under-Secretary's Report, *Ibid.*, Encl. 1 in 56, pp. 39ff.

CHAPTER 12

1. Letter of C. J. Watts in the Library of the late Dr Killie Campbell, Durban.
2. Stuart, *A History of the Zulu Rebellion*, p. 110.
3. Interview between the Governor and Dinuzulu, 21 May 1907. See *ibid.*, pp. 510 and 532.
4. Bryant, *Olden Times in Zululand and Natal*, p. 23.
5. Lugg, *Historic Natal and Zululand*, p. 113.
6. See Sir Garnet Wolseley's dispatch in B.B. C2482, p. 255.
7. See Binns, *The Last Zulu King*, Appendix C, p. 222.
8. *Report of Zululand Commission*, 1902–04, p. 3.
9. Brookes and Webb, *A History of Natal*, p. 186.
10. *B.B. of Native Affairs, Colony of Natal*, 1902, C.1.
11. Stuart, *A History of the Zulu Rebellion*, p. 483.
12. See C. R. Saunders's report in *B.B. of Native Affairs, Colony of Natal*, 1904, pp. 91 and 165.

CHAPTER 13

1. Stuart, *A History of the Zulu Rebellion*, p. 100.
2. *Ibid.*, p. 101.
3. *Ibid.*, p. 103.
4. *Ibid.*, pp. 104ff.; Brookes and Webb, *A History of Natal*, p. 220.
5. Perrett, *Dinuzulu and the Bambata Rebellion*, p. 28.
6. *Ibid.*, p. 61.
7. For a detailed account see Stuart, *A History of the Zulu Rebellion*, pp. 122ff.
8. *Ibid.*, p. 122.
9. Brookes and Webb, *A History of Natal*, p. 223.
10. *Ibid.*, p. 224.

CHAPTER 14

1. For an account of his life see Stuart, *A History of the Zulu Rebellion*, pp. 157ff.
2. This appears in Ngqengqengqe's evidence to be found in *Criminal Records, Special Court, 1908–09*, Vol. 1, *Rex vs Dinuzulu*.
3. Dinuzulu's evidence.
4. Evidence of Ngqengqengqe.

5. Evidence.
6. See Cakijana's evidence.
7. See Magwababa's evidence.
8. Evidence of Inspector Ottley who found the body.
9. Ngqengqengqe's evidence.
10. *Ibid.*
11. *Ibid.*
12. *Ibid.*
13. Cakijana's evidence.

## CHAPTER 15

1. Stuart, *A History of the Zulu Rebellion*, p. 214.
2. *Ibid.*
3. *Ibid.*, p. 298.
4. P. H. Holt, quoted from Brookes and Webb, *A History of Natal*, p. 224.

## CHAPTER 16

1. Stuart, *A History of the Zulu Rebellion*, p. 337.
2. *Ibid.*, p. 340.
3. Résumé of a letter from W. T. Robbins, son of W. C. Robbins, written to the late Dr Killie Campbell and now in her Durban Library.
4. Sir Charles Saunders's Diary, 19 August 1906.
5. *Ibid.*, 28 December 1906.
6. *Ibid.*, 30 and 31 December 1906.
7. Cakijana's evidence.
8. Stuart, *A History of the Zulu Rebellion*, p. 427.
9. Perrett, *Dinuzulu and the Bambata Rebellion*, p. 78, quoted from the report of the interview.
10. Stuart, *A History of the Zulu Rebellion*, pp. 510 and 532.
11. The chief and headmen of Vryheid District to Native Affairs Commission, January 1907; Stuart, *A History of the Zulu Rebellion*, pp. 532–3.
12. Brookes and Webb, *A History of Natal*, p. 225.
13. Harriette Colenso, Notes on Life of Dinuzulu, in the Library of the late Dr Killie Campbell, Durban.
14. Walker, *W. P. Schreiner*, p. 283.
15. *Ibid.*
16. This and much of the following information have been obtained from a document entitled 'Memorandum on Dinuzulu' by Eugene Renaud in the Library of the late Dr Killie Campbell, Durban.

CHAPTER 17

1. Renaud, 'Memorandum on Dinuzulu'.
2. Perrett, *Dinuzulu and the Bambata Rebellion*, p. 191.
3. Walker, *W. P. Schreiner*, p. 279.
4. *Ibid.*, p. 289.
5. *Ibid.*, p. 293.
6. *Ibid.*, p. 287.
7. *Ibid.*, p. 295.
8. Brookes and Webb, *A History of Natal*, p. 227.
9. *Ibid.*
10. Walker, *W. P. Schreiner*, p. 299.
11. Brookes and Webb, *A History of Natal*, p. 225.
12. The above extracts are taken from the *Criminal Records of the Attorney-General's Office, Special Court 1908–09*, Vol. 1, *Rex vs Dinuzulu*.
13. Walker, *W. P. Schreiner*, p. 302.

EPILOGUE

1. Walker, *W. P. Schreiner*, p. 337.

APPENDIX II: The Death of Cetshwayo

1. B.B. C4587, p. 8.
2. See *Natal Witness*, 12 Feb. 1884.
3. B.B. C4587, p. 8, para. 9.

APPENDIX III: Grant's Support of Boer Claims

1. B.B. C4645, No. 21, pp. 30–3.

APPENDIX IV: Proclamation No. 1, New Republic

1. B.B. C4214, Encl. 1 in 56; *Natal Witness*, 29 Aug. 1884; *Natal Mercury*, 2 Sept. 1884.

APPENDIX VI: Memorandum of Terms of Settlement between Sir A. E. Havelock, L. J. Meyer, P. R. Spies and D. J. Esselen

1. B.B. C4980, Encl. 2 in 42, p. 60.

# BIBLIOGRAPHY

*Annual Reports, Department of Native Affairs, Colony of Natal.* 1905, 1906.

BINNS, C. T. *The Last Zulu King. The Life and Death of Cetshwayo,* Longmans, London, 1963.

BLUE BOOK C2482. *Further Correspondence respecting the Affairs of South Africa. Correspondence re War 1879–80.*

BLUE BOOK C3705. *Further Correspondence respecting the Affairs of Zululand and Cetwayo,* July 1883.

BLUE BOOK C4037. *Further Correspondence re the Affairs of Zululand,* May 1884.

BLUE BOOK C4191. *Further Correspondence re the Affairs of Zululand,* August 1884.

BLUE BOOK C4214. *Further Correspondence re the Affairs of Zululand,* October 1884.

BLUE BOOK C4274. *Further Correspondence re the Affairs of Zululand,* February 1885.

BLUE BOOK C4587. *Further Correspondence re the Affairs of Zululand,* August 1885.

BLUE BOOK C4645. *Further Correspondence re the Affairs of Zululand,* February 1886.

BLUE BOOK C4913. *Further Correspondence re the Affairs of Zululand,* February 1887.

BLUE BOOK C4980. *Further Correspondence re the Affairs of Zululand,* February 1887.

BLUE BOOK C5143. *Further Correspondence re the Affairs of Zululand,* August 1887.

BLUE BOOK C5331. *Further Correspondence re the Affairs of Zululand,* March 1888.

BLUE BOOK C5522. *Further Correspondence re the Affairs of Zululand,* August 1888.

BLUE BOOK C5892. *Further Correspondence re the Affairs of Zululand,* February 1890.

BLUE BOOK C5893. *Further Correspondence re the Affairs of Zululand,* February 1890.

BLUE BOOK C6070. *Further Correspondence re the Affairs of Zululand,* June 1890.

BLUE BOOK C6487. *Correspondence respecting Responsible Government in Natal,* 1888–90.

# Bibliography

BLUE BOOK C6684. *Correspondence respecting Zululand Boundaries*, May 1892.

BLUE BOOK C8782. *Correspondence relating to the Affairs of Zululand*, 1895–1898.

BLUE BOOKS of *Native Affairs, Colony of Natal*. 1902, 1904.

BOSMAN, W. *The Natal Native Rebellion, 1906*, London.

BRAATVEDT, H. P. *Roaming Zululand with a Native Commissioner*, Shuter and Shooter, Pietermaritzburg, 1949.

BROOKES, E. H., and WEBB, C. DE B. *A History of Natal*, University of Natal Press, 1965.

BRUNNER, E. A. Extract from *Twentieth Century Impressions of Natal*, Lloyds Greater Britain Publishing Co., Natal, 1906.

BRYANT, A. T. *Olden Times in Zululand and Natal*, Longmans, London, 1929.

COLENSO, FRANCES. *Ruin of Zululand*, Ridgway, London, 1884. 2 vols.

COLENSO, HARRIETTE. 'The Case of Dinuzulu', *Universal Review*.

*Criminal Records, Special Court 1908–09*. Vol. 1, *Rex vs Dinuzulu*. Natal Archives, Pietermaritzburg.

ESCOMBE, HARRY. *A Remonstrance on behalf of the Zulu Chiefs, 1889*, City Printing Works, Pietermaritzburg, 1908.

GIBSON, J. Y. *Story of the Zulus*, P. Davis, Pietermaritzburg, 1903.

GRANT, WILLIAM. *Diary*. MS. in Natal Archives, Pietermaritzburg.

HATTERSLEY, A. F. *Later Annals of Natal*, Longmans, London, 1908.

LUGG, H. C. *Historic Natal and Zululand*, Shuter and Shooter, Pietermaritzburg, 1948.

Newspapers:
*Natal Witness*, 1884–1910
*Natal Mercury*, 1884–1910.
*Natal Advertiser*, 1883.
*Staats Courant*, 15 May 1884.

PERRETT, I. M. *Dinuzulu and the Bambata Rebellion*. Unpublished M.A. thesis, Natal University, 1960.

POWELL, W. J. 'The Zulu Rebellion 1906. Souvenir of the Transvaal Mounted Rifles', *Transvaal Leader*, Johannesburg, 1906.

REES, WYN. *Colenso Letters from Natal*, Shuter and Shooter, Pietermaritzburg, 1958.

RENAUD, EUGENE. 'Memorandum on Dinuzulu'. MS. in Library of the late Dr Killie Campbell, Durban.

SAMUELSON, R. C. *Long, Long Ago*, Knox Publishing Co., Durban, 1929.

SAUNDERS, SIR CHARLES. Private Diary for 1906 and Sundry Correspondence. Loaned by Mrs M. M. K. Robinson, his daughter.

SIEDLE, OTTO. *Story of Dinuzulu's Return from St Helena*. MS. in Library of the late Dr Killie Campbell, Durban.

## Bibliography

STUART, J. *A History of the Zulu Rebellion*, 1906, Macmillan, London, 1913.

WALKER, ERIC A. *History of Southern Africa*, Third Edition, Longmans, London, 1964.

WALKER, ERIC A. *W. P. Schreiner*, Oxford University Press, 1937.

# INDEX

# Index

British Government—*cont.*
with Sibebu, 33 and n., 40–2; and the Boers, 44; refusal to intervene, 48, 50, 61–2, 67, 72–3; reaction to these appeals, 73ff.; Havelock stresses her position, 79; claims to Zululand, 79, 82; threatens to send a Commission, 84; and Natal Legislative Council, 91–4; annexes Zululand, 96, 99–100; and D.'s trial, 138, 139; and alienation of Zulu lands, 171, 172; and Bambata's rebellion, 229; and D., 236, 248–9
Brown, Sergeant, 204
Browne, Gerald, and Maritzburg meetings, 79, 89
Buffalo River, 134
Bulwer, Sir Henry, urges annexation of Zululand, 7, 27; refuses to recognize D. as King, 9; and Osborn's demand for troops, 21 and n.; and Boer migrants, 24; and Sibebu, 27, 40–1, 43, 69; and Boer intervention, 44; and Grant, 46–7; and the Reserve, 50; knowledge of ceded territory, 56–7; succeeded by Havelock, 57, 70 and n., 73; rebukes Osborn, 60, 61; appeals to London for aid to Zulus, 61–2, 66; impression given by his despatches, 68–72; and land cessions, 69; and Cetshwayo's death, 260
Buntting, George, and Emakosini Valley, 272

Cakijana, 192; and Bambata, 194, 198–201, 204, 205; joins the rebels, 206, 213, 216; and Stainbank's murder, 214n.; and D., 229; murders Gence, 231–2; eludes arrest, 246–7; his surrender, 247–8; trial and sentence, 250–1
Calder, D., and D.'s trial, 251
Calverley, Sergeant W., 219n.; 222; and Bambata's death, 222–3, 279–80; and Sigananda, 223, 224n.; and Cakijana, 247–8
Capetown, 2, 3, 132–3
Cardew, Lieut. Col., Sub-Commissioner at Nqutu, 51n., 86; appeals for help, 67; on Boer meanness, 70; and Dabulamanzi's murder, 86–8; member of Boundary Commission, 89; and Usutu boundary dispute, 150
Carter, K. C., Hon. T. F., and D.'s trial, 251, 252
Celebantu, 55
Cetshwayo, King, 113, 142n.; his coronation, 1; conflict with British, 2; banishment and imprisonment, 2–3, 28n.; family reunion, 5; final defeat

and death, 5–6, 259–60; and Boers, 6; his posthumous son, 8 and n., 176; choice of his successor, 8ff., 30; his burial, 13–15, 16–17, 19, 257; Grant and, 44–5, 49; request to guard his grave, 59, 61; Bulwer and, 68; refuge at Enhlweni, 208–9; his grave site, 215, 216, 217; visit to Queen Victoria, 257
Ceza, D.'s stronghold, 118, 124, 131
Ceza mountain, 47, 48, 123, 127
Chamberlain, Joseph, suggests D.'s repatriation, 157; and incorporation of Zululand, 157–8
Clarke, Col., and D.'s surrender, 238, 243
Clarke, Sir Marshall, Resident Commissioner, 153; and D.'s return, 155–7, 161, 163, 165–6, 167
Colenbrander, Johann, his 'Stanger Disreputables', 22; Sibebu and, 26, 31, 33; and the Government, 31–2; and Bambata, 210
Colenso, Agnes, and D., 135–6, 159, 164, 232, 249
Colenso, Frances, on D., 5; on his arrival at Bishopstowe, 135
Colenso, Harriette, and D., 96, 131–2, 136, 138–9, 160, 237, 238, 239, 240, 248–9
Colenso, John William, Bishop of Natal, 3
Colonial Office, and Responsible Government for Natal, 152–3; and D.'s return to Zululand, 155–8
Combrink, John, mission to Sibebu, 25–6
Commission of Inquiry into Native Administration, 229, 234, 236
Committee of Dinuzulu's Volunteers, composition, 22 and n.; letter to Sibebu and Uhamu, 23, 25; ambitions in Zululand, 23–6; and D.'s coronation, 28–30; and Disputed Territory, 30–1, 32, 45; and Sibebu, 32, 33, 34
*Criminal Records: Rex vs. Dinuzulu,* 194n. 196n.
Cross, J. W., interpreter, 251

Dabulamanzi, 60; burial of Cetshwayo, 15, 16; clash with Osborn, 20–1; Grant and, 47; his murder, 86–8, 110
Daniels, Anthony, secretary to D., 152, 159, 164, 229, 275; his 'disclosures', 229, 230–1
David ka Zulu, 272
Darke, Grosvenor, adviser to Sibebu, 38, 40; Colenbrander and, 31–2
Dartnell, Col., 134

# Index